INTERNATIONAL TIME TABLES

by

Gary L. Fitzpatrick

The Scarecrow Press, Inc.
Metuchen, N.J., & London
1990

British Library Cataloguing-in-Publication data available

Library of Congress Cataloging-in-Publication Data

Fitzpatrick, Gary L., 1947-
    International time tables / by Gary L. Fitzpatrick.
       p.   cm.
    ISBN 0-8108-2341-1 (alk. paper)
    1. Time--Conversion tables. I. Title.
QB211.F56 1990
529'.7--dc20   90-37885

Introduction

International Time Tables makes it possible to determine time relationships of places around the world and to visualize those time relationships over the spectrum of a full day.

The tables are structured to provide time in both the 12- and 24-hour forms of notation. For places that observe Advanced Time, also known as Daylight Saving Time or Summer Time, separate tables are given for each period of the year. For places with multiple time zones, separate sets of tables are given for each time zone. The effect of the International Dateline on time relationships is also taken into account.

The basic principle of this volume is that the time under a specific column in one time table is directly comparable to the time under the same column for any other time table.

Example

Consider the following question: what time is it in Afghanistan when it is 10:00 PM, or 22:00 in 24-hour notation, in Albania on June 15? (Tables for these places are found on page 1.)

Step 1. Determine which of the two tables given for Albania is applicable for the question. Beneath the subheading "Standard Time," a note indicates that Standard Time is observed in that country from the last Sunday in September to the last Sunday in March. June 15 does not fall into that period, so the table for Advanced Time—the last Sunday in March to the last Sunday in September in this example—applies to the date June 15.

Step 2. In the table under "Advanced Time" for Albania, find the column that contains the entries 10:01 PM and 22:01. (The paragraph under the heading "Designation of Minutes" explains why the time is expressed as one minute after the hour instead of on the hour.) Note that the first line in this column is identified by the letter *i* within brackets. Also note that the bottom line gives the abbreviation "Sun" for Sunday.

Step 3. Find the table for Afghanistan. Only one table is given; the third line of notes indicates that Advanced Time is not observed.

Step 4. Locate column [i] in the Afghanistan table. The second line indicates the time 00:31 and the third line gives the time as 12:31 AM. The bottom line gives the abbreviation "Mon."

Step 5. The above steps yield the information that when it is 10:01 PM on June 15 in Albania, it is 12:31 AM on June 16 in Afghanistan. The time relationship is explicit, but the date in Afghanistan is inferred from the fact that the bottom line of the Albania table lists the day as "Sun" and the Afghanistan table lists it as "Mon." June 16 follows June 15, just as Monday follows Sunday.

This example covers a wide range of possible considerations in answering time questions. In particular, it demonstrates the ease with which time relationships can be deduced even when one of the places has its minute hand offset by 30 or 45 minutes compared to the majority of places in the world.

Countries with More Than One Time Zone

For countries with more than one time zone, it is necessary to consult the table for the appropriate part of the country. Textual descriptions under the name of the time zone provide enough information to make the determination in many cases. In others, it will be necessary to consult the map of world time zones. A separate time zone map of the Soviet Union is also provided. (See back cover.)

The United States has probably the most complex time zone boundaries of any country. There is no map that conveys accurately all the nuances of time zones in this country, for in some areas the boundary does not conform even to city or county boundaries, let alone state boundaries. For this edition, it was possible to give no more than the textual descriptions of the state and counties comprising a time zone.

For the countries of North America, the names of time zones have been used in the subheadings for those tables. In the tables for the Soviet Union, time zones are identified by Roman numerals that correspond to the identifiers on the time zone map of the Soviet Union. In Australia, time zones basically conform to first-order administrative boundaries as given. For other countries around the world, time zones are identified by the terms "Eastern," "Central," or "Western."

Dates of Changeover between Standard and Advanced Times

Advanced Time is a political issue, not a scientific one, and decisions regarding its observance are made in a political context. Consequently, there is no uniformity throughout the world on when Advanced Time will be observed or how much the clock will be retarded or advanced. Within any country, the observance of Advanced Time can be altered to reflect the needs of the nation. There is no international organization officially charged with maintaining records of the dates of changeover between Standard and Advanced times for the countries of the world.

The changeover between Standard and Advanced times has been given only to the nearest day, since that is the best level of information available for many countries. For a few countries, however, even that level of precision is not possible, for there are no set dates when clocks are switched between Standard and Advanced times; the decision when to switch is made each year. Based on a review of the changeovers between Standard and Advanced times in previous years, an approximate range in which future changeovers can be expected is given.

Users are cautioned to use discretion when consulting the tables for time on a date when one or both places involved are changing between Standard and Advanced times. Also, be especially cautious about time when dealing with a country that does not have precisely defined dates for the change between Standard and Advanced times.

Designation of Minutes

The tables give comparative time at a minute after the hour, half-hour, or three-quarter hour in order to avoid the ambiguity of the terms *midnight* and *noon*. There is no universally accepted convention as to whether midnight denotes the end of one day or the beginning of another. The term really refers to that one infinitesimally small moment that separates two days, and is therefore neither. Noon is equally ambiguous when giving time in the 12-hour form of notation; it is neither AM nor PM, but that moment that separates the two.

Helpful Hint for Using This Volume

Although this volume can be readily used to determine time relationships throughout the world, it is likely that the table of the users' local time zone will be consulted more frequently than any other. If that is indeed the case, then it may prove effective to photocopy the table (or tables, if Advanced Time is observed locally) for the local time zone and use it as a bookmark. Having the local time zone tables readily available eliminates one look-up and makes it possible to physically place two tables adjacent to each other.

Elements of an Individual Entry

The first line of an entry is the name of the country or geographic locale. If an island or archipelago is not close to the country to which it belongs, then it receives a separate entry. The Galapagos Islands and French Polynesia, for instance, are listed separately rather than with Ecuador or France.

Several islands in the Caribbean are listed separately as well as with the country to which they belong: Tobago will be found under its own listing as well as under Trinidad and Tobago, and the Grenadines are listed separately as well as under St. Vincent and the Grenadines. This decision reflects a belief that the political geography of this popular vacation region is not adequately understood by most people.

The elements that describe the number of time zones, the periods during which Standard Time and Advanced Time apply, and notes about what comprises a particular time zone are all self-explanatory.

The line beginning with the heading "Time Zone" requires some explanation. The first element following the heading is the time in 24-hour notation where the first time zone east of the International Dateline is zone 01:00. This corresponds to the notation given on the first of the two lines at the bottom of the "Standard Time Zones of the World" map. The second element of that line, given in parentheses, is the time of the zone given in terms of the number of hours by which it differs from the base time of the Coordinated Universal Time (UTC), which is equivalent to 12:00 hours at Greenwich, England. Zones to the west are assigned a negative value and those to the east a positive value. Zones in which the time is the same as at Greenwich are simply identified as "UTC". The term *UTC* is synonymous with the more common expression, "Greenwich Mean Time" (GMT). *UTC* is the term used by international bodies responsible for keeping precise time.

Sources of Information

The information on which the tables in this volume are based is found in a wide variety of sources. The most difficult information to find is that which concerns the dates during which Advanced Time is observed in the different countries of the world. Fortunately, most countries observing Advanced Time adhere to either of two major systems. The most commonly used is the European system, in which the last Sundays in March and September are dates of changeover. This system is prescribed in a directive issued by the Council of the European Community known as "Fifth Council Directive of 21 December 1988 on summertime arrangements." Except for the United Kingdom and Ireland, which are given specific exception to this directive, all the countries of Europe and many around the eastern and southern shores of the Mediterranean Sea observe these same dates for Standard and Advanced times.

The dates used for Standard and Advanced times in the United States are set forth in the Uniform Time Act. Application and enforcement of that legislation is the responsibility of the Department of Transportation.

For a few countries, information regarding the periods of Standard and Advanced times have been deduced from a list provided by the U. S. Naval Observatory in Washington, D.C., the agency in this country responsible for keeping precise time.

Historical Aspects of Time and Time Zones

Since *International Time Tables* is intended to serve one specific reference function, there will be no digression into a history of time keeping. Let it suffice to say that numerous books are available on myriad aspects of the subject. *Books in Print* lists several such volumes. Almanacs and encyclopedias also include information about time zones, the different types of time, etc.

Time Zone Maps

Atlases, almanacs, encyclopedias, and other reference works frequently include maps showing time zones. The map of world time zones in this volume is a reprint of that published each year in *The World Factbook* (Washington: Central Intelligence Agency, annual). The map showing time zones of the Soviet Union is also a reproduction of a map by the Central Intelligence Agency.

Gary L. Fitzpatrick
Alexandria, Virginia

ABU DHABI
Number of Time Zones: *1*
Standard Time: *Applicable for the entire year*
Advanced Time: *Not observed*
Time Zone: *16:00 (+4hrs UTC)*

[a]	[b]	[c]	[d]	[e]	[f]	[g]	[h]	[i]	[j]	[k]	[l]	[m]	[n]	[o]	[p]	[q]	[r]	[s]	[t]	[u]	[v]	[w]	[x]
16:01	17:01	18:01	19:01	20:01	21:01	22:01	23:01	00:01	01:01	02:01	03:01	04:01	05:01	06:01	07:01	08:01	09:01	10:01	11:01	12:01	13:01	14:01	15:01
4^{01}_{pm}	5^{01}_{pm}	6^{01}_{pm}	7^{01}_{pm}	8^{01}_{pm}	9^{01}_{pm}	10^{01}_{pm}	11^{01}_{pm}	12^{01}_{am}	1^{01}_{am}	2^{01}_{am}	3^{01}_{am}	4^{01}_{am}	5^{01}_{am}	6^{01}_{am}	7^{01}_{am}	8^{01}_{am}	9^{01}_{am}	10^{01}_{am}	11^{01}_{am}	12^{01}_{pm}	1^{01}_{pm}	2^{01}_{pm}	3^{01}_{pm}
Sun	Sun	Sun	Sun	Sun	Sun	Sun	Sun	Mon	Mon	Mon	Mon	Mon	Mon	Mon	Mon	Mon	Mon	Mon	Mon	Mon	Mon	Mon	Mon

AFGHANISTAN
Number of Time Zones: *1*
Standard Time: *Applicable for the entire year*
Advanced Time: *Not observed*
Time Zone: *16:30 (+4hrs 30mins UTC)*

[a]	[b]	[c]	[d]	[e]	[f]	[g]	[h]	[i]	[j]	[k]	[l]	[m]	[n]	[o]	[p]	[q]	[r]	[s]	[t]	[u]	[v]	[w]	[x]
16:31	17:31	18:31	19:31	20:31	21:31	22:31	23:31	00:31	01:31	02:31	03:31	04:31	05:31	06:31	07:31	08:31	09:31	10:31	11:31	12:31	13:31	14:31	15:31
4^{31}_{pm}	5^{31}_{pm}	6^{31}_{pm}	7^{31}_{pm}	8^{31}_{pm}	9^{31}_{pm}	10^{31}_{pm}	11^{31}_{pm}	12^{31}_{am}	1^{31}_{am}	2^{31}_{am}	3^{31}_{am}	4^{31}_{am}	5^{31}_{am}	6^{31}_{am}	7^{31}_{am}	8^{31}_{am}	9^{31}_{am}	10^{31}_{am}	11^{31}_{am}	12^{31}_{pm}	1^{31}_{pm}	2^{31}_{pm}	3^{31}_{pm}
Sun	Sun	Sun	Sun	Sun	Sun	Sun	Sun	Mon	Mon	Mon	Mon	Mon	Mon	Mon	Mon	Mon	Mon	Mon	Mon	Mon	Mon	Mon	Mon

ALBANIA
Number of Time Zones: *1*

Standard Time
Period: *Last Sunday in September to Last Sunday in March*
Time Zone: *13:00 (+1hr UTC)*

[a]	[b]	[c]	[d]	[e]	[f]	[g]	[h]	[i]	[j]	[k]	[l]	[m]	[n]	[o]	[p]	[q]	[r]	[s]	[t]	[u]	[v]	[w]	[x]
13:01	14:01	15:01	16:01	17:01	18:01	19:01	20:01	21:01	22:01	23:01	00:01	01:01	02:01	03:01	04:01	05:01	06:01	07:01	08:01	09:01	10:01	11:01	12:01
1^{01}_{pm}	2^{01}_{pm}	3^{01}_{pm}	4^{01}_{pm}	5^{01}_{pm}	6^{01}_{pm}	7^{01}_{pm}	8^{01}_{pm}	9^{01}_{pm}	10^{01}_{pm}	11^{01}_{pm}	12^{01}_{am}	1^{01}_{am}	2^{01}_{am}	3^{01}_{am}	4^{01}_{am}	5^{01}_{am}	6^{01}_{am}	7^{01}_{am}	8^{01}_{am}	9^{01}_{am}	10^{01}_{am}	11^{01}_{am}	12^{01}_{pm}
Sun	Sun	Sun	Sun	Sun	Sun	Sun	Sun	Sun	Sun	Sun	Mon	Mon	Mon	Mon	Mon	Mon	Mon	Mon	Mon	Mon	Mon	Mon	Mon

Advanced Time
Period: *Last Sunday in March to Last Sunday in September*
Time Zone: *14:00 (+2hrs UTC)*

[a]	[b]	[c]	[d]	[e]	[f]	[g]	[h]	[i]	[j]	[k]	[l]	[m]	[n]	[o]	[p]	[q]	[r]	[s]	[t]	[u]	[v]	[w]	[x]
14:01	15:01	16:01	17:01	18:01	19:01	20:01	21:01	22:01	23:01	00:01	01:01	02:01	03:01	04:01	05:01	06:01	07:01	08:01	09:01	10:01	11:01	12:01	13:01
2^{01}_{pm}	3^{01}_{pm}	4^{01}_{pm}	5^{01}_{pm}	6^{01}_{pm}	7^{01}_{pm}	8^{01}_{pm}	9^{01}_{pm}	10^{01}_{pm}	11^{01}_{pm}	12^{01}_{am}	1^{01}_{am}	2^{01}_{am}	3^{01}_{am}	4^{01}_{am}	5^{01}_{am}	6^{01}_{am}	7^{01}_{am}	8^{01}_{am}	9^{01}_{am}	10^{01}_{am}	11^{01}_{am}	12^{01}_{pm}	1^{01}_{pm}
Sun	Sun	Sun	Sun	Sun	Sun	Sun	Sun	Sun	Sun	Mon	Mon	Mon	Mon	Mon	Mon	Mon	Mon	Mon	Mon	Mon	Mon	Mon	Mon

Note: Advanced Time = Daylight Saving Time = Summer Time

ALGERIA

Number of Time Zones: *1*
Standard Time: *Applicable for the entire year*
Advanced Time: *Not observed*
Time Zone: *13:00 (+1hr UTC)*

[a]	[b]	[c]	[d]	[e]	[f]	[g]	[h]	[i]	[j]	[k]	[l]	[m]	[n]	[o]	[p]	[q]	[r]	[s]	[t]	[u]	[v]	[w]	[x]
13:01	14:01	15:01	16:01	17:01	18:01	19:01	20:01	21:01	22:01	23:01	00:01	01:01	02:01	03:01	04:01	05:01	06:01	07:01	08:01	09:01	10:01	11:01	12:01
1^{01}_{pm}	2^{01}_{pm}	3^{01}_{pm}	4^{01}_{pm}	5^{01}_{pm}	6^{01}_{pm}	7^{01}_{pm}	8^{01}_{pm}	9^{01}_{pm}	10^{01}_{pm}	11^{01}_{pm}	12^{01}_{am}	1^{01}_{am}	2^{01}_{am}	3^{01}_{am}	4^{01}_{am}	5^{01}_{am}	6^{01}_{am}	7^{01}_{am}	8^{01}_{am}	9^{01}_{am}	10^{01}_{am}	11^{01}_{am}	12^{01}_{pm}
Sun	Sun	Sun	Sun	Sun	Sun	Sun	Sun	Sun	Sun	Sun	Mon	Mon	Mon	Mon	Mon	Mon	Mon	Mon	Mon	Mon	Mon	Mon	Mon

AMERICAN SAMOA

Number of Time Zones: *1*
Standard Time: *Applicable for the entire year*
Advanced Time: *Not observed*
Time Zone: *01:00 (-11hrs UTC)*

[a]	[b]	[c]	[d]	[e]	[f]	[g]	[h]	[i]	[j]	[k]	[l]	[m]	[n]	[o]	[p]	[q]	[r]	[s]	[t]	[u]	[v]	[w]	[x]
01:01	02:01	03:01	04:01	05:01	06:01	07:01	08:01	09:01	10:01	11:01	12:01	13:01	14:01	15:01	16:01	17:01	18:01	19:01	20:01	21:01	22:01	23:01	00:01
1^{01}_{am}	2^{01}_{am}	3^{01}_{am}	4^{01}_{am}	5^{01}_{am}	6^{01}_{am}	7^{01}_{am}	8^{01}_{am}	9^{01}_{am}	10^{01}_{am}	11^{01}_{am}	12^{01}_{pm}	1^{01}_{pm}	2^{01}_{pm}	3^{01}_{pm}	4^{01}_{pm}	5^{01}_{pm}	6^{01}_{pm}	7^{01}_{pm}	8^{01}_{pm}	9^{01}_{pm}	10^{01}_{pm}	11^{01}_{pm}	12^{01}_{am}
Sun	Sun	Sun	Sun	Sun	Sun	Sun	Sun	Sun	Sun	Sun	Sun	Sun	Sun	Sun	Sun	Sun	Sun	Sun	Sun	Sun	Sun	Sun	Mon

ANDAMAN ISLANDS

Number of Time Zones: *1*
Standard Time: *Applicable for the entire year*
Advanced Time: *Not observed*
Time Zone: *17:30 (+5hrs 30mins UTC)*

[a]	[b]	[c]	[d]	[e]	[f]	[g]	[h]	[i]	[j]	[k]	[l]	[m]	[n]	[o]	[p]	[q]	[r]	[s]	[t]	[u]	[v]	[w]	[x]
17:31	18:31	19:31	20:31	21:31	22:31	23:31	00:31	01:31	02:31	03:31	04:31	05:31	06:31	07:31	08:31	09:31	10:31	11:31	12:31	13:31	14:31	15:31	16:31
5^{31}_{pm}	6^{31}_{pm}	7^{31}_{pm}	8^{31}_{pm}	9^{31}_{pm}	10^{31}_{pm}	11^{31}_{pm}	12^{31}_{am}	1^{31}_{am}	2^{31}_{am}	3^{31}_{am}	4^{31}_{am}	5^{31}_{am}	6^{31}_{am}	7^{31}_{am}	8^{31}_{am}	9^{31}_{am}	10^{31}_{am}	11^{31}_{am}	12^{31}_{pm}	1^{31}_{pm}	2^{31}_{pm}	3^{31}_{pm}	4^{31}_{pm}
Sun	Sun	Sun	Sun	Sun	Sun	Sun	Mon	Mon	Mon	Mon	Mon	Mon	Mon	Mon	Mon	Mon	Mon	Mon	Mon	Mon	Mon	Mon	Mon

Note: Advanced Time = Daylight Saving Time = Summer Time

ANDORRA
Number of Time Zones: *1*

Standard Time
Period: *Last Sunday in September to Last Sunday in March*
Time Zone: *13:00 (+1hr UTC)*

[a]	[b]	[c]	[d]	[e]	[f]	[g]	[h]	[i]	[j]	[k]	[l]	[m]	[n]	[o]	[p]	[q]	[r]	[s]	[t]	[u]	[v]	[w]	[x]
13:01	14:01	15:01	16:01	17:01	18:01	19:01	20:01	21:01	22:01	23:01	00:01	01:01	02:01	03:01	04:01	05:01	06:01	07:01	08:01	09:01	10:01	11:01	12:01
1^{01}_{pm}	2^{01}_{pm}	3^{01}_{pm}	4^{01}_{pm}	5^{01}_{pm}	6^{01}_{pm}	7^{01}_{pm}	8^{01}_{pm}	9^{01}_{pm}	10^{01}_{pm}	11^{01}_{pm}	12^{01}_{am}	1^{01}_{am}	2^{01}_{am}	3^{01}_{am}	4^{01}_{am}	5^{01}_{am}	6^{01}_{am}	7^{01}_{am}	8^{01}_{am}	9^{01}_{am}	10^{01}_{am}	11^{01}_{am}	12^{01}_{pm}
Sun	Sun	Sun	Sun	Sun	Sun	Sun	Sun	Sun	Sun	Sun	Mon	Mon	Mon	Mon	Mon	Mon	Mon	Mon	Mon	Mon	Mon	Mon	Mon

Advanced Time
Period: *Last Sunday in March to Last Sunday in September*
Time Zone: *14:00 (+2hrs UTC)*

[a]	[b]	[c]	[d]	[e]	[f]	[g]	[h]	[i]	[j]	[k]	[l]	[m]	[n]	[o]	[p]	[q]	[r]	[s]	[t]	[u]	[v]	[w]	[x]
14:01	15:01	16:01	17:01	18:01	19:01	20:01	21:01	22:01	23:01	00:01	01:01	02:01	03:01	04:01	05:01	06:01	07:01	08:01	09:01	10:01	11:01	12:01	13:01
2^{01}_{pm}	3^{01}_{pm}	4^{01}_{pm}	5^{01}_{pm}	6^{01}_{pm}	7^{01}_{pm}	8^{01}_{pm}	9^{01}_{pm}	10^{01}_{pm}	11^{01}_{pm}	12^{01}_{am}	1^{01}_{am}	2^{01}_{am}	3^{01}_{am}	4^{01}_{am}	5^{01}_{am}	6^{01}_{am}	7^{01}_{am}	8^{01}_{am}	9^{01}_{am}	10^{01}_{am}	11^{01}_{am}	12^{01}_{pm}	1^{01}_{pm}
Sun	Sun	Sun	Sun	Sun	Sun	Sun	Sun	Sun	Sun	Mon	Mon	Mon	Mon	Mon	Mon	Mon	Mon	Mon	Mon	Mon	Mon	Mon	Mon

ANGOLA
Number of Time Zones: *1*
Standard Time: *Applicable for the entire year*
Advanced Time: *Not observed*
Time Zone: *13:00 (+1hr UTC)*

[a]	[b]	[c]	[d]	[e]	[f]	[g]	[h]	[i]	[j]	[k]	[l]	[m]	[n]	[o]	[p]	[q]	[r]	[s]	[t]	[u]	[v]	[w]	[x]
13:01	14:01	15:01	16:01	17:01	18:01	19:01	20:01	21:01	22:01	23:01	00:01	01:01	02:01	03:01	04:01	05:01	06:01	07:01	08:01	09:01	10:01	11:01	12:01
1^{01}_{pm}	2^{01}_{pm}	3^{01}_{pm}	4^{01}_{pm}	5^{01}_{pm}	6^{01}_{pm}	7^{01}_{pm}	8^{01}_{pm}	9^{01}_{pm}	10^{01}_{pm}	11^{01}_{pm}	12^{01}_{am}	1^{01}_{am}	2^{01}_{am}	3^{01}_{am}	4^{01}_{am}	5^{01}_{am}	6^{01}_{am}	7^{01}_{am}	8^{01}_{am}	9^{01}_{am}	10^{01}_{am}	11^{01}_{am}	12^{01}_{pm}
Sun	Sun	Sun	Sun	Sun	Sun	Sun	Sun	Sun	Sun	Sun	Mon	Mon	Mon	Mon	Mon	Mon	Mon	Mon	Mon	Mon	Mon	Mon	Mon

ANGUILLA
Number of Time Zones: *1*
Standard Time: *Applicable for the entire year*
Advanced Time: *Not observed*
Time Zone: *08:00 (-4hrs UTC)*

[a]	[b]	[c]	[d]	[e]	[f]	[g]	[h]	[i]	[j]	[k]	[l]	[m]	[n]	[o]	[p]	[q]	[r]	[s]	[t]	[u]	[v]	[w]	[x]
08:01	09:01	10:01	11:01	12:01	13:01	14:01	15:01	16:01	17:01	18:01	19:01	20:01	21:01	22:01	23:01	00:01	01:01	02:01	03:01	04:01	05:01	06:01	07:01
8^{01}_{am}	9^{01}_{am}	10^{01}_{am}	11^{01}_{am}	12^{01}_{pm}	1^{01}_{pm}	2^{01}_{pm}	3^{01}_{pm}	4^{01}_{pm}	5^{01}_{pm}	6^{01}_{pm}	7^{01}_{pm}	8^{01}_{pm}	9^{01}_{pm}	10^{01}_{pm}	11^{01}_{pm}	12^{01}_{am}	1^{01}_{am}	2^{01}_{am}	3^{01}_{am}	4^{01}_{am}	5^{01}_{am}	6^{01}_{am}	7^{01}_{am}
Sun	Sun	Sun	Sun	Sun	Sun	Sun	Sun	Sun	Sun	Sun	Sun	Sun	Sun	Sun	Sun	Sun	Mon	Mon	Mon	Mon	Mon	Mon	Mon

Note: Advanced Time = Daylight Saving Time = Summer Time

ANTIGUA
Number of Time Zones: *1*
Standard Time: *Applicable for the entire year*
Advanced Time: *Not observed*
Time Zone: *08:00 (-4hrs UTC)*

[a]	[b]	[c]	[d]	[e]	[f]	[g]	[h]	[i]	[j]	[k]	[l]	[m]	[n]	[o]	[p]	[q]	[r]	[s]	[t]	[u]	[v]	[w]	[x]
08:01	09:01	10:01	11:01	12:01	13:01	14:01	15:01	16:01	17:01	18:01	19:01	20:01	21:01	22:01	23:01	00:01	01:01	02:01	03:01	04:01	05:01	06:01	07:0
8^{01}_{am}	9^{01}_{am}	10^{01}_{am}	11^{01}_{am}	12^{01}_{pm}	1^{01}_{pm}	2^{01}_{pm}	3^{01}_{pm}	4^{01}_{pm}	5^{01}_{pm}	6^{01}_{pm}	7^{01}_{pm}	8^{01}_{pm}	9^{01}_{pm}	10^{01}_{pm}	11^{01}_{pm}	12^{01}_{am}	1^{01}_{am}	2^{01}_{am}	3^{01}_{am}	4^{01}_{am}	5^{01}_{am}	6^{01}_{am}	7_{a}
Sun	Sun	Sun	Sun	Sun	Sun	Sun	Sun	Sun	Sun	Sun	Sun	Sun	Sun	Sun	Sun	Mon	Mon	Mon	Mon	Mon	Mon	Mon	Mo

ARGENTINA
Number of Time Zones: *1*
Standard Time: *Applicable for the entire year*
Advanced Time: *Not observed*
Time Zone: *09:00 (-3hrs UTC)*

[a]	[b]	[c]	[d]	[e]	[f]	[g]	[h]	[i]	[j]	[k]	[l]	[m]	[n]	[o]	[p]	[q]	[r]	[s]	[t]	[u]	[v]	[w]	[x]
09:01	10:01	11:01	12:01	13:01	14:01	15:01	16:01	17:01	18:01	19:01	20:01	21:01	22:01	23:01	00:01	01:01	02:01	03:01	04:01	05:01	06:01	07:01	08:0
9^{01}_{am}	10^{01}_{am}	11^{01}_{am}	12^{01}_{pm}	1^{01}_{pm}	2^{01}_{pm}	3^{01}_{pm}	4^{01}_{pm}	5^{01}_{pm}	6^{01}_{pm}	7^{01}_{pm}	8^{01}_{pm}	9^{01}_{pm}	10^{01}_{pm}	11^{01}_{pm}	12^{01}_{am}	1^{01}_{am}	2^{01}_{am}	3^{01}_{am}	4^{01}_{am}	5^{01}_{am}	6^{01}_{am}	7^{01}_{am}	8^{01}_{am}
Sun	Sun	Sun	Sun	Sun	Sun	Sun	Sun	Sun	Sun	Sun	Sun	Sun	Sun	Sun	Mon	Mon	Mon	Mon	Mon	Mon	Mon	Mon	Mon

ARUBA
Number of Time Zones: *1*
Standard Time: *Applicable for the entire year*
Advanced Time: *Not observed*
Time Zone: *08:00 (-4hrs UTC)*

[a]	[b]	[c]	[d]	[e]	[f]	[g]	[h]	[i]	[j]	[k]	[l]	[m]	[n]	[o]	[p]	[q]	[r]	[s]	[t]	[u]	[v]	[w]	[x]
08:01	09:01	10:01	11:01	12:01	13:01	14:01	15:01	16:01	17:01	18:01	19:01	20:01	21:01	22:01	23:01	00:01	01:01	02:01	03:01	04:01	05:01	06:01	07:01
8^{01}_{am}	9^{01}_{am}	10^{01}_{am}	11^{01}_{am}	12^{01}_{pm}	1^{01}_{pm}	2^{01}_{pm}	3^{01}_{pm}	4^{01}_{pm}	5^{01}_{pm}	6^{01}_{pm}	7^{01}_{pm}	8^{01}_{pm}	9^{01}_{pm}	10^{01}_{pm}	11^{01}_{pm}	12^{01}_{am}	1^{01}_{am}	2^{01}_{am}	3^{01}_{am}	4^{01}_{am}	5^{01}_{am}	6^{01}_{am}	7^{01}_{am}
Sun	Sun	Sun	Sun	Sun	Sun	Sun	Sun	Sun	Sun	Sun	Sun	Sun	Sun	Sun	Sun	Mon	Mon	Mon	Mon	Mon	Mon	Mon	Mon

ASCENSION ISLAND
Number of Time Zones: *1*
Standard Time: *Applicable for the entire year*
Advanced Time: *Not observed*
Time Zone: *12:00 (UTC)*

[a]	[b]	[c]	[d]	[e]	[f]	[g]	[h]	[i]	[j]	[k]	[l]	[m]	[n]	[o]	[p]	[q]	[r]	[s]	[t]	[u]	[v]	[w]	[x]
12:01	13:01	14:01	15:01	16:01	17:01	18:01	19:01	20:01	21:01	22:01	23:01	00:01	01:01	02:01	03:01	04:01	05:01	06:01	07:01	08:01	09:01	10:01	11:01
12^{01}_{pm}	1^{01}_{pm}	2^{01}_{pm}	3^{01}_{pm}	4^{01}_{pm}	5^{01}_{pm}	6^{01}_{pm}	7^{01}_{pm}	8^{01}_{pm}	9^{01}_{pm}	10^{01}_{pm}	11^{01}_{pm}	12^{01}_{am}	1^{01}_{am}	2^{01}_{am}	3^{01}_{am}	4^{01}_{am}	5^{01}_{am}	6^{01}_{am}	7^{01}_{am}	8^{01}_{am}	9^{01}_{am}	10^{01}_{am}	11^{01}_{am}
Sun	Sun	Sun	Sun	Sun	Sun	Sun	Sun	Sun	Sun	Sun	Sun	Mon	Mon	Mon	Mon	Mon	Mon	Mon	Mon	Mon	Mon	Mon	Mon

Note: Advanced Time = Daylight Saving Time = Summer Time

AUSTRALIA
Number of Time Zones: *3*
Note: *Advanced Time observed irregularly*
     See Reference Map I for graphic depiction of time zones

QUEENSLAND
Standard Time: *Applicable for entire year*
Advanced Time: *Not observed*
Time Zone: *22:00 (+10hrs UTC)*

[a]	[b]	[c]	[d]	[e]	[f]	[g]	[h]	[i]	[j]	[k]	[l]	[m]	[n]	[o]	[p]	[q]	[r]	[s]	[t]	[u]	[v]	[w]	[x]
:01	23:01	00:01	01:01	02:01	03:01	04:01	05:01	06:01	07:01	08:01	09:01	10:01	11:01	12:01	13:01	14:01	15:01	16:01	17:01	18:01	19:01	20:01	21:01
0^{01}_{pm}	11^{01}_{pm}	12^{01}_{am}	1^{01}_{am}	2^{01}_{am}	3^{01}_{am}	4^{01}_{am}	5^{01}_{am}	6^{01}_{am}	7^{01}_{am}	8^{01}_{am}	9^{01}_{am}	10^{01}_{am}	11^{01}_{am}	12^{01}_{pm}	1^{01}_{pm}	2^{01}_{pm}	3^{01}_{pm}	4^{01}_{pm}	5^{01}_{pm}	6^{01}_{pm}	7^{01}_{pm}	8^{01}_{pm}	9^{01}_{pm}
Sun	Sun	Mon	Mon	Mon	Mon	Mon	Mon	Mon	Mon	Mon	Mon	Mon	Mon	Mon	Mon	Mon	Mon	Mon	Mon	Mon	Mon	Mon	Mon

NEW SOUTH WALES, VICTORIA, TASMANIA, & AUSTRALIAN CAPITAL TERRITORY
Note: Excludes portion of New South Wales around town of Broken Hill

Standard Time
Period: *First Sunday in March to Last Sunday in October*
Time Zone: *22:00 (+10hrs UTC)*

[a]	[b]	[c]	[d]	[e]	[f]	[g]	[h]	[i]	[j]	[k]	[l]	[m]	[n]	[o]	[p]	[q]	[r]	[s]	[t]	[u]	[v]	[w]	[x]
2:01	23:01	00:01	01:01	02:01	03:01	04:01	05:01	06:01	07:01	08:01	09:01	10:01	11:01	12:01	13:01	14:01	15:01	16:01	17:01	18:01	19:01	20:01	21:01
0^{01}_{pm}	11^{01}_{pm}	12^{01}_{am}	1^{01}_{am}	2^{01}_{am}	3^{01}_{am}	4^{01}_{am}	5^{01}_{am}	6^{01}_{am}	7^{01}_{am}	8^{01}_{am}	9^{01}_{am}	10^{01}_{am}	11^{01}_{am}	12^{01}_{pm}	1^{01}_{pm}	2^{01}_{pm}	3^{01}_{pm}	4^{01}_{pm}	5^{01}_{pm}	6^{01}_{pm}	7^{01}_{pm}	8^{01}_{pm}	9^{01}_{pm}
Sun	Sun	Mon	Mon	Mon	Mon	Mon	Mon	Mon	Mon	Mon	Mon	Mon	Mon	Mon	Mon	Mon	Mon	Mon	Mon	Mon	Mon	Mon	Mon

Advanced Time
Period: *Last Sunday in October to First Sunday in March*
Time Zone: *23:00 (+11hrs UTC)*

[a]	[b]	[c]	[d]	[e]	[f]	[g]	[h]	[i]	[j]	[k]	[l]	[m]	[n]	[o]	[p]	[q]	[r]	[s]	[t]	[u]	[v]	[w]	[x]
3:01	00:01	01:01	02:01	03:01	04:01	05:01	06:01	07:01	08:01	09:01	10:01	11:01	12:01	13:01	14:01	15:01	16:01	17:01	18:01	19:01	20:01	21:01	22:01
1^{01}_{pm}	12^{01}_{am}	1^{01}_{am}	2^{01}_{am}	3^{01}_{am}	4^{01}_{am}	5^{01}_{am}	6^{01}_{am}	7^{01}_{am}	8^{01}_{am}	9^{01}_{am}	10^{01}_{am}	11^{01}_{am}	12^{01}_{pm}	1^{01}_{pm}	2^{01}_{pm}	3^{01}_{pm}	4^{01}_{pm}	5^{01}_{pm}	6^{01}_{pm}	7^{01}_{pm}	8^{01}_{pm}	9^{01}_{pm}	10^{01}_{pm}
Sun	Mon	Mon	Mon	Mon	Mon	Mon	Mon	Mon	Mon	Mon	Mon	Mon	Mon	Mon	Mon	Mon	Mon	Mon	Mon	Mon	Mon	Mon	Mon

Note: Advanced Time = Daylight Saving Time = Summer Time

AUSTRALIA *(Continued)*

SOUTH AUSTRALIA
Note: *Includes area in New South Wales around town of Broken Hill*

Standard Time
Period: *First Sunday in March to Last Sunday in October*
Time Zone: *21:30 (+9hrs 30mins UTC)*

[a]	[b]	[c]	[d]	[e]	[f]	[g]	[h]	[i]	[j]	[k]	[l]	[m]	[n]	[o]	[p]	[q]	[r]	[s]	[t]	[u]	[v]	[w]	[
21:31	22:31	23:31	00:31	01:31	02:31	03:31	04:31	05:31	06:31	07:31	08:31	09:31	10:31	11:31	12:31	13:31	14:31	15:31	16:31	17:31	18:31	19:31	20:
9^{31}_{pm}	10^{31}_{pm}	11^{31}_{pm}	12^{31}_{am}	1^{31}_{am}	2^{31}_{am}	3^{31}_{am}	4^{31}_{am}	5^{31}_{am}	6^{31}_{am}	7^{31}_{am}	8^{31}_{am}	9^{31}_{am}	10^{31}_{am}	11^{31}_{am}	12^{31}_{pm}	1^{31}_{pm}	2^{31}_{pm}	3^{31}_{pm}	4^{31}_{pm}	5^{31}_{pm}	6^{31}_{pm}	7^{31}_{pm}	8
Sun	Sun	Sun	Mon	Mon	Mon	Mon	Mon	Mon	Mon	Mon	Mon	Mon	Mon	Mon	Mon	Mon	Mon	Mon	Mon	Mon	Mon	Mon	M

Advanced Time
Period: *Last Sunday in October to First Sunday in March*
Time Zone: *22:30 (+10hrs 30mins UTC)*

[a]	[b]	[c]	[d]	[e]	[f]	[g]	[h]	[i]	[j]	[k]	[l]	[m]	[n]	[o]	[p]	[q]	[r]	[s]	[t]	[u]	[v]	[w]	[
22:31	23:31	00:31	01:31	02:31	03:31	04:31	05:31	06:31	07:31	08:31	09:31	10:31	11:31	12:31	13:31	14:31	15:31	16:31	17:31	18:31	19:31	20:31	21:
10^{31}_{pm}	11^{31}_{pm}	12^{31}_{am}	1^{31}_{am}	2^{31}_{am}	3^{31}_{am}	4^{31}_{am}	5^{31}_{am}	6^{31}_{am}	7^{31}_{am}	8^{31}_{am}	9^{31}_{am}	10^{31}_{am}	11^{31}_{am}	12^{31}_{pm}	1^{31}_{pm}	2^{31}_{pm}	3^{31}_{pm}	4^{31}_{pm}	5^{31}_{pm}	6^{31}_{pm}	7^{31}_{pm}	8^{31}_{pm}	9
Sun	Sun	Mon	Mon	Mon	Mon	Mon	Mon	Mon	Mon	Mon	Mon	Mon	Mon	Mon	Mon	Mon	Mon	Mon	Mon	Mon	Mon	Mon	M

NORTHERN TERRITORY
Standard Time: *Applicable for entire year*
Advanced Time: *Not observed*
Time Zone: *21:30 (+9hrs 30mins UTC)*

[a]	[b]	[c]	[d]	[e]	[f]	[g]	[h]	[i]	[j]	[k]	[l]	[m]	[n]	[o]	[p]	[q]	[r]	[s]	[t]	[u]	[v]	[w]	[
21:31	22:31	23:31	00:31	01:31	02:31	03:31	04:31	05:31	06:31	07:31	08:31	09:31	10:31	11:31	12:31	13:31	14:31	15:31	16:31	17:31	18:31	19:31	20:
9^{31}_{pm}	10^{31}_{pm}	11^{31}_{pm}	12^{31}_{am}	1^{31}_{am}	2^{31}_{am}	3^{31}_{am}	4^{31}_{am}	5^{31}_{am}	6^{31}_{am}	7^{31}_{am}	8^{31}_{am}	9^{31}_{am}	10^{31}_{am}	11^{31}_{am}	12^{31}_{pm}	1^{31}_{pm}	2^{31}_{pm}	3^{31}_{pm}	4^{31}_{pm}	5^{31}_{pm}	6^{31}_{pm}	7^{31}_{pm}	8
Sun	Sun	Sun	Mon	Mon	Mon	Mon	Mon	Mon	Mon	Mon	Mon	Mon	Mon	Mon	Mon	Mon	Mon	Mon	Mon	Mon	Mon	Mon	M

WESTERN AUSTRALIA
Standard Time: *Applicable for entire year*
Advanced Time: *Not observed*
Time Zone: *20:00 (+8hrs UTC)*

[a]	[b]	[c]	[d]	[e]	[f]	[g]	[h]	[i]	[j]	[k]	[l]	[m]	[n]	[o]	[p]	[q]	[r]	[s]	[t]	[u]	[v]	[w]	[
20:01	21:01	22:01	23:01	00:01	01:01	02:01	03:01	04:01	05:01	06:01	07:01	08:01	09:01	10:01	11:01	12:01	13:01	14:01	15:01	16:01	17:01	18:01	19:0
8^{01}_{pm}	9^{01}_{pm}	10^{01}_{pm}	11^{01}_{pm}	12^{01}_{am}	1^{01}_{am}	2^{01}_{am}	3^{01}_{am}	4^{01}_{am}	5^{01}_{am}	6^{01}_{am}	7^{01}_{am}	8^{01}_{am}	9^{01}_{am}	10^{01}_{am}	11^{01}_{am}	12^{01}_{pm}	1^{01}_{pm}	2^{01}_{pm}	3^{01}_{pm}	4^{01}_{pm}	5^{01}_{pm}	6^{01}_{pm}	7^{0}_{p}
Sun	Sun	Sun	Sun	Mon	Mon	Mon	Mon	Mon	Mon	Mon	Mon	Mon	Mon	Mon	Mon	Mon	Mon	Mon	Mon	Mon	Mon	Mon	Mo

Note: Advanced Time = Daylight Saving Time = Summer Time

BARBADOS
Number of Time Zones: *1*
Standard Time: *Applicable for the entire year*
Advanced Time: *Not observed*
Time Zone: *08:00 (-4hrs UTC)*

[a]	[b]	[c]	[d]	[e]	[f]	[g]	[h]	[i]	[j]	[k]	[l]	[m]	[n]	[o]	[p]	[q]	[r]	[s]	[t]	[u]	[v]	[w]	[x]
08:01	09:01	10:01	11:01	12:01	13:01	14:01	15:01	16:01	17:01	18:01	19:01	20:01	21:01	22:01	23:01	00:01	01:01	02:01	03:01	04:01	05:01	06:01	07:01
8^{01}_{am}	9^{01}_{am}	10^{01}_{am}	11^{01}_{am}	12^{01}_{pm}	1^{01}_{pm}	2^{01}_{pm}	3^{01}_{pm}	4^{01}_{pm}	5^{01}_{pm}	6^{01}_{pm}	7^{01}_{pm}	8^{01}_{pm}	9^{01}_{pm}	10^{01}_{pm}	11^{01}_{pm}	12^{01}_{am}	1^{01}_{am}	2^{01}_{am}	3^{01}_{am}	4^{01}_{am}	5^{01}_{am}	6^{01}_{am}	7^{01}_{am}
Sun	Sun	Sun	Sun	Sun	Sun	Sun	Sun	Sun	Sun	Sun	Sun	Sun	Sun	Sun	Sun	Mon	Mon	Mon	Mon	Mon	Mon	Mon	Mon

BARBUDA
Number of Time Zones: *1*
Standard Time: *Applicable for the entire year*
Advanced Time: *Not observed*
Time Zone: *08:00 (-4hrs UTC)*

[a]	[b]	[c]	[d]	[e]	[f]	[g]	[h]	[i]	[j]	[k]	[l]	[m]	[n]	[o]	[p]	[q]	[r]	[s]	[t]	[u]	[v]	[w]	[x]
08:01	09:01	10:01	11:01	12:01	13:01	14:01	15:01	16:01	17:01	18:01	19:01	20:01	21:01	22:01	23:01	00:01	01:01	02:01	03:01	04:01	05:01	06:01	07:01
8^{01}_{am}	9^{01}_{am}	10^{01}_{am}	11^{01}_{am}	12^{01}_{pm}	1^{01}_{pm}	2^{01}_{pm}	3^{01}_{pm}	4^{01}_{pm}	5^{01}_{pm}	6^{01}_{pm}	7^{01}_{pm}	8^{01}_{pm}	9^{01}_{pm}	10^{01}_{pm}	11^{01}_{pm}	12^{01}_{am}	1^{01}_{am}	2^{01}_{am}	3^{01}_{am}	4^{01}_{am}	5^{01}_{am}	6^{01}_{am}	7^{01}_{am}
Sun	Sun	Sun	Sun	Sun	Sun	Sun	Sun	Sun	Sun	Sun	Sun	Sun	Sun	Sun	Sun	Mon	Mon	Mon	Mon	Mon	Mon	Mon	Mon

BELGIUM
Number of Time Zones: *1*

Standard Time
Period: *Last Sunday in September to Last Sunday in March*
Time Zone: *13:00 (+1hr UTC)*

[a]	[b]	[c]	[d]	[e]	[f]	[g]	[h]	[i]	[j]	[k]	[l]	[m]	[n]	[o]	[p]	[q]	[r]	[s]	[t]	[u]	[v]	[w]	[x]
13:01	14:01	15:01	16:01	17:01	18:01	19:01	20:01	21:01	22:01	23:01	00:01	01:01	02:01	03:01	04:01	05:01	06:01	07:01	08:01	09:01	10:01	11:01	12:01
1^{01}_{pm}	2^{01}_{pm}	3^{01}_{pm}	4^{01}_{pm}	5^{01}_{pm}	6^{01}_{pm}	7^{01}_{pm}	8^{01}_{pm}	9^{01}_{pm}	10^{01}_{pm}	11^{01}_{pm}	12^{01}_{am}	1^{01}_{am}	2^{01}_{am}	3^{01}_{am}	4^{01}_{am}	5^{01}_{am}	6^{01}_{am}	7^{01}_{am}	8^{01}_{am}	9^{01}_{am}	10^{01}_{am}	11^{01}_{am}	12^{01}_{pm}
Sun	Sun	Sun	Sun	Sun	Sun	Sun	Sun	Sun	Sun	Sun	Mon	Mon	Mon	Mon	Mon	Mon	Mon	Mon	Mon	Mon	Mon	Mon	Mon

Advanced Time
Period: *Last Sunday in March to Last Sunday in September*
Time Zone: *14:00 (+2hrs UTC)*

[a]	[b]	[c]	[d]	[e]	[f]	[g]	[h]	[i]	[j]	[k]	[l]	[m]	[n]	[o]	[p]	[q]	[r]	[s]	[t]	[u]	[v]	[w]	[x]
14:01	15:01	16:01	17:01	18:01	19:01	20:01	21:01	22:01	23:01	00:01	01:01	02:01	03:01	04:01	05:01	06:01	07:01	08:01	09:01	10:01	11:01	12:01	13:01
2^{01}_{pm}	3^{01}_{pm}	4^{01}_{pm}	5^{01}_{pm}	6^{01}_{pm}	7^{01}_{pm}	8^{01}_{pm}	9^{01}_{pm}	10^{01}_{pm}	11^{01}_{pm}	12^{01}_{am}	1^{01}_{am}	2^{01}_{am}	3^{01}_{am}	4^{01}_{am}	5^{01}_{am}	6^{01}_{am}	7^{01}_{am}	8^{01}_{am}	9^{01}_{am}	10^{01}_{am}	11^{01}_{am}	12^{01}_{pm}	1^{01}_{pm}
Sun	Sun	Sun	Sun	Sun	Sun	Sun	Sun	Sun	Sun	Mon	Mon	Mon	Mon	Mon	Mon	Mon	Mon	Mon	Mon	Mon	Mon	Mon	Mon

Note: Advanced Time = Daylight Saving Time = Summer Time

BELIZE

Number of Time Zones: *1*
Standard Time: *Applicable for the entire year*
Advanced Time: *Not observed*
Time Zone: *06:00 (-6hrs UTC)*

[a]	[b]	[c]	[d]	[e]	[f]	[g]	[h]	[i]	[j]	[k]	[l]	[m]	[n]	[o]	[p]	[q]	[r]	[s]	[t]	[u]	[v]	[w]	[x]
06:01	07:01	08:01	09:01	10:01	11:01	12:01	13:01	14:01	15:01	16:01	17:01	18:01	19:01	20:01	21:01	22:01	23:01	00:01	01:01	02:01	03:01	04:01	05:01
6_{am}^{01}	7_{am}^{01}	8_{am}^{01}	9_{am}^{01}	10_{am}^{01}	11_{am}^{01}	12_{pm}^{01}	1_{pm}^{01}	2_{pm}^{01}	3_{pm}^{01}	4_{pm}^{01}	5_{pm}^{01}	6_{pm}^{01}	7_{pm}^{01}	8_{pm}^{01}	9_{pm}^{01}	10_{pm}^{01}	11_{pm}^{01}	12_{am}^{01}	1_{am}^{01}	2_{am}^{01}	3_{am}^{01}	4_{am}^{01}	5_{am}^{01}
Sun	Sun	Sun	Sun	Sun	Sun	Sun	Sun	Sun	Sun	Sun	Sun	Sun	Sun	Sun	Sun	Sun	Sun	Mon	Mon	Mon	Mon	Mon	Mon

BENIN

Number of Time Zones: *1*
Standard Time: *Applicable for the entire year*
Advanced Time: *Not observed*
Time Zone: *13:00 (+1hr UTC)*

[a]	[b]	[c]	[d]	[e]	[f]	[g]	[h]	[i]	[j]	[k]	[l]	[m]	[n]	[o]	[p]	[q]	[r]	[s]	[t]	[u]	[v]	[w]	[x]
13:01	14:01	15:01	16:01	17:01	18:01	19:01	20:01	21:01	22:01	23:01	00:01	01:01	02:01	03:01	04:01	05:01	06:01	07:01	08:01	09:01	10:01	11:01	12:01
1_{pm}^{01}	2_{pm}^{01}	3_{pm}^{01}	4_{pm}^{01}	5_{pm}^{01}	6_{pm}^{01}	7_{pm}^{01}	8_{pm}^{01}	9_{pm}^{01}	10_{pm}^{01}	11_{pm}^{01}	12_{am}^{01}	1_{am}^{01}	2_{am}^{01}	3_{am}^{01}	4_{am}^{01}	5_{am}^{01}	6_{am}^{01}	7_{am}^{01}	8_{am}^{01}	9_{am}^{01}	10_{am}^{01}	11_{am}^{01}	12_{pm}^{01}
Sun	Sun	Sun	Sun	Sun	Sun	Sun	Sun	Sun	Sun	Sun	Mon	Mon	Mon	Mon	Mon	Mon	Mon	Mon	Mon	Mon	Mon	Mon	Mon

BERMUDA

Number of Time Zones: *1*

Standard Time

Period: *Last Sunday in October to First Sunday in April*
Time Zone: *08:00 (-4hrs UTC)*

[a]	[b]	[c]	[d]	[e]	[f]	[g]	[h]	[i]	[j]	[k]	[l]	[m]	[n]	[o]	[p]	[q]	[r]	[s]	[t]	[u]	[v]	[w]	[x]
08:01	09:01	10:01	11:01	12:01	13:01	14:01	15:01	16:01	17:01	18:01	19:01	20:01	21:01	22:01	23:01	00:01	01:01	02:01	03:01	04:01	05:01	06:01	07:01
8_{am}^{01}	9_{am}^{01}	10_{am}^{01}	11_{am}^{01}	12_{pm}^{01}	1_{pm}^{01}	2_{pm}^{01}	3_{pm}^{01}	4_{pm}^{01}	5_{pm}^{01}	6_{pm}^{01}	7_{pm}^{01}	8_{pm}^{01}	9_{pm}^{01}	10_{pm}^{01}	11_{pm}^{01}	12_{am}^{01}	1_{am}^{01}	2_{am}^{01}	3_{am}^{01}	4_{am}^{01}	5_{am}^{01}	6_{am}^{01}	7_{am}^{01}
Sun	Sun	Sun	Sun	Sun	Sun	Sun	Sun	Sun	Sun	Sun	Sun	Sun	Sun	Sun	Sun	Mon	Mon	Mon	Mon	Mon	Mon	Mon	Mon

Advanced Time

Period: *First Sunday in April to Last Sunday in October*
Time Zone: *09:00 (-3hrs UTC)*

[a]	[b]	[c]	[d]	[e]	[f]	[g]	[h]	[i]	[j]	[k]	[l]	[m]	[n]	[o]	[p]	[q]	[r]	[s]	[t]	[u]	[v]	[w]	[x]
09:01	10:01	11:01	12:01	13:01	14:01	15:01	16:01	17:01	18:01	19:01	20:01	21:01	22:01	23:01	00:01	01:01	02:01	03:01	04:01	05:01	06:01	07:01	08:01
9_{am}^{01}	10_{am}^{01}	11_{am}^{01}	12_{pm}^{01}	1_{pm}^{01}	2_{pm}^{01}	3_{pm}^{01}	4_{pm}^{01}	5_{pm}^{01}	6_{pm}^{01}	7_{pm}^{01}	8_{pm}^{01}	9_{pm}^{01}	10_{pm}^{01}	11_{pm}^{01}	12_{am}^{01}	1_{am}^{01}	2_{am}^{01}	3_{am}^{01}	4_{am}^{01}	5_{am}^{01}	6_{am}^{01}	7_{am}^{01}	8_{am}^{01}
Sun	Sun	Sun	Sun	Sun	Sun	Sun	Sun	Sun	Sun	Sun	Sun	Sun	Sun	Sun	Mon	Mon	Mon	Mon	Mon	Mon	Mon	Mon	Mon

Note: Advanced Time = Daylight Saving Time = Summer Time

BHUTAN

Number of Time Zones: *1*
Standard Time: *Applicable for the entire year*
Advanced Time: *Not observed*
Time Zone: *18:00 (+6hrs UTC)*

[a]	[b]	[c]	[d]	[e]	[f]	[g]	[h]	[i]	[j]	[k]	[l]	[m]	[n]	[o]	[p]	[q]	[r]	[s]	[t]	[u]	[v]	[w]	[x]
:01	19:01	20:01	21:01	22:01	23:01	00:01	01:01	02:01	03:01	04:01	05:01	06:01	07:01	08:01	09:01	10:01	11:01	12:01	13:01	14:01	15:01	16:01	17:01
6^{01}_{pm}	7^{01}_{pm}	8^{01}_{pm}	9^{01}_{pm}	10^{01}_{pm}	11^{01}_{pm}	12^{01}_{am}	1^{01}_{am}	2^{01}_{am}	3^{01}_{am}	4^{01}_{am}	5^{01}_{am}	6^{01}_{am}	7^{01}_{am}	8^{01}_{am}	9^{01}_{am}	10^{01}_{am}	11^{01}_{am}	12^{01}_{pm}	1^{01}_{pm}	2^{01}_{pm}	3^{01}_{pm}	4^{01}_{pm}	5^{01}_{pm}
Sun	Sun	Sun	Sun	Sun	Sun	Mon	Mon	Mon	Mon	Mon	Mon	Mon	Mon	Mon	Mon	Mon	Mon	Mon	Mon	Mon	Mon	Mon	Mon

BOLIVIA

Number of Time Zones: *1*
Standard Time: *Applicable for the entire year*
Advanced Time: *Not observed*
Time Zone: *08:00 (-4hrs UTC)*

[a]	[b]	[c]	[d]	[e]	[f]	[g]	[h]	[i]	[j]	[k]	[l]	[m]	[n]	[o]	[p]	[q]	[r]	[s]	[t]	[u]	[v]	[w]	[x]
:01	09:01	10:01	11:01	12:01	13:01	14:01	15:01	16:01	17:01	18:01	19:01	20:01	21:01	22:01	23:01	00:01	01:01	02:01	03:01	04:01	05:01	06:01	07:01
8^{01}_{am}	9^{01}_{am}	10^{01}_{am}	11^{01}_{am}	12^{01}_{pm}	1^{01}_{pm}	2^{01}_{pm}	3^{01}_{pm}	4^{01}_{pm}	5^{01}_{pm}	6^{01}_{pm}	7^{01}_{pm}	8^{01}_{pm}	9^{01}_{pm}	10^{01}_{pm}	11^{01}_{pm}	12^{01}_{am}	1^{01}_{am}	2^{01}_{am}	3^{01}_{am}	4^{01}_{am}	5^{01}_{am}	6^{01}_{am}	7^{01}_{am}
Sun	Sun	Sun	Sun	Sun	Sun	Sun	Sun	Sun	Sun	Sun	Sun	Sun	Sun	Sun	Sun	Mon	Mon	Mon	Mon	Mon	Mon	Mon	Mon

BONAIRE

Number of Time Zones: *1*
Standard Time: *Applicable for the entire year*
Advanced Time: *Not observed*
Time Zone: *08:00 (-4hrs UTC)*

[a]	[b]	[c]	[d]	[e]	[f]	[g]	[h]	[i]	[j]	[k]	[l]	[m]	[n]	[o]	[p]	[q]	[r]	[s]	[t]	[u]	[v]	[w]	[x]
:01	09:01	10:01	11:01	12:01	13:01	14:01	15:01	16:01	17:01	18:01	19:01	20:01	21:01	22:01	23:01	00:01	01:01	02:01	03:01	04:01	05:01	06:01	07:01
8^{01}_{am}	9^{01}_{am}	10^{01}_{am}	11^{01}_{am}	12^{01}_{pm}	1^{01}_{pm}	2^{01}_{pm}	3^{01}_{pm}	4^{01}_{pm}	5^{01}_{pm}	6^{01}_{pm}	7^{01}_{pm}	8^{01}_{pm}	9^{01}_{pm}	10^{01}_{pm}	11^{01}_{pm}	12^{01}_{am}	1^{01}_{am}	2^{01}_{am}	3^{01}_{am}	4^{01}_{am}	5^{01}_{am}	6^{01}_{am}	7^{01}_{am}
Sun	Sun	Sun	Sun	Sun	Sun	Sun	Sun	Sun	Sun	Sun	Sun	Sun	Sun	Sun	Sun	Mon	Mon	Mon	Mon	Mon	Mon	Mon	Mon

BONIN ISLANDS

Number of Time Zones: *1*
Standard Time: *Applicable for the entire year*
Advanced Time: *Not observed*
Time Zone: *22:00 (+10hrs UTC)*

[a]	[b]	[c]	[d]	[e]	[f]	[g]	[h]	[i]	[j]	[k]	[l]	[m]	[n]	[o]	[p]	[q]	[r]	[s]	[t]	[u]	[v]	[w]	[x]
:01	23:01	00:01	01:01	02:01	03:01	04:01	05:01	06:01	07:01	08:01	09:01	10:01	11:01	12:01	13:01	14:01	15:01	16:01	17:01	18:01	19:01	20:01	21:01
10^{01}_{pm}	11^{01}_{pm}	12^{01}_{am}	1^{01}_{am}	2^{01}_{am}	3^{01}_{am}	4^{01}_{am}	5^{01}_{am}	6^{01}_{am}	7^{01}_{am}	8^{01}_{am}	9^{01}_{am}	10^{01}_{am}	11^{01}_{am}	12^{01}_{pm}	1^{01}_{pm}	2^{01}_{pm}	3^{01}_{pm}	4^{01}_{pm}	5^{01}_{pm}	6^{01}_{pm}	7^{01}_{pm}	8^{01}_{pm}	9^{01}_{pm}
Sun	Sun	Mon	Mon	Mon	Mon	Mon	Mon	Mon	Mon	Mon	Mon	Mon	Mon	Mon	Mon	Mon	Mon	Mon	Mon	Mon	Mon	Mon	Mon

Note: Advanced Time = Daylight Saving Time = Summer Time

BOTSWANA

Number of Time Zones: *1*
Standard Time: *Applicable for the entire year*
Advanced Time: *Not observed*
Time Zone: *14:00 (+2hrs UTC)*

[a]	[b]	[c]	[d]	[e]	[f]	[g]	[h]	[i]	[j]	[k]	[l]	[m]	[n]	[o]	[p]	[q]	[r]	[s]	[t]	[u]	[v]	[w]	[x]
14:01	15:01	16:01	17:01	18:01	19:01	20:01	21:01	22:01	23:01	00:01	01:01	02:01	03:01	04:01	05:01	06:01	07:01	08:01	09:01	10:01	11:01	12:01	13:0
2^{01}_{pm}	3^{01}_{pm}	4^{01}_{pm}	5^{01}_{pm}	6^{01}_{pm}	7^{01}_{pm}	8^{01}_{pm}	9^{01}_{pm}	10^{01}_{pm}	11^{01}_{pm}	12^{01}_{am}	1^{01}_{am}	2^{01}_{am}	3^{01}_{am}	4^{01}_{am}	5^{01}_{am}	6^{01}_{am}	7^{01}_{am}	8^{01}_{am}	9^{01}_{am}	10^{01}_{am}	11^{01}_{am}	12^{01}_{pm}	1^{0}_{p}
Sun	Sun	Sun	Sun	Sun	Sun	Sun	Sun	Sun	Sun	Mon	Mon	Mon	Mon	Mon	Mon	Mon	Mon	Mon	Mon	Mon	Mon	Mon	Mo

BRAZIL

Number of Time Zones: *3*
Notes: *Dates for changes between Standard and Advanced Times vary yearly*
See Reference Map I for graphic depiction of time zones

EASTERN TIME ZONE

Note: *Comprises the Federal District and all the seaboard states except the western half of Para*

Standard Time

Period: *Varies: March/April to Mid-October*
Time Zone: *09:00 (-3hrs UTC)*

[a]	[b]	[c]	[d]	[e]	[f]	[g]	[h]	[i]	[j]	[k]	[l]	[m]	[n]	[o]	[p]	[q]	[r]	[s]	[t]	[u]	[v]	[w]	[x]
09:01	10:01	11:01	12:01	13:01	14:01	15:01	16:01	17:01	18:01	19:01	20:01	21:01	22:01	23:01	00:01	01:01	02:01	03:01	04:01	05:01	06:01	07:01	08:0
9^{01}_{am}	10^{01}_{am}	11^{01}_{am}	12^{01}_{pm}	1^{01}_{pm}	2^{01}_{pm}	3^{01}_{pm}	4^{01}_{pm}	5^{01}_{pm}	6^{01}_{pm}	7^{01}_{pm}	8^{01}_{pm}	9^{01}_{pm}	10^{01}_{pm}	11^{01}_{pm}	12^{01}_{am}	1^{01}_{am}	2^{01}_{am}	3^{01}_{am}	4^{01}_{am}	5^{01}_{am}	6^{01}_{am}	7^{01}_{am}	8^{01}_{ar}
Sun	Sun	Sun	Sun	Sun	Sun	Sun	Sun	Sun	Sun	Sun	Sun	Sun	Sun	Sun	Sun	Mon	Mon	Mon	Mon	Mon	Mon	Mon	Mon	Mor

Advanced Time

Period: *Varies: Mid-October to March/April*
Time Zone: *10:00 (-2hrs UTC)*

[a]	[b]	[c]	[d]	[e]	[f]	[g]	[h]	[i]	[j]	[k]	[l]	[m]	[n]	[o]	[p]	[q]	[r]	[s]	[t]	[u]	[v]	[w]	[x]
10:01	11:01	12:01	13:01	14:01	15:01	16:01	17:01	18:01	19:01	20:01	21:01	22:01	23:01	00:01	01:01	02:01	03:01	04:01	05:01	06:01	07:01	08:01	09:01
10^{01}_{am}	11^{01}_{am}	12^{01}_{pm}	1^{01}_{pm}	2^{01}_{pm}	3^{01}_{pm}	4^{01}_{pm}	5^{01}_{pm}	6^{01}_{pm}	7^{01}_{pm}	8^{01}_{pm}	9^{01}_{pm}	10^{01}_{pm}	11^{01}_{pm}	12^{01}_{am}	1^{01}_{am}	2^{01}_{am}	3^{01}_{am}	4^{01}_{am}	5^{01}_{am}	6^{01}_{am}	7^{01}_{am}	8^{01}_{am}	9^{01}_{am}
Sun	Sun	Sun	Sun	Sun	Sun	Sun	Sun	Sun	Sun	Sun	Sun	Sun	Sun	Sun	Mon	Mon	Mon	Mon	Mon	Mon	Mon	Mon	Mon

Note: Advanced Time = Daylight Saving Time = Summer Time

BRAZIL *(Continued)*

CENTRAL TIME ZONE

Note: *Comprises western half of Para and the central states (Amazon Valley) except the western sixth of Amazonas*

Standard Time

Period: *Varies: March/April to Mid-October*
Time Zone: *08:00 (-4hrs UTC)*

[a]	[b]	[c]	[d]	[e]	[f]	[g]	[h]	[i]	[j]	[k]	[l]	[m]	[n]	[o]	[p]	[q]	[r]	[s]	[t]	[u]	[v]	[w]	[x]
08:01	09:01	10:01	11:01	12:01	13:01	14:01	15:01	16:01	17:01	18:01	19:01	20:01	21:01	22:01	23:01	00:01	01:01	02:01	03:01	04:01	05:01	06:01	07:01
8^{01}_{am}	9^{01}_{am}	10^{01}_{am}	11^{01}_{am}	12^{01}_{pm}	1^{01}_{pm}	2^{01}_{pm}	3^{01}_{pm}	4^{01}_{pm}	5^{01}_{pm}	6^{01}_{pm}	7^{01}_{pm}	8^{01}_{pm}	9^{01}_{pm}	10^{01}_{pm}	11^{01}_{pm}	12^{01}_{am}	1^{01}_{am}	2^{01}_{am}	3^{01}_{am}	4^{01}_{am}	5^{01}_{am}	6^{01}_{am}	7^{01}_{am}
Sun	Sun	Sun	Sun	Sun	Sun	Sun	Sun	Sun	Sun	Sun	Sun	Sun	Sun	Sun	Sun	Sun	Mon	Mon	Mon	Mon	Mon	Mon	Mon

Advanced Time

Period: *Varies: Mid-October to March/April*
Time Zone: *09:00 (-3hrs UTC)*

[a]	[b]	[c]	[d]	[e]	[f]	[g]	[h]	[i]	[j]	[k]	[l]	[m]	[n]	[o]	[p]	[q]	[r]	[s]	[t]	[u]	[v]	[w]	[x]
09:01	10:01	11:01	12:01	13:01	14:01	15:01	16:01	17:01	18:01	19:01	20:01	21:01	22:01	23:01	00:01	01:01	02:01	03:01	04:01	05:01	06:01	07:01	08:01
9^{01}_{am}	10^{01}_{am}	11^{01}_{am}	12^{01}_{pm}	1^{01}_{pm}	2^{01}_{pm}	3^{01}_{pm}	4^{01}_{pm}	5^{01}_{pm}	6^{01}_{pm}	7^{01}_{pm}	8^{01}_{pm}	9^{01}_{pm}	10^{01}_{pm}	11^{01}_{pm}	12^{01}_{am}	1^{01}_{am}	2^{01}_{am}	3^{01}_{am}	4^{01}_{am}	5^{01}_{am}	6^{01}_{am}	7^{01}_{am}	8^{01}_{am}
Sun	Sun	Sun	Sun	Sun	Sun	Sun	Sun	Sun	Sun	Sun	Sun	Sun	Sun	Sun	Sun	Mon	Mon	Mon	Mon	Mon	Mon	Mon	Mon

WESTERN TIME ZONE

Note: *Comprises western sixth of Amazonas and the state of Acre*

Standard Time

Period: *Varies: March/April to Mid-October*
Time Zone: *07:00 (-5hrs UTC)*

[a]	[b]	[c]	[d]	[e]	[f]	[g]	[h]	[i]	[j]	[k]	[l]	[m]	[n]	[o]	[p]	[q]	[r]	[s]	[t]	[u]	[v]	[w]	[x]
07:01	08:01	09:01	10:01	11:01	12:01	13:01	14:01	15:01	16:01	17:01	18:01	19:01	20:01	21:01	22:01	23:01	00:01	01:01	02:01	03:01	04:01	05:01	06:01
7^{01}_{am}	8^{01}_{am}	9^{01}_{am}	10^{01}_{am}	11^{01}_{am}	12^{01}_{pm}	1^{01}_{pm}	2^{01}_{pm}	3^{01}_{pm}	4^{01}_{pm}	5^{01}_{pm}	6^{01}_{pm}	7^{01}_{pm}	8^{01}_{pm}	9^{01}_{pm}	10^{01}_{pm}	11^{01}_{pm}	12^{01}_{am}	1^{01}_{am}	2^{01}_{am}	3^{01}_{am}	4^{01}_{am}	5^{01}_{am}	6^{01}_{am}
Sun	Sun	Sun	Sun	Sun	Sun	Sun	Sun	Sun	Sun	Sun	Sun	Sun	Sun	Sun	Sun	Sun	Mon	Mon	Mon	Mon	Mon	Mon	Mon

Advanced Time

Period: *Varies: Mid-October to March/April*
Time Zone: *08:00 (-4hrs UTC)*

[a]	[b]	[c]	[d]	[e]	[f]	[g]	[h]	[i]	[j]	[k]	[l]	[m]	[n]	[o]	[p]	[q]	[r]	[s]	[t]	[u]	[v]	[w]	[x]
08:01	09:01	10:01	11:01	12:01	13:01	14:01	15:01	16:01	17:01	18:01	19:01	20:01	21:01	22:01	23:01	00:01	01:01	02:01	03:01	04:01	05:01	06:01	07:01
8^{01}_{am}	9^{01}_{am}	10^{01}_{am}	11^{01}_{am}	12^{01}_{pm}	1^{01}_{pm}	2^{01}_{pm}	3^{01}_{pm}	4^{01}_{pm}	5^{01}_{pm}	6^{01}_{pm}	7^{01}_{pm}	8^{01}_{pm}	9^{01}_{pm}	10^{01}_{pm}	11^{01}_{pm}	12^{01}_{am}	1^{01}_{am}	2^{01}_{am}	3^{01}_{am}	4^{01}_{am}	5^{01}_{am}	6^{01}_{am}	7^{01}_{am}
Sun	Sun	Sun	Sun	Sun	Sun	Sun	Sun	Sun	Sun	Sun	Sun	Sun	Sun	Sun	Sun	Sun	Mon	Mon	Mon	Mon	Mon	Mon	Mon

Note: Advanced Time = Daylight Saving Time = Summer Time

BRUNEI
Number of Time Zones: *1*
Standard Time: *Applicable for the entire year*
Advanced Time: *Not observed*
Time Zone: *20:00 (+8hrs UTC)*

[a]	[b]	[c]	[d]	[e]	[f]	[g]	[h]	[i]	[j]	[k]	[l]	[m]	[n]	[o]	[p]	[q]	[r]	[s]	[t]	[u]	[v]	[w]	[x]
20:01	21:01	22:01	23:01	00:01	01:01	02:01	03:01	04:01	05:01	06:01	07:01	08:01	09:01	10:01	11:01	12:01	13:01	14:01	15:01	16:01	17:01	18:01	19:01
8^{01}_{pm}	9^{01}_{pm}	10^{01}_{pm}	11^{01}_{pm}	12^{01}_{am}	1^{01}_{am}	2^{01}_{am}	3^{01}_{am}	4^{01}_{am}	5^{01}_{am}	6^{01}_{am}	7^{01}_{am}	8^{01}_{am}	9^{01}_{am}	10^{01}_{am}	11^{01}_{am}	12^{01}_{pm}	1^{01}_{pm}	2^{01}_{pm}	3^{01}_{pm}	4^{01}_{pm}	5^{01}_{pm}	6^{01}_{pm}	7^{01}_{pm}
Sun	Sun	Sun	Sun	Mon	Mon	Mon	Mon	Mon	Mon	Mon	Mon	Mon	Mon	Mon	Mon	Mon	Mon	Mon	Mon	Mon	Mon	Mon	Mon

BULGARIA
Number of Time Zones: *1*

Standard Time
Period: *Last Sunday in September to Last Sunday in March*
Time Zone: *14:00 (+2hrs UTC)*

[a]	[b]	[c]	[d]	[e]	[f]	[g]	[h]	[i]	[j]	[k]	[l]	[m]	[n]	[o]	[p]	[q]	[r]	[s]	[t]	[u]	[v]	[w]	[x]
14:01	15:01	16:01	17:01	18:01	19:01	20:01	21:01	22:01	23:01	00:01	01:01	02:01	03:01	04:01	05:01	06:01	07:01	08:01	09:01	10:01	11:01	12:01	13:01
2^{01}_{pm}	3^{01}_{pm}	4^{01}_{pm}	5^{01}_{pm}	6^{01}_{pm}	7^{01}_{pm}	8^{01}_{pm}	9^{01}_{pm}	10^{01}_{pm}	11^{01}_{pm}	12^{01}_{am}	1^{01}_{am}	2^{01}_{am}	3^{01}_{am}	4^{01}_{am}	5^{01}_{am}	6^{01}_{am}	7^{01}_{am}	8^{01}_{am}	9^{01}_{am}	10^{01}_{am}	11^{01}_{am}	12^{01}_{pm}	1^{01}_{pm}
Sun	Sun	Sun	Sun	Sun	Sun	Sun	Sun	Sun	Sun	Mon	Mon	Mon	Mon	Mon	Mon	Mon	Mon	Mon	Mon	Mon	Mon	Mon	Mon

Advanced Time
Period: *Last Sunday in March to Last Sunday in September*
Time Zone: *15:00 (+3hrs UTC)*

[a]	[b]	[c]	[d]	[e]	[f]	[g]	[h]	[i]	[j]	[k]	[l]	[m]	[n]	[o]	[p]	[q]	[r]	[s]	[t]	[u]	[v]	[w]	[x]
15:01	16:01	17:01	18:01	19:01	20:01	21:01	22:01	23:01	00:01	01:01	02:01	03:01	04:01	05:01	06:01	07:01	08:01	09:01	10:01	11:01	12:01	13:01	14:01
3^{01}_{pm}	4^{01}_{pm}	5^{01}_{pm}	6^{01}_{pm}	7^{01}_{pm}	8^{01}_{pm}	9^{01}_{pm}	10^{01}_{pm}	11^{01}_{pm}	12^{01}_{am}	1^{01}_{am}	2^{01}_{am}	3^{01}_{am}	4^{01}_{am}	5^{01}_{am}	6^{01}_{am}	7^{01}_{am}	8^{01}_{am}	9^{01}_{am}	10^{01}_{am}	11^{01}_{am}	12^{01}_{pm}	1^{01}_{pm}	2^{01}_{pm}
Sun	Sun	Sun	Sun	Sun	Sun	Sun	Sun	Sun	Mon	Mon	Mon	Mon	Mon	Mon	Mon	Mon	Mon	Mon	Mon	Mon	Mon	Mon	Mon

BURKINA
Number of Time Zones: *1*
Standard Time: *Applicable for the entire year*
Advanced Time: *Not observed*
Time Zone: *12:00 (UTC)*

[a]	[b]	[c]	[d]	[e]	[f]	[g]	[h]	[i]	[j]	[k]	[l]	[m]	[n]	[o]	[p]	[q]	[r]	[s]	[t]	[u]	[v]	[w]	[x]
12:01	13:01	14:01	15:01	16:01	17:01	18:01	19:01	20:01	21:01	22:01	23:01	00:01	01:01	02:01	03:01	04:01	05:01	06:01	07:01	08:01	09:01	10:01	11:01
12^{01}_{pm}	1^{01}_{pm}	2^{01}_{pm}	3^{01}_{pm}	4^{01}_{pm}	5^{01}_{pm}	6^{01}_{pm}	7^{01}_{pm}	8^{01}_{pm}	9^{01}_{pm}	10^{01}_{pm}	11^{01}_{pm}	12^{01}_{am}	1^{01}_{am}	2^{01}_{am}	3^{01}_{am}	4^{01}_{am}	5^{01}_{am}	6^{01}_{am}	7^{01}_{am}	8^{01}_{am}	9^{01}_{am}	10^{01}_{am}	11^{01}_{am}
Sun	Sun	Sun	Sun	Sun	Sun	Sun	Sun	Sun	Sun	Sun	Sun	Mon	Mon	Mon	Mon	Mon	Mon	Mon	Mon	Mon	Mon	Mon	Mon

Note: Advanced Time = Daylight Saving Time = Summer Time

BURMA

Number of Time Zones: *1*
Standard Time: *Applicable for the entire year*
Advanced Time: *Not observed*
Time Zone: *18:30 (+6hrs 30mins UTC)*

[a]	[b]	[c]	[d]	[e]	[f]	[g]	[h]	[i]	[j]	[k]	[l]	[m]	[n]	[o]	[p]	[q]	[r]	[s]	[t]	[u]	[v]	[w]	[x]
18:31	19:31	20:31	21:31	22:31	23:31	00:31	01:31	02:31	03:31	04:31	05:31	06:31	07:31	08:31	09:31	10:31	11:31	12:31	13:31	14:31	15:31	16:31	17:31
6^{31}_{pm}	7^{31}_{pm}	8^{31}_{pm}	9^{31}_{pm}	10^{31}_{pm}	11^{31}_{pm}	12^{31}_{am}	1^{31}_{am}	2^{31}_{am}	3^{31}_{am}	4^{31}_{am}	5^{31}_{am}	6^{31}_{am}	7^{31}_{am}	8^{31}_{am}	9^{31}_{am}	10^{31}_{am}	11^{31}_{am}	12^{31}_{pm}	1^{31}_{pm}	2^{31}_{pm}	3^{31}_{pm}	4^{31}_{pm}	5^{31}_{pm}
Sun	Sun	Sun	Sun	Sun	Sun	Mon	Mon	Mon	Mon	Mon	Mon	Mon	Mon	Mon	Mon	Mon	Mon	Mon	Mon	Mon	Mon	Mon	Mon

BURUNDI

Number of Time Zones: *1*
Standard Time: *Applicable for the entire year*
Advanced Time: *Not observed*
Time Zone: *14:00 (+2hrs UTC)*

[a]	[b]	[c]	[d]	[e]	[f]	[g]	[h]	[i]	[j]	[k]	[l]	[m]	[n]	[o]	[p]	[q]	[r]	[s]	[t]	[u]	[v]	[w]	[x]
14:01	15:01	16:01	17:01	18:01	19:01	20:01	21:01	22:01	23:01	00:01	01:01	02:01	03:01	04:01	05:01	06:01	07:01	08:01	09:01	10:01	11:01	12:01	13:01
2^{01}_{pm}	3^{01}_{pm}	4^{01}_{pm}	5^{01}_{pm}	6^{01}_{pm}	7^{01}_{pm}	8^{01}_{pm}	9^{01}_{pm}	10^{01}_{pm}	11^{01}_{pm}	12^{01}_{am}	1^{01}_{am}	2^{01}_{am}	3^{01}_{am}	4^{01}_{am}	5^{01}_{am}	6^{01}_{am}	7^{01}_{am}	8^{01}_{am}	9^{01}_{am}	10^{01}_{am}	11^{01}_{am}	12^{01}_{pm}	1^{01}_{pm}
Sun	Sun	Sun	Sun	Sun	Sun	Sun	Sun	Sun	Sun	Mon	Mon	Mon	Mon	Mon	Mon	Mon	Mon	Mon	Mon	Mon	Mon	Mon	Mon

CAMBODIA

Number of Time Zones: *1*
Standard Time: *Applicable for the entire year*
Advanced Time: *Not observed*
Time Zone: *19:00 (+7hrs UTC)*

[a]	[b]	[c]	[d]	[e]	[f]	[g]	[h]	[i]	[j]	[k]	[l]	[m]	[n]	[o]	[p]	[q]	[r]	[s]	[t]	[u]	[v]	[w]	[x]
19:01	20:01	21:01	22:01	23:01	00:01	01:01	02:01	03:01	04:01	05:01	06:01	07:01	08:01	09:01	10:01	11:01	12:01	13:01	14:01	15:01	16:01	17:01	18:01
7^{01}_{pm}	8^{01}_{pm}	9^{01}_{pm}	10^{01}_{pm}	11^{01}_{pm}	12^{01}_{am}	1^{01}_{am}	2^{01}_{am}	3^{01}_{am}	4^{01}_{am}	5^{01}_{am}	6^{01}_{am}	7^{01}_{am}	8^{01}_{am}	9^{01}_{am}	10^{01}_{am}	11^{01}_{am}	12^{01}_{pm}	1^{01}_{pm}	2^{01}_{pm}	3^{01}_{pm}	4^{01}_{pm}	5^{01}_{pm}	6^{01}_{pm}
Sun	Sun	Sun	Sun	Sun	Mon	Mon	Mon	Mon	Mon	Mon	Mon	Mon	Mon	Mon	Mon	Mon	Mon	Mon	Mon	Mon	Mon	Mon	Mon

CAMEROON

Number of Time Zones: *1*
Standard Time: *Applicable for the entire year*
Advanced Time: *Not observed*
Time Zone: *13:00 (+1hr UTC)*

[a]	[b]	[c]	[d]	[e]	[f]	[g]	[h]	[i]	[j]	[k]	[l]	[m]	[n]	[o]	[p]	[q]	[r]	[s]	[t]	[u]	[v]	[w]	[x]
13:01	14:01	15:01	16:01	17:01	18:01	19:01	20:01	21:01	22:01	23:01	00:01	01:01	02:01	03:01	04:01	05:01	06:01	07:01	08:01	09:01	10:01	11:01	12:01
1^{01}_{pm}	2^{01}_{pm}	3^{01}_{pm}	4^{01}_{pm}	5^{01}_{pm}	6^{01}_{pm}	7^{01}_{pm}	8^{01}_{pm}	9^{01}_{pm}	10^{01}_{pm}	11^{01}_{pm}	12^{01}_{am}	1^{01}_{am}	2^{01}_{am}	3^{01}_{am}	4^{01}_{am}	5^{01}_{am}	6^{01}_{am}	7^{01}_{am}	8^{01}_{am}	9^{01}_{am}	10^{01}_{am}	11^{01}_{am}	12^{01}_{pm}
Sun	Sun	Sun	Sun	Sun	Sun	Sun	Sun	Sun	Sun	Sun	Mon	Mon	Mon	Mon	Mon	Mon	Mon	Mon	Mon	Mon	Mon	Mon	Mon

Note: Advanced Time = Daylight Saving Time = Summer Time

CANADA
Number of Time Zones: *6*
Notes: *Advanced Time observed*

NEWFOUNDLAND TIME ZONE
Note: *Comprises the island of Newfoundland*

Standard Time
Period: *Last Sunday in October to Last Sunday in April*
Time Zone: *08:30 (-3hrs 30mins UTC)*

[a]	[b]	[c]	[d]	[e]	[f]	[g]	[h]	[i]	[j]	[k]	[l]	[m]	[n]	[o]	[p]	[q]	[r]	[s]	[t]	[u]	[v]	[w]	[x]
08:31	09:31	10:31	11:31	12:31	13:31	14:31	15:31	16:31	17:31	18:31	19:31	20:31	21:31	22:31	23:31	00:31	01:31	02:31	03:31	04:31	05:31	06:31	07:3
8^{31}_{am}	9^{31}_{am}	10^{31}_{am}	11^{31}_{am}	12^{31}_{pm}	1^{31}_{pm}	2^{31}_{pm}	3^{31}_{pm}	4^{31}_{pm}	5^{31}_{pm}	6^{31}_{pm}	7^{31}_{pm}	8^{31}_{pm}	9^{31}_{pm}	10^{31}_{pm}	11^{31}_{pm}	12^{31}_{am}	1^{31}_{am}	2^{31}_{am}	3^{31}_{am}	4^{31}_{am}	5^{31}_{am}	6^{31}_{am}	7^{3}_{a}
Sun	Sun	Sun	Sun	Sun	Sun	Sun	Sun	Sun	Sun	Sun	Sun	Sun	Sun	Sun	Sun	Sun	Mon	Mon	Mon	Mon	Mon	Mon	Mo

Advanced Time
Period: *Last Sunday in April to Last Sunday in October*
Time Zone: *10:30 (-1hr 30mins UTC)*

[a]	[b]	[c]	[d]	[e]	[f]	[g]	[h]	[i]	[j]	[k]	[l]	[m]	[n]	[o]	[p]	[q]	[r]	[s]	[t]	[u]	[v]	[w]	[x]
10:31	11:31	12:31	13:31	14:31	15:31	16:31	17:31	18:31	19:31	20:31	21:31	22:31	23:31	00:31	01:31	02:31	03:31	04:31	05:31	06:31	07:31	08:31	09:3
10^{31}_{am}	11^{31}_{am}	12^{31}_{pm}	1^{31}_{pm}	2^{31}_{pm}	3^{31}_{pm}	4^{31}_{pm}	5^{31}_{pm}	6^{31}_{pm}	7^{31}_{pm}	8^{31}_{pm}	9^{31}_{pm}	10^{31}_{pm}	11^{31}_{pm}	12^{31}_{am}	1^{31}_{am}	2^{31}_{am}	3^{31}_{am}	4^{31}_{am}	5^{31}_{am}	6^{31}_{am}	7^{31}_{am}	8^{31}_{am}	9^{3}_{a}
Sun	Sun	Sun	Sun	Sun	Sun	Sun	Sun	Sun	Sun	Sun	Sun	Sun	Sun	Sun	Mon	Mon	Mon	Mon	Mon	Mon	Mon	Mon	Mon

ATLANTIC TIME ZONE
Note: *Comprises Nova Scotia, New Brunswick, Prince Edward Island, Labrador, and the far eastern portions of Quebec and Northwest Territories*

Standard Time
Period: *Last Sunday in October to Last Sunday in April*
Time Zone: *08:00 (-4hrs UTC)*

[a]	[b]	[c]	[d]	[e]	[f]	[g]	[h]	[i]	[j]	[k]	[l]	[m]	[n]	[o]	[p]	[q]	[r]	[s]	[t]	[u]	[v]	[w]	[x]
08:01	09:01	10:01	11:01	12:01	13:01	14:01	15:01	16:01	17:01	18:01	19:01	20:01	21:01	22:01	23:01	00:01	01:01	02:01	03:01	04:01	05:01	06:01	07:01
8^{01}_{am}	9^{01}_{am}	10^{01}_{am}	11^{01}_{am}	12^{01}_{pm}	1^{01}_{pm}	2^{01}_{pm}	3^{01}_{pm}	4^{01}_{pm}	5^{01}_{pm}	6^{01}_{pm}	7^{01}_{pm}	8^{01}_{pm}	9^{01}_{pm}	10^{01}_{pm}	11^{01}_{pm}	12^{01}_{am}	1^{01}_{am}	2^{01}_{am}	3^{01}_{am}	4^{01}_{am}	5^{01}_{am}	6^{01}_{am}	7^{01}_{am}
Sun	Sun	Sun	Sun	Sun	Sun	Sun	Sun	Sun	Sun	Sun	Sun	Sun	Sun	Sun	Sun	Sun	Mon	Mon	Mon	Mon	Mon	Mon	Mon

Advanced Time
Period: *Last Sunday in April to Last Sunday in October*
Time Zone: *09:00 (-3hrs UTC)*

[a]	[b]	[c]	[d]	[e]	[f]	[g]	[h]	[i]	[j]	[k]	[l]	[m]	[n]	[o]	[p]	[q]	[r]	[s]	[t]	[u]	[v]	[w]	[x]
09:01	10:01	11:01	12:01	13:01	14:01	15:01	16:01	17:01	18:01	19:01	20:01	21:01	22:01	23:01	00:01	01:01	02:01	03:01	04:01	05:01	06:01	07:01	08:01
9^{01}_{am}	10^{01}_{am}	11^{01}_{am}	12^{01}_{pm}	1^{01}_{pm}	2^{01}_{pm}	3^{01}_{pm}	4^{01}_{pm}	5^{01}_{pm}	6^{01}_{pm}	7^{01}_{pm}	8^{01}_{pm}	9^{01}_{pm}	10^{01}_{pm}	11^{01}_{pm}	12^{01}_{am}	1^{01}_{am}	2^{01}_{am}	3^{01}_{am}	4^{01}_{am}	5^{01}_{am}	6^{01}_{am}	7^{01}_{am}	8^{01}_{am}
Sun	Sun	Sun	Sun	Sun	Sun	Sun	Sun	Sun	Sun	Sun	Sun	Sun	Sun	Sun	Mon	Mon	Mon	Mon	Mon	Mon	Mon	Mon	Mon

Note: Advanced Time = Daylight Saving Time = Summer Time

CANADA *(Continued)*

EASTERN TIME ZONE

Note: *Comprises most of Quebec, eastern half of Ontario, and part of Northwest Territories*

Standard Time

Period: *Last Sunday in October to Last Sunday in April*
Time Zone: *07:00 (-5hrs UTC)*

[a]	[b]	[c]	[d]	[e]	[f]	[g]	[h]	[i]	[j]	[k]	[l]	[m]	[n]	[o]	[p]	[q]	[r]	[s]	[t]	[u]	[v]	[w]	[x]
07:01	08:01	09:01	10:01	11:01	12:01	13:01	14:01	15:01	16:01	17:01	18:01	19:01	20:01	21:01	22:01	23:01	00:01	01:01	02:01	03:01	04:01	05:01	06:01
7^{01}_{am}	8^{01}_{am}	9^{01}_{am}	10^{01}_{am}	11^{01}_{am}	12^{01}_{pm}	1^{01}_{pm}	2^{01}_{pm}	3^{01}_{pm}	4^{01}_{pm}	5^{01}_{pm}	6^{01}_{pm}	7^{01}_{pm}	8^{01}_{pm}	9^{01}_{pm}	10^{01}_{pm}	11^{01}_{pm}	12^{01}_{am}	1^{01}_{am}	2^{01}_{am}	3^{01}_{am}	4^{01}_{am}	5^{01}_{am}	6^{01}_{am}
Sun	Sun	Sun	Sun	Sun	Sun	Sun	Sun	Sun	Sun	Sun	Sun	Sun	Sun	Sun	Sun	Sun	Mon	Mon	Mon	Mon	Mon	Mon	Mon

Advanced Time

Period: *Last Sunday in April to Last Sunday in October*
Time Zone: *08:00 (-4hrs UTC)*

[a]	[b]	[c]	[d]	[e]	[f]	[g]	[h]	[i]	[j]	[k]	[l]	[m]	[n]	[o]	[p]	[q]	[r]	[s]	[t]	[u]	[v]	[w]	[x]
08:01	09:01	10:01	11:01	12:01	13:01	14:01	15:01	16:01	17:01	18:01	19:01	20:01	21:01	22:01	23:01	00:01	01:01	02:01	03:01	04:01	05:01	06:01	07:01
8^{01}_{am}	9^{01}_{am}	10^{01}_{am}	11^{01}_{am}	12^{01}_{pm}	1^{01}_{pm}	2^{01}_{pm}	3^{01}_{pm}	4^{01}_{pm}	5^{01}_{pm}	6^{01}_{pm}	7^{01}_{pm}	8^{01}_{pm}	9^{01}_{pm}	10^{01}_{pm}	11^{01}_{pm}	12^{01}_{am}	1^{01}_{am}	2^{01}_{am}	3^{01}_{am}	4^{01}_{am}	5^{01}_{am}	6^{01}_{am}	7^{01}_{am}
Sun	Sun	Sun	Sun	Sun	Sun	Sun	Sun	Sun	Sun	Sun	Sun	Sun	Sun	Sun	Sun	Mon	Mon	Mon	Mon	Mon	Mon	Mon	Mon

CENTRAL TIME ZONE

Note: *Comprises western half of Ontario, all of Manitoba, southern and northeastern parts of Saskatchewan, and part of Northwest Territories*

Standard Time

Period: *Last Sunday in October to Last Sunday in April*
Time Zone: *06:00 (-6hrs UTC)*

[a]	[b]	[c]	[d]	[e]	[f]	[g]	[h]	[i]	[j]	[k]	[l]	[m]	[n]	[o]	[p]	[q]	[r]	[s]	[t]	[u]	[v]	[w]	[x]
06:01	07:01	08:01	09:01	10:01	11:01	12:01	13:01	14:01	15:01	16:01	17:01	18:01	19:01	20:01	21:01	22:01	23:01	00:01	01:01	02:01	03:01	04:01	05:01
6^{01}_{am}	7^{01}_{am}	8^{01}_{am}	9^{01}_{am}	10^{01}_{am}	11^{01}_{am}	12^{01}_{pm}	1^{01}_{pm}	2^{01}_{pm}	3^{01}_{pm}	4^{01}_{pm}	5^{01}_{pm}	6^{01}_{pm}	7^{01}_{pm}	8^{01}_{pm}	9^{01}_{pm}	10^{01}_{pm}	11^{01}_{pm}	12^{01}_{am}	1^{01}_{am}	2^{01}_{am}	3^{01}_{am}	4^{01}_{am}	5^{01}_{am}
Sun	Sun	Sun	Sun	Sun	Sun	Sun	Sun	Sun	Sun	Sun	Sun	Sun	Sun	Sun	Sun	Sun	Sun	Mon	Mon	Mon	Mon	Mon	Mon

Advanced Time

Period: *Last Sunday in April to Last Sunday in October*
Time Zone: *07:00 (-5hrs UTC)*

[a]	[b]	[c]	[d]	[e]	[f]	[g]	[h]	[i]	[j]	[k]	[l]	[m]	[n]	[o]	[p]	[q]	[r]	[s]	[t]	[u]	[v]	[w]	[x]
07:01	08:01	09:01	10:01	11:01	12:01	13:01	14:01	15:01	16:01	17:01	18:01	19:01	20:01	21:01	22:01	23:01	00:01	01:01	02:01	03:01	04:01	05:01	06:01
7^{01}_{am}	8^{01}_{am}	9^{01}_{am}	10^{01}_{am}	11^{01}_{am}	12^{01}_{pm}	1^{01}_{pm}	2^{01}_{pm}	3^{01}_{pm}	4^{01}_{pm}	5^{01}_{pm}	6^{01}_{pm}	7^{01}_{pm}	8^{01}_{pm}	9^{01}_{pm}	10^{01}_{pm}	11^{01}_{pm}	12^{01}_{am}	1^{01}_{am}	2^{01}_{am}	3^{01}_{am}	4^{01}_{am}	5^{01}_{am}	6^{01}_{am}
Sun	Sun	Sun	Sun	Sun	Sun	Sun	Sun	Sun	Sun	Sun	Sun	Sun	Sun	Sun	Sun	Sun	Mon	Mon	Mon	Mon	Mon	Mon	Mon

Note: Advanced Time = Daylight Saving Time = Summer Time

CANADA *(Continued)*

MOUNTAIN TIME ZONE
Note: *Comprises the northwest part of Saskatchewan, all of Alberta, northeastern part of British Columbia, and western half of Northwest Territories*

Standard Time
Period: *Last Sunday in October to Last Sunday in April*
Time Zone: *05:00 (-7hrs UTC)*

[a]	[b]	[c]	[d]	[e]	[f]	[g]	[h]	[i]	[j]	[k]	[l]	[m]	[n]	[o]	[p]	[q]	[r]	[s]	[t]	[u]	[v]	[w]
05:01	06:01	07:01	08:01	09:01	10:01	11:01	12:01	13:01	14:01	15:01	16:01	17:01	18:01	19:01	20:01	21:01	22:01	23:01	00:01	01:01	02:01	03:01	04
5^{01}_{am}	6^{01}_{am}	7^{01}_{am}	8^{01}_{am}	9^{01}_{am}	10^{01}_{am}	11^{01}_{am}	12^{01}_{pm}	1^{01}_{pm}	2^{01}_{pm}	3^{01}_{pm}	4^{01}_{pm}	5^{01}_{pm}	6^{01}_{pm}	7^{01}_{pm}	8^{01}_{pm}	9^{01}_{pm}	10^{01}_{pm}	11^{01}_{pm}	12^{01}_{am}	1^{01}_{am}	2^{01}_{am}	3^{01}_{am}
Sun	Sun	Sun	Sun	Sun	Sun	Sun	Sun	Sun	Sun	Sun	Sun	Sun	Sun	Sun	Sun	Sun	Sun	Sun	Mon	Mon	Mon	Mon

Advanced Time
Period: *Last Sunday in April to Last Sunday in October*
Time Zone: *06:00 (-6hrs UTC)*

[a]	[b]	[c]	[d]	[e]	[f]	[g]	[h]	[i]	[j]	[k]	[l]	[m]	[n]	[o]	[p]	[q]	[r]	[s]	[t]	[u]	[v]	[w]
06:01	07:01	08:01	09:01	10:01	11:01	12:01	13:01	14:01	15:01	16:01	17:01	18:01	19:01	20:01	21:01	22:01	23:01	00:01	01:01	02:01	03:01	04:01	05
6^{01}_{am}	7^{01}_{am}	8^{01}_{am}	9^{01}_{am}	10^{01}_{am}	11^{01}_{am}	12^{01}_{pm}	1^{01}_{pm}	2^{01}_{pm}	3^{01}_{pm}	4^{01}_{pm}	5^{01}_{pm}	6^{01}_{pm}	7^{01}_{pm}	8^{01}_{pm}	9^{01}_{pm}	10^{01}_{pm}	11^{01}_{pm}	12^{01}_{am}	1^{01}_{am}	2^{01}_{am}	3^{01}_{am}	4^{01}_{am}
Sun	Sun	Sun	Sun	Sun	Sun	Sun	Sun	Sun	Sun	Sun	Sun	Sun	Sun	Sun	Sun	Sun	Sun	Sun	Mon	Mon	Mon	Mon

PACIFIC TIME ZONE
Note: *Comprises most of British Columbia and all of Yukon*

Standard Time
Period: *Last Sunday in October to Last Sunday in April*
Time Zone: *04:00 (-8hrs UTC)*

[a]	[b]	[c]	[d]	[e]	[f]	[g]	[h]	[i]	[j]	[k]	[l]	[m]	[n]	[o]	[p]	[q]	[r]	[s]	[t]	[u]	[v]	[w]
04:01	05:01	06:01	07:01	08:01	09:01	10:01	11:01	12:01	13:01	14:01	15:01	16:01	17:01	18:01	19:01	20:01	21:01	22:01	23:01	00:01	01:01	02:01	03
4^{01}_{am}	5^{01}_{am}	6^{01}_{am}	7^{01}_{am}	8^{01}_{am}	9^{01}_{am}	10^{01}_{am}	11^{01}_{am}	12^{01}_{pm}	1^{01}_{pm}	2^{01}_{pm}	3^{01}_{pm}	4^{01}_{pm}	5^{01}_{pm}	6^{01}_{pm}	7^{01}_{pm}	8^{01}_{pm}	9^{01}_{pm}	10^{01}_{pm}	11^{01}_{pm}	12^{01}_{am}	1^{01}_{am}	2^{01}_{am}
Sun	Sun	Sun	Sun	Sun	Sun	Sun	Sun	Sun	Sun	Sun	Sun	Sun	Sun	Sun	Sun	Sun	Sun	Sun	Sun	Mon	Mon	Mon

Advanced Time
Period: *Last Sunday in April to Last Sunday in October*
Time Zone: *05:00 (-7hrs UTC)*

[a]	[b]	[c]	[d]	[e]	[f]	[g]	[h]	[i]	[j]	[k]	[l]	[m]	[n]	[o]	[p]	[q]	[r]	[s]	[t]	[u]	[v]	[w]
05:01	06:01	07:01	08:01	09:01	10:01	11:01	12:01	13:01	14:01	15:01	16:01	17:01	18:01	19:01	20:01	21:01	22:01	23:01	00:01	01:01	02:01	03:01	04
5^{01}_{am}	6^{01}_{am}	7^{01}_{am}	8^{01}_{am}	9^{01}_{am}	10^{01}_{am}	11^{01}_{am}	12^{01}_{pm}	1^{01}_{pm}	2^{01}_{pm}	3^{01}_{pm}	4^{01}_{pm}	5^{01}_{pm}	6^{01}_{pm}	7^{01}_{pm}	8^{01}_{pm}	9^{01}_{pm}	10^{01}_{pm}	11^{01}_{pm}	12^{01}_{am}	1^{01}_{am}	2^{01}_{am}	3^{01}_{am}
Sun	Sun	Sun	Sun	Sun	Sun	Sun	Sun	Sun	Sun	Sun	Sun	Sun	Sun	Sun	Sun	Sun	Sun	Sun	Mon	Mon	Mon	Mon

Note: Advanced Time = Daylight Saving Time = Summer Time

CANARY ISLANDS
Number of Time Zones: *1*

Standard Time
Period: *Last Sunday in September to Last Sunday in March*
Time Zone: *12:00 (UTC)*

[a]	[b]	[c]	[d]	[e]	[f]	[g]	[h]	[i]	[j]	[k]	[l]	[m]	[n]	[o]	[p]	[q]	[r]	[s]	[t]	[u]	[v]	[w]	[x]
2:01	13:01	14:01	15:01	16:01	17:01	18:01	19:01	20:01	21:01	22:01	23:01	00:01	01:01	02:01	03:01	04:01	05:01	06:01	07:01	08:01	09:01	10:01	11:01
12_{pm}^{01}	1_{pm}^{01}	2_{pm}^{01}	3_{pm}^{01}	4_{pm}^{01}	5_{pm}^{01}	6_{pm}^{01}	7_{pm}^{01}	8_{pm}^{01}	9_{pm}^{01}	10_{pm}^{01}	11_{pm}^{01}	12_{am}^{01}	1_{am}^{01}	2_{am}^{01}	3_{am}^{01}	4_{am}^{01}	5_{am}^{01}	6_{am}^{01}	7_{am}^{01}	8_{am}^{01}	9_{am}^{01}	10_{am}^{01}	11_{am}^{01}
Sun	Sun	Sun	Sun	Sun	Sun	Sun	Sun	Sun	Sun	Sun	Sun	Sun	Mon	Mon	Mon	Mon	Mon	Mon	Mon	Mon	Mon	Mon	Mon

Advanced Time
Period: *Last Sunday in March to Last Sunday in September*
Time Zone: *13:00 (+1hr UTC)*

[a]	[b]	[c]	[d]	[e]	[f]	[g]	[h]	[i]	[j]	[k]	[l]	[m]	[n]	[o]	[p]	[q]	[r]	[s]	[t]	[u]	[v]	[w]	[x]
13:01	14:01	15:01	16:01	17:01	18:01	19:01	20:01	21:01	22:01	23:01	00:01	01:01	02:01	03:01	04:01	05:01	06:01	07:01	08:01	09:01	10:01	11:01	12:01
1_{pm}^{01}	2_{pm}^{01}	3_{pm}^{01}	4_{pm}^{01}	5_{pm}^{01}	6_{pm}^{01}	7_{pm}^{01}	8_{pm}^{01}	9_{pm}^{01}	10_{pm}^{01}	11_{pm}^{01}	12_{am}^{01}	1_{am}^{01}	2_{am}^{01}	3_{am}^{01}	4_{am}^{01}	5_{am}^{01}	6_{am}^{01}	7_{am}^{01}	8_{am}^{01}	9_{am}^{01}	10_{am}^{01}	11_{am}^{01}	12_{pm}^{01}
Sun	Sun	Sun	Sun	Sun	Sun	Sun	Sun	Sun	Sun	Sun	Mon	Mon	Mon	Mon	Mon	Mon	Mon	Mon	Mon	Mon	Mon	Mon	Mon

CAPE VERDE
Number of Time Zones: *1*
Standard Time: *Applicable for the entire year*
Advanced Time: *Not observed*
Time Zone: *11:00 (-1hr UTC)*

[a]	[b]	[c]	[d]	[e]	[f]	[g]	[h]	[i]	[j]	[k]	[l]	[m]	[n]	[o]	[p]	[q]	[r]	[s]	[t]	[u]	[v]	[w]	[x]
11:01	12:01	13:01	14:01	15:01	16:01	17:01	18:01	19:01	20:01	21:01	22:01	23:01	00:01	01:01	02:01	03:01	04:01	05:01	06:01	07:01	08:01	09:01	10:01
11_{am}^{01}	12_{pm}^{01}	1_{pm}^{01}	2_{pm}^{01}	3_{pm}^{01}	4_{pm}^{01}	5_{pm}^{01}	6_{pm}^{01}	7_{pm}^{01}	8_{pm}^{01}	9_{pm}^{01}	10_{pm}^{01}	11_{pm}^{01}	12_{am}^{01}	1_{am}^{01}	2_{am}^{01}	3_{am}^{01}	4_{am}^{01}	5_{am}^{01}	6_{am}^{01}	7_{am}^{01}	8_{am}^{01}	9_{am}^{01}	10_{am}^{01}
Sun	Sun	Sun	Sun	Sun	Sun	Sun	Sun	Sun	Sun	Sun	Sun	Sun	Mon	Mon	Mon	Mon	Mon	Mon	Mon	Mon	Mon	Mon	Mon

CAYMAN ISLANDS
Number of Time Zones: *1*
Standard Time: *Applicable for the entire year*
Advanced Time: *Not observed*
Time Zone: *07:00 (-5hrs UTC)*

[a]	[b]	[c]	[d]	[e]	[f]	[g]	[h]	[i]	[j]	[k]	[l]	[m]	[n]	[o]	[p]	[q]	[r]	[s]	[t]	[u]	[v]	[w]	[x]
07:01	08:01	09:01	10:01	11:01	12:01	13:01	14:01	15:01	16:01	17:01	18:01	19:01	20:01	21:01	22:01	23:01	00:01	01:01	02:01	03:01	04:01	05:01	06:01
7_{am}^{01}	8_{am}^{01}	9_{am}^{01}	10_{am}^{01}	11_{am}^{01}	12_{pm}^{01}	1_{pm}^{01}	2_{pm}^{01}	3_{pm}^{01}	4_{pm}^{01}	5_{pm}^{01}	6_{pm}^{01}	7_{pm}^{01}	8_{pm}^{01}	9_{pm}^{01}	10_{pm}^{01}	11_{pm}^{01}	12_{am}^{01}	1_{am}^{01}	2_{am}^{01}	3_{am}^{01}	4_{am}^{01}	5_{am}^{01}	6_{am}^{01}
Sun	Sun	Sun	Sun	Sun	Sun	Sun	Sun	Sun	Sun	Sun	Sun	Sun	Sun	Sun	Sun	Sun	Mon	Mon	Mon	Mon	Mon	Mon	Mon

Note: Advanced Time = Daylight Saving Time = Summer Time

CENTRAL AFRICAN REPUBLIC
Number of Time Zones: *1*
Standard Time: *Applicable for the entire year*
Advanced Time: *Not observed*
Time Zone: *13:00 (+1hr UTC)*

[a]	[b]	[c]	[d]	[e]	[f]	[g]	[h]	[i]	[j]	[k]	[l]	[m]	[n]	[o]	[p]	[q]	[r]	[s]	[t]	[u]	[v]	[w]	[x]
13:01	14:01	15:01	16:01	17:01	18:01	19:01	20:01	21:01	22:01	23:01	00:01	01:01	02:01	03:01	04:01	05:01	06:01	07:01	08:01	09:01	10:01	11:01	12:01
1^{01}_{pm}	2^{01}_{pm}	3^{01}_{pm}	4^{01}_{pm}	5^{01}_{pm}	6^{01}_{pm}	7^{01}_{pm}	8^{01}_{pm}	9^{01}_{pm}	10^{01}_{pm}	11^{01}_{pm}	12^{01}_{am}	1^{01}_{am}	2^{01}_{am}	3^{01}_{am}	4^{01}_{am}	5^{01}_{am}	6^{01}_{am}	7^{01}_{am}	8^{01}_{am}	9^{01}_{am}	10^{01}_{am}	11^{01}_{am}	12^{01}_{pm}
Sun	Sun	Sun	Sun	Sun	Sun	Sun	Sun	Sun	Sun	Sun	Mon	Mon	Mon	Mon	Mon	Mon	Mon	Mon	Mon	Mon	Mon	Mon	Mon

CHAD
Number of Time Zones: *1*
Standard Time: *Applicable for the entire year*
Advanced Time: *Not observed*
Time Zone: *13:00 (+1hr UTC)*

[a]	[b]	[c]	[d]	[e]	[f]	[g]	[h]	[i]	[j]	[k]	[l]	[m]	[n]	[o]	[p]	[q]	[r]	[s]	[t]	[u]	[v]	[w]	[x]
13:01	14:01	15:01	16:01	17:01	18:01	19:01	20:01	21:01	22:01	23:01	00:01	01:01	02:01	03:01	04:01	05:01	06:01	07:01	08:01	09:01	10:01	11:01	12:01
1^{01}_{pm}	2^{01}_{pm}	3^{01}_{pm}	4^{01}_{pm}	5^{01}_{pm}	6^{01}_{pm}	7^{01}_{pm}	8^{01}_{pm}	9^{01}_{pm}	10^{01}_{pm}	11^{01}_{pm}	12^{01}_{am}	1^{01}_{am}	2^{01}_{am}	3^{01}_{am}	4^{01}_{am}	5^{01}_{am}	6^{01}_{am}	7^{01}_{am}	8^{01}_{am}	9^{01}_{am}	10^{01}_{am}	11^{01}_{am}	12^{01}_{pm}
Sun	Sun	Sun	Sun	Sun	Sun	Sun	Sun	Sun	Sun	Sun	Mon	Mon	Mon	Mon	Mon	Mon	Mon	Mon	Mon	Mon	Mon	Mon	Mon

CHATHAM ISLANDS
Number of Time Zones: *1*

Standard Time
Period: *First Sunday in March to Last Sunday in October*
Time Zone: *24:45 (+12hrs 45mins UTC)*

[a]	[b]	[c]	[d]	[e]	[f]	[g]	[h]	[i]	[j]	[k]	[l]	[m]	[n]	[o]	[p]	[q]	[r]	[s]	[t]	[u]	[v]	[w]	[x]
00:46	01:46	02:46	03:46	04:46	05:46	06:46	07:46	08:46	09:46	10:46	11:46	12:46	13:46	14:46	15:46	16:46	17:46	18:46	19:46	20:46	21:46	22:46	23:46
12^{46}_{am}	1^{46}_{am}	2^{46}_{am}	3^{46}_{am}	4^{46}_{am}	5^{46}_{am}	6^{46}_{am}	7^{46}_{am}	8^{46}_{am}	9^{46}_{am}	10^{46}_{am}	11^{46}_{am}	12^{46}_{pm}	1^{46}_{pm}	2^{46}_{pm}	3^{46}_{pm}	4^{46}_{pm}	5^{46}_{pm}	6^{45}_{pm}	7^{46}_{pm}	8^{46}_{pm}	9^{46}_{pm}	10^{46}_{pm}	11^{46}_{pm}
Mon	Mon	Mon	Mon	Mon	Mon	Mon	Mon	Mon	Mon	Mon	Mon	Mon	Mon	Mon	Mon	Mon	Mon	Mon	Mon	Mon	Mon	Mon	Mon

Advanced Time
Period: *Last Sunday in October to First Sunday in March*
Time Zone: *25:45 (+13hrs 45mins UTC)*

[a]	[b]	[c]	[d]	[e]	[f]	[g]	[h]	[i]	[j]	[k]	[l]	[m]	[n]	[o]	[p]	[q]	[r]	[s]	[t]	[u]	[v]	[w]	[x]
01:46	02:46	03:46	04:46	05:46	06:46	07:46	08:46	09:46	10:46	11:46	12:46	13:46	14:46	15:46	16:46	17:46	18:46	19:46	20:46	21:46	22:46	23:46	00:46
1^{46}_{am}	2^{46}_{am}	3^{46}_{am}	4^{46}_{am}	5^{46}_{am}	6^{46}_{am}	7^{46}_{am}	8^{46}_{am}	9^{46}_{am}	10^{46}_{am}	11^{46}_{am}	12^{46}_{pm}	1^{46}_{pm}	2^{46}_{pm}	3^{46}_{pm}	4^{46}_{pm}	5^{46}_{pm}	6^{46}_{pm}	7^{46}_{pm}	8^{46}_{pm}	9^{46}_{pm}	10^{46}_{pm}	11^{46}_{pm}	12^{46}_{am}
Mon	Mon	Mon	Mon	Mon	Mon	Mon	Mon	Mon	Mon	Mon	Mon	Mon	Mon	Mon	Mon	Mon	Mon	Mon	Mon	Mon	Mon	Mon	Tue

Note: Advanced Time = Daylight Saving Time = Summer Time

CHILE
Number of Time Zones: *1*

Standard Time
Period: *Second Sunday in March to Second Sunday in October*
Time Zone: *08:00 (-4hrs UTC)*

[a]	[b]	[c]	[d]	[e]	[f]	[g]	[h]	[i]	[j]	[k]	[l]	[m]	[n]	[o]	[p]	[q]	[r]	[s]	[t]	[u]	[v]	[w]	[x]
08:01	09:01	10:01	11:01	12:01	13:01	14:01	15:01	16:01	17:01	18:01	19:01	20:01	21:01	22:01	23:01	00:01	01:01	02:01	03:01	04:01	05:01	06:01	07:01
8^{01}_{am}	9^{01}_{am}	10^{01}_{am}	11^{01}_{am}	12^{01}_{pm}	1^{01}_{pm}	2^{01}_{pm}	3^{01}_{pm}	4^{01}_{pm}	5^{01}_{pm}	6^{01}_{pm}	7^{01}_{pm}	8^{01}_{pm}	9^{01}_{pm}	10^{01}_{pm}	11^{01}_{pm}	12^{01}_{am}	1^{01}_{am}	2^{01}_{am}	3^{01}_{am}	4^{01}_{am}	5^{01}_{am}	6^{01}_{am}	7^{01}_{am}
Sun	Sun	Sun	Sun	Sun	Sun	Sun	Sun	Sun	Sun	Sun	Sun	Sun	Sun	Sun	Sun	Mon	Mon	Mon	Mon	Mon	Mon	Mon	Mon

Advanced Time
Period: *Second Sunday in October to Second Sunday in March*
Time Zone: *09:00 (-3hrs UTC)*

[a]	[b]	[c]	[d]	[e]	[f]	[g]	[h]	[i]	[j]	[k]	[l]	[m]	[n]	[o]	[p]	[q]	[r]	[s]	[t]	[u]	[v]	[w]	[x]
09:01	10:01	11:01	12:01	13:01	14:01	15:01	16:01	17:01	18:01	19:01	20:01	21:01	22:01	23:01	00:01	01:01	02:01	03:01	04:01	05:01	06:01	07:01	08:01
9^{01}_{am}	10^{01}_{am}	11^{01}_{am}	12^{01}_{pm}	1^{01}_{pm}	2^{01}_{pm}	3^{01}_{pm}	4^{01}_{pm}	5^{01}_{pm}	6^{01}_{pm}	7^{01}_{pm}	8^{01}_{pm}	9^{01}_{pm}	10^{01}_{pm}	11^{01}_{pm}	12^{01}_{am}	1^{01}_{am}	2^{01}_{am}	3^{01}_{am}	4^{01}_{am}	5^{01}_{am}	6^{01}_{am}	7^{01}_{am}	8^{01}_{am}
Sun	Sun	Sun	Sun	Sun	Sun	Sun	Sun	Sun	Sun	Sun	Sun	Sun	Sun	Sun	Mon	Mon	Mon	Mon	Mon	Mon	Mon	Mon	Mon

CHINA
Number of Time Zones: *1*

Standard Time
Period: *Second Sunday in September to Third Sunday in April*
Time Zone: *20:00 (+8hrs UTC)*

[a]	[b]	[c]	[d]	[e]	[f]	[g]	[h]	[i]	[j]	[k]	[l]	[m]	[n]	[o]	[p]	[q]	[r]	[s]	[t]	[u]	[v]	[w]	[x]
20:01	21:01	22:01	23:01	00:01	01:01	02:01	03:01	04:01	05:01	06:01	07:01	08:01	09:01	10:01	11:01	12:01	13:01	14:01	15:01	16:01	17:01	18:01	19:01
8^{01}_{pm}	9^{01}_{pm}	10^{01}_{pm}	11^{01}_{pm}	12^{01}_{am}	1^{01}_{am}	2^{01}_{am}	3^{01}_{am}	4^{01}_{am}	5^{01}_{am}	6^{01}_{am}	7^{01}_{am}	8^{01}_{am}	9^{01}_{am}	10^{01}_{am}	11^{01}_{am}	12^{01}_{pm}	1^{01}_{pm}	2^{01}_{pm}	3^{01}_{pm}	4^{01}_{pm}	5^{01}_{pm}	6^{01}_{pm}	7^{01}_{pm}
Sun	Sun	Sun	Sun	Mon	Mon	Mon	Mon	Mon	Mon	Mon	Mon	Mon	Mon	Mon	Mon	Mon	Mon	Mon	Mon	Mon	Mon	Mon	Mon

Advanced Time
Period: *Third Sunday in April to Second Sunday in September*
Time Zone: *21:00 (+9hrs UTC)*

[a]	[b]	[c]	[d]	[e]	[f]	[g]	[h]	[i]	[j]	[k]	[l]	[m]	[n]	[o]	[p]	[q]	[r]	[s]	[t]	[u]	[v]	[w]	[x]
21:01	22:01	23:01	00:01	01:01	02:01	03:01	04:01	05:01	06:01	07:01	08:01	09:01	10:01	11:01	12:01	13:01	14:01	15:01	16:01	17:01	18:01	19:01	20:01
9^{01}_{pm}	10^{01}_{pm}	11^{01}_{pm}	12^{01}_{am}	1^{01}_{am}	2^{01}_{am}	3^{01}_{am}	4^{01}_{am}	5^{01}_{am}	6^{01}_{am}	7^{01}_{am}	8^{01}_{am}	9^{01}_{am}	10^{01}_{am}	11^{01}_{am}	12^{01}_{pm}	1^{01}_{pm}	2^{01}_{pm}	3^{01}_{pm}	4^{01}_{pm}	5^{01}_{pm}	6^{01}_{pm}	7^{01}_{pm}	8^{01}_{pm}
Sun	Sun	Sun	Mon	Mon	Mon	Mon	Mon	Mon	Mon	Mon	Mon	Mon	Mon	Mon	Mon	Mon	Mon	Mon	Mon	Mon	Mon	Mon	Mon

Note: Advanced Time = Daylight Saving Time = Summer Time

CHRISTMAS ISLAND (Indian Ocean)
Number of Time Zones: *1*
Standard Time: *Applicable for the entire year*
Advanced Time: *Not observed*
Time Zone: *19:00 (+7hrs UTC)*

[a]	[b]	[c]	[d]	[e]	[f]	[g]	[h]	[i]	[j]	[k]	[l]	[m]	[n]	[o]	[p]	[q]	[r]	[s]	[t]	[u]	[v]	[w]	
19:01	20:01	21:01	22:01	23:01	00:01	01:01	02:01	03:01	04:01	05:01	06:01	07:01	08:01	09:01	10:01	11:01	12:01	13:01	14:01	15:01	16:01	17:01	18:
7^{01}_{pm}	8^{01}_{pm}	9^{01}_{pm}	10^{01}_{pm}	11^{01}_{pm}	12^{01}_{am}	1^{01}_{am}	2^{01}_{am}	3^{01}_{am}	4^{01}_{am}	5^{01}_{am}	6^{01}_{am}	7^{01}_{am}	8^{01}_{am}	9^{01}_{am}	10^{01}_{am}	11^{01}_{am}	12^{01}_{pm}	1^{01}_{pm}	2^{01}_{pm}	3^{01}_{pm}	4^{01}_{pm}	5^{01}_{pm}	
Sun	Sun	Sun	Sun	Sun	Mon	Mon	Mon	Mon	Mon	Mon	Mon	Mon	Mon	Mon	Mon	Mon	Mon	Mon	Mon	Mon	Mon	Mon	M

COCOS (KEELING) ISLANDS
Number of Time Zones: *1*
Standard Time: *Applicable for the entire year*
Advanced Time: *Not observed*
Time Zone: *18:30 (+6hrs UTC)*

[a]	[b]	[c]	[d]	[e]	[f]	[g]	[h]	[i]	[j]	[k]	[l]	[m]	[n]	[o]	[p]	[q]	[r]	[s]	[t]	[u]	[v]	[w]	[
18:31	19:31	20:31	21:31	22:31	23:31	00:31	01:31	02:31	03:31	04:31	05:31	06:31	07:31	08:31	09:31	10:31	11:31	12:31	13:31	14:31	15:31	16:31	17:
6^{31}_{pm}	7^{31}_{pm}	8^{31}_{pm}	9^{31}_{pm}	10^{31}_{pm}	11^{31}_{pm}	12^{31}_{am}	1^{31}_{am}	2^{31}_{am}	3^{31}_{am}	4^{31}_{am}	5^{31}_{am}	6^{31}_{am}	7^{31}_{am}	8^{31}_{am}	9^{31}_{am}	10^{31}_{am}	11^{31}_{am}	12^{31}_{pm}	1^{31}_{pm}	2^{31}_{pm}	3^{31}_{pm}	4^{31}_{pm}	5
Sun	Sun	Sun	Sun	Sun	Sun	Mon	Mon	Mon	Mon	Mon	Mon	Mon	Mon	Mon	Mon	Mon	Mon	Mon	Mon	Mon	Mon	Mon	M

COLOMBIA
Number of Time Zones: *1*
Standard Time: *Applicable for the entire year*
Advanced Time: *Not observed*
Time Zone: *07:00 (-5hrs UTC)*

[a]	[b]	[c]	[d]	[e]	[f]	[g]	[h]	[i]	[j]	[k]	[l]	[m]	[n]	[o]	[p]	[q]	[r]	[s]	[t]	[u]	[v]	[w]	[x
07:01	08:01	09:01	10:01	11:01	12:01	13:01	14:01	15:01	16:01	17:01	18:01	19:01	20:01	21:01	22:01	23:01	00:01	01:01	02:01	03:01	04:01	05:01	06:
7^{01}_{am}	8^{01}_{am}	9^{01}_{am}	10^{01}_{am}	11^{01}_{am}	12^{01}_{pm}	1^{01}_{pm}	2^{01}_{pm}	3^{01}_{pm}	4^{01}_{pm}	5^{01}_{pm}	6^{01}_{pm}	7^{01}_{pm}	8^{01}_{pm}	9^{01}_{pm}	10^{01}_{pm}	11^{01}_{pm}	12^{01}_{am}	1^{01}_{am}	2^{01}_{am}	3^{01}_{am}	4^{01}_{am}	5^{01}_{am}	6
Sun	Sun	Sun	Sun	Sun	Sun	Sun	Sun	Sun	Sun	Sun	Sun	Sun	Sun	Sun	Sun	Sun	Mon	Mon	Mon	Mon	Mon	Mon	Mo

COMOROS
Number of Time Zones: *1*
Standard Time: *Applicable for the entire year*
Advanced Time: *Not observed*
Time Zone: *15:00 (+3hrs UTC)*

[a]	[b]	[c]	[d]	[e]	[f]	[g]	[h]	[i]	[j]	[k]	[l]	[m]	[n]	[o]	[p]	[q]	[r]	[s]	[t]	[u]	[v]	[w]	[x
15:01	16:01	17:01	18:01	19:01	20:01	21:01	22:01	23:01	00:01	01:01	02:01	03:01	04:01	05:01	06:01	07:01	08:01	09:01	10:01	11:01	12:01	13:01	14:0
3^{01}_{pm}	4^{01}_{pm}	5^{01}_{pm}	6^{01}_{pm}	7^{01}_{pm}	8^{01}_{pm}	9^{01}_{pm}	10^{01}_{pm}	11^{01}_{pm}	12^{01}_{am}	1^{01}_{am}	2^{01}_{am}	3^{01}_{am}	4^{01}_{am}	5^{01}_{am}	6^{01}_{am}	7^{01}_{am}	8^{01}_{am}	9^{01}_{am}	10^{01}_{am}	11^{01}_{am}	12^{01}_{pm}	1^{01}_{pm}	2^{0}_{p}
Sun	Sun	Sun	Sun	Sun	Sun	Sun	Sun	Sun	Mon	Mon	Mon	Mon	Mon	Mon	Mon	Mon	Mon	Mon	Mon	Mon	Mon	Mon	Mo

Note: Advanced Time = Daylight Saving Time = Summer Time

CONGO

Number of Time Zones: *1*
Standard Time: *Applicable for the entire year*
Advanced Time: *Not observed*
Time Zone: *13:00 (+1hr UTC)*

[a]	[b]	[c]	[d]	[e]	[f]	[g]	[h]	[i]	[j]	[k]	[l]	[m]	[n]	[o]	[p]	[q]	[r]	[s]	[t]	[u]	[v]	[w]	[x]
13:01	14:01	15:01	16:01	17:01	18:01	19:01	20:01	21:01	22:01	23:01	00:01	01:01	02:01	03:01	04:01	05:01	06:01	07:01	08:01	09:01	10:01	11:01	12:01
1^{01}_{pm}	2^{01}_{pm}	3^{01}_{pm}	4^{01}_{pm}	5^{01}_{pm}	6^{01}_{pm}	7^{01}_{pm}	8^{01}_{pm}	9^{01}_{pm}	10^{01}_{pm}	11^{01}_{pm}	12^{01}_{am}	1^{01}_{am}	2^{01}_{am}	3^{01}_{am}	4^{01}_{am}	5^{01}_{am}	6^{01}_{am}	7^{01}_{am}	8^{01}_{am}	9^{01}_{am}	10^{01}_{am}	11^{01}_{am}	12^{01}_{pm}
Sun	Sun	Sun	Sun	Sun	Sun	Sun	Sun	Sun	Sun	Sun	Mon	Mon	Mon	Mon	Mon	Mon	Mon	Mon	Mon	Mon	Mon	Mon	Mon

COOK ISLANDS

Number of Time Zones: *1*

Standard Time

Period: *First Sunday in March to Last Sunday in October*
Time Zone: *02:00 (-10hrs UTC)*

[a]	[b]	[c]	[d]	[e]	[f]	[g]	[h]	[i]	[j]	[k]	[l]	[m]	[n]	[o]	[p]	[q]	[r]	[s]	[t]	[u]	[v]	[w]	[x]
02:01	03:01	04:01	05:01	06:01	07:01	08:01	09:01	10:01	11:01	12:01	13:01	14:01	15:01	16:01	17:01	18:01	19:01	20:01	21:01	22:01	23:01	00:01	01:01
2^{01}_{am}	3^{01}_{am}	4^{01}_{am}	5^{01}_{am}	6^{01}_{am}	7^{01}_{am}	8^{01}_{am}	9^{01}_{am}	10^{01}_{am}	11^{01}_{am}	12^{01}_{pm}	1^{01}_{pm}	2^{01}_{pm}	3^{01}_{pm}	4^{01}_{pm}	5^{01}_{pm}	6^{01}_{pm}	7^{01}_{pm}	8^{01}_{pm}	9^{01}_{pm}	10^{01}_{pm}	11^{01}_{pm}	12^{01}_{am}	1^{01}_{am}
Sun	Sun	Sun	Sun	Sun	Sun	Sun	Sun	Sun	Sun	Sun	Sun	Sun	Sun	Sun	Sun	Sun	Sun	Sun	Sun	Sun	Sun	Mon	Mon

Advanced Time

Period: *Last Sunday in October to First Sunday in March*
Time Zone: *03:00 (-9hrs UTC)*

[a]	[b]	[c]	[d]	[e]	[f]	[g]	[h]	[i]	[j]	[k]	[l]	[m]	[n]	[o]	[p]	[q]	[r]	[s]	[t]	[u]	[v]	[w]	[x]
03:01	04:01	05:01	06:01	07:01	08:01	09:01	10:01	11:01	12:01	13:01	14:01	15:01	16:01	17:01	18:01	19:01	20:01	21:01	22:01	23:01	00:01	01:01	02:01
3^{01}_{am}	4^{01}_{am}	5^{01}_{am}	6^{01}_{am}	7^{01}_{am}	8^{01}_{am}	9^{01}_{am}	10^{01}_{am}	11^{01}_{am}	12^{01}_{pm}	1^{01}_{pm}	2^{01}_{pm}	3^{01}_{pm}	4^{01}_{pm}	5^{01}_{pm}	6^{01}_{pm}	7^{01}_{pm}	8^{01}_{pm}	9^{01}_{pm}	10^{01}_{pm}	11^{01}_{pm}	12^{01}_{am}	1^{01}_{am}	2^{01}_{am}
Sun	Sun	Sun	Sun	Sun	Sun	Sun	Sun	Sun	Sun	Sun	Sun	Sun	Sun	Sun	Sun	Sun	Sun	Sun	Sun	Sun	Mon	Mon	Mon

COSTA RICA

Number of Time Zones: *1*
Standard Time: *Applicable for the entire year*
Advanced Time: *Not observed*
Time Zone: *06:00 (-6hrs UTC)*

[a]	[b]	[c]	[d]	[e]	[f]	[g]	[h]	[i]	[j]	[k]	[l]	[m]	[n]	[o]	[p]	[q]	[r]	[s]	[t]	[u]	[v]	[w]	[x]
06:01	07:01	08:01	09:01	10:01	11:01	12:01	13:01	14:01	15:01	16:01	17:01	18:01	19:01	20:01	21:01	22:01	23:01	00:01	01:01	02:01	03:01	04:01	05:01
6^{01}_{am}	7^{01}_{am}	8^{01}_{am}	9^{01}_{am}	10^{01}_{am}	11^{01}_{am}	12^{01}_{pm}	1^{01}_{pm}	2^{01}_{pm}	3^{01}_{pm}	4^{01}_{pm}	5^{01}_{pm}	6^{01}_{pm}	7^{01}_{pm}	8^{01}_{pm}	9^{01}_{pm}	10^{01}_{pm}	11^{01}_{pm}	12^{01}_{am}	1^{01}_{am}	2^{01}_{am}	3^{01}_{am}	4^{01}_{am}	5^{01}_{am}
Sun	Sun	Sun	Sun	Sun	Sun	Sun	Sun	Sun	Sun	Sun	Sun	Sun	Sun	Sun	Sun	Sun	Sun	Mon	Mon	Mon	Mon	Mon	Mon

Note: Advanced Time = Daylight Saving Time = Summer Time

CUBA

Number of Time Zones: *1*

Standard Time

Period: *Varies: Mid-October to Mid/Late March*
Time Zone: *07:00 (-5hrs UTC)*

[a]	[b]	[c]	[d]	[e]	[f]	[g]	[h]	[i]	[j]	[k]	[l]	[m]	[n]	[o]	[p]	[q]	[r]	[s]	[t]	[u]	[v]	[w]	[x]
07:01	08:01	09:01	10:01	11:01	12:01	13:01	14:01	15:01	16:01	17:01	18:01	19:01	20:01	21:01	22:01	23:01	00:01	01:01	02:01	03:01	04:01	05:01	06:01
7^{01}_{am}	8^{01}_{am}	9^{01}_{am}	10^{01}_{am}	11^{01}_{am}	12^{01}_{pm}	1^{01}_{pm}	2^{01}_{pm}	3^{01}_{pm}	4^{01}_{pm}	5^{01}_{pm}	6^{01}_{pm}	7^{01}_{pm}	8^{01}_{pm}	9^{01}_{pm}	10^{01}_{pm}	11^{01}_{pm}	12^{01}_{am}	1^{01}_{am}	2^{01}_{am}	3^{01}_{am}	4^{01}_{am}	5^{01}_{am}	6^{01}_{am}
Sun	Sun	Sun	Sun	Sun	Sun	Sun	Sun	Sun	Sun	Sun	Sun	Sun	Sun	Sun	Sun	Sun	Mon	Mon	Mon	Mon	Mon	Mon	Mon

Advanced Time

Period: *Varies: Mid/Late March to Mid-October*
Time Zone: *08:00 (-4hrs UTC)*

[a]	[b]	[c]	[d]	[e]	[f]	[g]	[h]	[i]	[j]	[k]	[l]	[m]	[n]	[o]	[p]	[q]	[r]	[s]	[t]	[u]	[v]	[w]	[x]
08:01	09:01	10:01	11:01	12:01	13:01	14:01	15:01	16:01	17:01	18:01	19:01	20:01	21:01	22:01	23:01	00:01	01:01	02:01	03:01	04:01	05:01	06:01	07:01
8^{01}_{am}	9^{01}_{am}	10^{01}_{am}	11^{01}_{am}	12^{01}_{pm}	1^{01}_{pm}	2^{01}_{pm}	3^{01}_{pm}	4^{01}_{pm}	5^{01}_{pm}	6^{01}_{pm}	7^{01}_{pm}	8^{01}_{pm}	9^{01}_{pm}	10^{01}_{pm}	11^{01}_{pm}	12^{01}_{am}	1^{01}_{am}	2^{01}_{am}	3^{01}_{am}	4^{01}_{am}	5^{01}_{am}	6^{01}_{am}	7^{01}_{am}
Sun	Sun	Sun	Sun	Sun	Sun	Sun	Sun	Sun	Sun	Sun	Sun	Sun	Sun	Sun	Sun	Mon	Mon	Mon	Mon	Mon	Mon	Mon	Mon

CURACAO

Number of Time Zones: *1*
Standard Time: *Applicable for the entire year*
Advanced Time: *Not observed*
Time Zone: *08:00 (-4hrs UTC)*

[a]	[b]	[c]	[d]	[e]	[f]	[g]	[h]	[i]	[j]	[k]	[l]	[m]	[n]	[o]	[p]	[q]	[r]	[s]	[t]	[u]	[v]	[w]	[x]
08:01	09:01	10:01	11:01	12:01	13:01	14:01	15:01	16:01	17:01	18:01	19:01	20:01	21:01	22:01	23:01	00:01	01:01	02:01	03:01	04:01	05:01	06:01	07:01
8^{01}_{am}	9^{01}_{am}	10^{01}_{am}	11^{01}_{am}	12^{01}_{pm}	1^{01}_{pm}	2^{01}_{pm}	3^{01}_{pm}	4^{01}_{pm}	5^{01}_{pm}	6^{01}_{pm}	7^{01}_{pm}	8^{01}_{pm}	9^{01}_{pm}	10^{01}_{pm}	11^{01}_{pm}	12^{01}_{am}	1^{01}_{am}	2^{01}_{am}	3^{01}_{am}	4^{01}_{am}	5^{01}_{am}	6^{01}_{am}	7^{01}_{am}
Sun	Sun	Sun	Sun	Sun	Sun	Sun	Sun	Sun	Sun	Sun	Sun	Sun	Sun	Sun	Sun	Mon	Mon	Mon	Mon	Mon	Mon	Mon	Mon

Note: Advanced Time = Daylight Saving Time = Summer Time

CYPRUS
Number of Time Zones: *1*

Standard Time
Period: *Last Sunday in September to Last Sunday in March*
Time Zone: *14:00 (+2hrs UTC)*

[a]	[b]	[c]	[d]	[e]	[f]	[g]	[h]	[i]	[j]	[k]	[l]	[m]	[n]	[o]	[p]	[q]	[r]	[s]	[t]	[u]	[v]	[w]	[x]
14:01	15:01	16:01	17:01	18:01	19:01	20:01	21:01	22:01	23:01	00:01	01:01	02:01	03:01	04:01	05:01	06:01	07:01	08:01	09:01	10:01	11:01	12:01	13:01
2:01pm	3:01pm	4:01pm	5:01pm	6:01pm	7:01pm	8:01pm	9:01pm	10:01pm	11:01pm	12:01am	1:01am	2:01am	3:01am	4:01am	5:01am	6:01am	7:01am	8:01am	9:01am	10:01am	11:01am	12:01pm	1:01pm
Sun	Sun	Sun	Sun	Sun	Sun	Sun	Sun	Sun	Sun	Mon	Mon	Mon	Mon	Mon	Mon	Mon	Mon	Mon	Mon	Mon	Mon	Mon	Mon

Advanced Time
Period: *Last Sunday in March to Last Sunday in September*
Time Zone: *15:00 (+3hrs UTC)*

[a]	[b]	[c]	[d]	[e]	[f]	[g]	[h]	[i]	[j]	[k]	[l]	[m]	[n]	[o]	[p]	[q]	[r]	[s]	[t]	[u]	[v]	[w]	[x]
15:01	16:01	17:01	18:01	19:01	20:01	21:01	22:01	23:01	00:01	01:01	02:01	03:01	04:01	05:01	06:01	07:01	08:01	09:01	10:01	11:01	12:01	13:01	14:01
3:01pm	4:01pm	5:01pm	6:01pm	7:01pm	8:01pm	9:01pm	10:01pm	11:01pm	12:01am	1:01am	2:01am	3:01am	4:01am	5:01am	6:01am	7:01am	8:01am	9:01am	10:01am	11:01am	12:01pm	1:01pm	2:01pm
Sun	Sun	Sun	Sun	Sun	Sun	Sun	Sun	Sun	Mon	Mon	Mon	Mon	Mon	Mon	Mon	Mon	Mon	Mon	Mon	Mon	Mon	Mon	Mon

CZECHOSLOVAKIA
Number of Time Zones: *1*

Standard Time
Period: *Last Sunday in September to Last Sunday in March*
Time Zone: *13:00 (+1hr UTC)*

[a]	[b]	[c]	[d]	[e]	[f]	[g]	[h]	[i]	[j]	[k]	[l]	[m]	[n]	[o]	[p]	[q]	[r]	[s]	[t]	[u]	[v]	[w]	[x]
13:01	14:01	15:01	16:01	17:01	18:01	19:01	20:01	21:01	22:01	23:01	00:01	01:01	02:01	03:01	04:01	05:01	06:01	07:01	08:01	09:01	10:01	11:01	12:01
1:01pm	2:01pm	3:01pm	4:01pm	5:01pm	6:01pm	7:01pm	8:01pm	9:01pm	10:01pm	11:01pm	12:01am	1:01am	2:01am	3:01am	4:01am	5:01am	6:01am	7:01am	8:01am	9:01am	10:01am	11:01am	12:01pm
Sun	Sun	Sun	Sun	Sun	Sun	Sun	Sun	Sun	Sun	Sun	Mon	Mon	Mon	Mon	Mon	Mon	Mon	Mon	Mon	Mon	Mon	Mon	Mon

Advanced Time
Period: *Last Sunday in March to Last Sunday in September*
Time Zone: *14:00 (+2hrs UTC)*

[a]	[b]	[c]	[d]	[e]	[f]	[g]	[h]	[i]	[j]	[k]	[l]	[m]	[n]	[o]	[p]	[q]	[r]	[s]	[t]	[u]	[v]	[w]	[x]
14:01	15:01	16:01	17:01	18:01	19:01	20:01	21:01	22:01	23:01	00:01	01:01	02:01	03:01	04:01	05:01	06:01	07:01	08:01	09:01	10:01	11:01	12:01	13:01
2:01pm	3:01pm	4:01pm	5:01pm	6:01pm	7:01pm	8:01pm	9:01pm	10:01pm	11:01pm	12:01am	1:01am	2:01am	3:01am	4:01am	5:01am	6:01am	7:01am	8:01am	9:01am	10:01am	11:01am	12:01pm	1:01pm
Sun	Sun	Sun	Sun	Sun	Sun	Sun	Sun	Sun	Sun	Mon	Mon	Mon	Mon	Mon	Mon	Mon	Mon	Mon	Mon	Mon	Mon	Mon	Mon

Note: Advanced Time = Daylight Saving Time = Summer Time

DENMARK
Number of Time Zones: *1*

Standard Time
Period: *Last Sunday in September to Last Sunday in March*
Time Zone: *13:00 (+1hr UTC)*

[a]	[b]	[c]	[d]	[e]	[f]	[g]	[h]	[i]	[j]	[k]	[l]	[m]	[n]	[o]	[p]	[q]	[r]	[s]	[t]	[u]	[v]	[w]	[x
13:01	14:01	15:01	16:01	17:01	18:01	19:01	20:01	21:01	22:01	23:01	00:01	01:01	02:01	03:01	04:01	05:01	06:01	07:01	08:01	09:01	10:01	11:01	12:0
1^{01}_{pm}	2^{01}_{pm}	3^{01}_{pm}	4^{01}_{pm}	5^{01}_{pm}	6^{01}_{pm}	7^{01}_{pm}	8^{01}_{pm}	9^{01}_{pm}	10^{01}_{pm}	11^{01}_{pm}	12^{01}_{am}	1^{01}_{am}	2^{01}_{am}	3^{01}_{am}	4^{01}_{am}	5^{01}_{am}	6^{01}_{am}	7^{01}_{am}	8^{01}_{am}	9^{01}_{am}	10^{01}_{am}	11^{01}_{am}	$12^{}_{p}$
Sun	Sun	Sun	Sun	Sun	Sun	Sun	Sun	Sun	Sun	Sun	Mon	Mon	Mon	Mon	Mon	Mon	Mon	Mon	Mon	Mon	Mon	Mon	Mo

Advanced Time
Period: *Last Sunday in March to Last Sunday in September*
Time Zone: *14:00 (+2hrs UTC)*

[a]	[b]	[c]	[d]	[e]	[f]	[g]	[h]	[i]	[j]	[k]	[l]	[m]	[n]	[o]	[p]	[q]	[r]	[s]	[t]	[u]	[v]	[w]	[x
14:01	15:01	16:01	17:01	18:01	19:01	20:01	21:01	22:01	23:01	00:01	01:01	02:01	03:01	04:01	05:01	06:01	07:01	08:01	09:01	10:01	11:01	12:01	13:0
2^{01}_{pm}	3^{01}_{pm}	4^{01}_{pm}	5^{01}_{pm}	6^{01}_{pm}	7^{01}_{pm}	8^{01}_{pm}	9^{01}_{pm}	10^{01}_{pm}	11^{01}_{pm}	12^{01}_{am}	1^{01}_{am}	2^{01}_{am}	3^{01}_{am}	4^{01}_{am}	5^{01}_{am}	6^{01}_{am}	7^{01}_{am}	8^{01}_{am}	9^{01}_{am}	10^{01}_{am}	11^{01}_{am}	12^{01}_{pm}	$1^{}_{p}$
Sun	Sun	Sun	Sun	Sun	Sun	Sun	Sun	Sun	Sun	Mon	Mon	Mon	Mon	Mon	Mon	Mon	Mon	Mon	Mon	Mon	Mon	Mon	Mo

DIEGO GARCIA ISLAND (British Indian Ocean Territory)
Number of Time Zones: *1*
Standard Time: *Applicable for the entire year*
Advanced Time: *Not observed*
Time Zone: *17:00 (+5hrs UTC)*

[a]	[b]	[c]	[d]	[e]	[f]	[g]	[h]	[i]	[j]	[k]	[l]	[m]	[n]	[o]	[p]	[q]	[r]	[s]	[t]	[u]	[v]	[w]	[x
17:01	18:01	19:01	20:01	21:01	22:01	23:01	00:01	01:01	02:01	03:01	04:01	05:01	06:01	07:01	08:01	09:01	10:01	11:01	12:01	13:01	14:01	15:01	16:01
5^{01}_{pm}	6^{01}_{pm}	7^{01}_{pm}	8^{01}_{pm}	9^{01}_{pm}	10^{01}_{pm}	11^{01}_{pm}	12^{01}_{am}	1^{01}_{am}	2^{01}_{am}	3^{01}_{am}	4^{01}_{am}	5^{01}_{am}	6^{01}_{am}	7^{01}_{am}	8^{01}_{am}	9^{01}_{am}	10^{01}_{am}	11^{01}_{am}	12^{01}_{pm}	1^{01}_{pm}	2^{01}_{pm}	3^{01}_{pm}	4^{01}_{pm}
Sun	Sun	Sun	Sun	Sun	Sun	Sun	Mon	Mon	Mon	Mon	Mon	Mon	Mon	Mon	Mon	Mon	Mon	Mon	Mon	Mon	Mon	Mon	Mon

DJIBOUTI
Number of Time Zones: *1*
Standard Time: *Applicable for the entire year*
Advanced Time: *Not observed*
Time Zone: *15:00 (+3hrs UTC)*

[a]	[b]	[c]	[d]	[e]	[f]	[g]	[h]	[i]	[j]	[k]	[l]	[m]	[n]	[o]	[p]	[q]	[r]	[s]	[t]	[u]	[v]	[w]	[x
15:01	16:01	17:01	18:01	19:01	20:01	21:01	22:01	23:01	00:01	01:01	02:01	03:01	04:01	05:01	06:01	07:01	08:01	09:01	10:01	11:01	12:01	13:01	14:01
3^{01}_{pm}	4^{01}_{pm}	5^{01}_{pm}	6^{01}_{pm}	7^{01}_{pm}	8^{01}_{pm}	9^{01}_{pm}	10^{01}_{pm}	11^{01}_{pm}	12^{01}_{am}	1^{01}_{am}	2^{01}_{am}	3^{01}_{am}	4^{01}_{am}	5^{01}_{am}	6^{01}_{am}	7^{01}_{am}	8^{01}_{am}	9^{01}_{am}	10^{01}_{am}	11^{01}_{am}	12^{01}_{pm}	1^{01}_{pm}	2^{01}_{pm}
Sun	Sun	Sun	Sun	Sun	Sun	Sun	Sun	Sun	Mon	Mon	Mon	Mon	Mon	Mon	Mon	Mon	Mon	Mon	Mon	Mon	Mon	Mon	Mon

Note: Advanced Time = Daylight Saving Time = Summer Time

DOMINICA
Number of Time Zones: *1*
Standard Time: *Applicable for the entire year*
Advanced Time: *Not observed*
Time Zone: *08:00 (-4hrs UTC)*

[a]	[b]	[c]	[d]	[e]	[f]	[g]	[h]	[i]	[j]	[k]	[l]	[m]	[n]	[o]	[p]	[q]	[r]	[s]	[t]	[u]	[v]	[w]	[x]
:01	09:01	10:01	11:01	12:01	13:01	14:01	15:01	16:01	17:01	18:01	19:01	20:01	21:01	22:01	23:01	00:01	01:01	02:01	03:01	04:01	05:01	06:01	07:01
8^{01}_{am}	9^{01}_{am}	10^{01}_{am}	11^{01}_{am}	12^{01}_{pm}	1^{01}_{pm}	2^{01}_{pm}	3^{01}_{pm}	4^{01}_{pm}	5^{01}_{pm}	6^{01}_{pm}	7^{01}_{pm}	8^{01}_{pm}	9^{01}_{pm}	10^{01}_{pm}	11^{01}_{pm}	12^{01}_{am}	1^{01}_{am}	2^{01}_{am}	3^{01}_{am}	4^{01}_{am}	5^{01}_{am}	6^{01}_{am}	7^{01}_{am}
Sun	Sun	Sun	Sun	Sun	Sun	Sun	Sun	Sun	Sun	Sun	Sun	Sun	Sun	Sun	Sun	Mon	Mon	Mon	Mon	Mon	Mon	Mon	Mon

DOMINICAN REPUBLIC
Number of Time Zones: *1*
Standard Time: *Applicable for the entire year*
Advanced Time: *Not observed*
Time Zone: *08:00 (-4hrs UTC)*

[a]	[b]	[c]	[d]	[e]	[f]	[g]	[h]	[i]	[j]	[k]	[l]	[m]	[n]	[o]	[p]	[q]	[r]	[s]	[t]	[u]	[v]	[w]	[x]
:01	09:01	10:01	11:01	12:01	13:01	14:01	15:01	16:01	17:01	18:01	19:01	20:01	21:01	22:01	23:01	00:01	01:01	02:01	03:01	04:01	05:01	06:01	07:01
8^{01}_{am}	9^{01}_{am}	10^{01}_{am}	11^{01}_{am}	12^{01}_{pm}	1^{01}_{pm}	2^{01}_{pm}	3^{01}_{pm}	4^{01}_{pm}	5^{01}_{pm}	6^{01}_{pm}	7^{01}_{pm}	8^{01}_{pm}	9^{01}_{pm}	10^{01}_{pm}	11^{01}_{pm}	12^{01}_{am}	1^{01}_{am}	2^{01}_{am}	3^{01}_{am}	4^{01}_{am}	5^{01}_{am}	6^{01}_{am}	7^{01}_{am}
Sun	Sun	Sun	Sun	Sun	Sun	Sun	Sun	Sun	Sun	Sun	Sun	Sun	Sun	Sun	Sun	Mon	Mon	Mon	Mon	Mon	Mon	Mon	Mon

DUBAI
Number of Time Zones: *1*
Standard Time: *Applicable for the entire year*
Advanced Time: *Not observed*
Time Zone: *16:00 (+4hrs UTC)*

[a]	[b]	[c]	[d]	[e]	[f]	[g]	[h]	[i]	[j]	[k]	[l]	[m]	[n]	[o]	[p]	[q]	[r]	[s]	[t]	[u]	[v]	[w]	[x]
:01	17:01	18:01	19:01	20:01	21:01	22:01	23:01	00:01	01:01	02:01	03:01	04:01	05:01	06:01	07:01	08:01	09:01	10:01	11:01	12:01	13:01	14:01	15:01
4^{01}_{pm}	5^{01}_{pm}	6^{01}_{pm}	7^{01}_{pm}	8^{01}_{pm}	9^{01}_{pm}	10^{01}_{pm}	11^{01}_{pm}	12^{01}_{am}	1^{01}_{am}	2^{01}_{am}	3^{01}_{am}	4^{01}_{am}	5^{01}_{am}	6^{01}_{am}	7^{01}_{am}	8^{01}_{am}	9^{01}_{am}	10^{01}_{am}	11^{01}_{am}	12^{01}_{pm}	1^{01}_{pm}	2^{01}_{pm}	3^{01}_{pm}
Sun	Sun	Sun	Sun	Sun	Sun	Sun	Sun	Mon	Mon	Mon	Mon	Mon	Mon	Mon	Mon	Mon	Mon	Mon	Mon	Mon	Mon	Mon	Mon

Note: Advanced Time = Daylight Saving Time = Summer Time

EASTER ISLAND
Number of Time Zones: *1*

Standard Time
Period: *Second Sunday in March to Second Sunday in October*
Time Zone: *06:00 (-6hrs UTC)*

[a]	[b]	[c]	[d]	[e]	[f]	[g]	[h]	[i]	[j]	[k]	[l]	[m]	[n]	[o]	[p]	[q]	[r]	[s]	[t]	[u]	[v]	[w]	[x]
06:01	07:01	08:01	09:01	10:01	11:01	12:01	13:01	14:01	15:01	16:01	17:01	18:01	19:01	20:01	21:01	22:01	23:01	00:01	01:01	02:01	03:01	04:01	05:01
6^{01}_{am}	7^{01}_{am}	8^{01}_{am}	9^{01}_{am}	10^{01}_{am}	11^{01}_{am}	12^{01}_{pm}	1^{01}_{pm}	2^{01}_{pm}	3^{01}_{pm}	4^{01}_{pm}	5^{01}_{pm}	6^{01}_{pm}	7^{01}_{pm}	8^{01}_{pm}	9^{01}_{pm}	10^{01}_{pm}	11^{01}_{pm}	12^{01}_{am}	1^{01}_{am}	2^{01}_{am}	3^{01}_{am}	4^{01}_{am}	5^{01}_{am}
Sun	Sun	Sun	Sun	Sun	Sun	Sun	Sun	Sun	Sun	Sun	Sun	Sun	Sun	Sun	Sun	Sun	Sun	Mon	Mon	Mon	Mon	Mon	Mon

Advanced Time
Period: *Second Sunday in October to Second Sunday in March*
Time Zone: *07:00 (-5hrs UTC)*

[a]	[b]	[c]	[d]	[e]	[f]	[g]	[h]	[i]	[j]	[k]	[l]	[m]	[n]	[o]	[p]	[q]	[r]	[s]	[t]	[u]	[v]	[w]	[x]
07:01	08:01	09:01	10:01	11:01	12:01	13:01	14:01	15:01	16:01	17:01	18:01	19:01	20:01	21:01	22:01	23:01	00:01	01:01	02:01	03:01	04:01	05:01	06:01
7^{01}_{am}	8^{01}_{am}	9^{01}_{am}	10^{01}_{am}	11^{01}_{am}	12^{01}_{pm}	1^{01}_{pm}	2^{01}_{pm}	3^{01}_{pm}	4^{01}_{pm}	5^{01}_{pm}	6^{01}_{pm}	7^{01}_{pm}	8^{01}_{pm}	9^{01}_{pm}	10^{01}_{pm}	11^{01}_{pm}	12^{01}_{am}	1^{01}_{am}	2^{01}_{am}	3^{01}_{am}	4^{01}_{am}	5^{01}_{am}	6^{01}_{am}
Sun	Sun	Sun	Sun	Sun	Sun	Sun	Sun	Sun	Sun	Sun	Sun	Sun	Sun	Sun	Sun	Sun	Mon	Mon	Mon	Mon	Mon	Mon	Mon

ECUADOR
Number of Time Zones: *1*
Standard Time: *Applicable for the entire year*
Advanced Time: *Not observed*
Time Zone: *07:00 (-5hrs UTC)*

[a]	[b]	[c]	[d]	[e]	[f]	[g]	[h]	[i]	[j]	[k]	[l]	[m]	[n]	[o]	[p]	[q]	[r]	[s]	[t]	[u]	[v]	[w]	[x]
07:01	08:01	09:01	10:01	11:01	12:01	13:01	14:01	15:01	16:01	17:01	18:01	19:01	20:01	21:01	22:01	23:01	00:01	01:01	02:01	03:01	04:01	05:01	06:01
7^{01}_{am}	8^{01}_{am}	9^{01}_{am}	10^{01}_{am}	11^{01}_{am}	12^{01}_{pm}	1^{01}_{pm}	2^{01}_{pm}	3^{01}_{pm}	4^{01}_{pm}	5^{01}_{pm}	6^{01}_{pm}	7^{01}_{pm}	8^{01}_{pm}	9^{01}_{pm}	10^{01}_{pm}	11^{01}_{pm}	12^{01}_{am}	1^{01}_{am}	2^{01}_{am}	3^{01}_{am}	4^{01}_{am}	5^{01}_{am}	6^{01}_{am}
Sun	Sun	Sun	Sun	Sun	Sun	Sun	Sun	Sun	Sun	Sun	Sun	Sun	Sun	Sun	Sun	Sun	Mon	Mon	Mon	Mon	Mon	Mon	Mon

Note: Advanced Time = Daylight Saving Time = Summer Time

EGYPT
Number of Time Zones: *1*

Standard Time
Period: *September 30 to May 15 (Approximate)*
Time Zone: *14:00 (+2hrs UTC)*

[a]	[b]	[c]	[d]	[e]	[f]	[g]	[h]	[i]	[j]	[k]	[l]	[m]	[n]	[o]	[p]	[q]	[r]	[s]	[t]	[u]	[v]	[w]	[x]
14:01	15:01	16:01	17:01	18:01	19:01	20:01	21:01	22:01	23:01	00:01	01:01	02:01	03:01	04:01	05:01	06:01	07:01	08:01	09:01	10:01	11:01	12:01	13:01
2^{01}_{pm}	3^{01}_{pm}	4^{01}_{pm}	5^{01}_{pm}	6^{01}_{pm}	7^{01}_{pm}	8^{01}_{pm}	9^{01}_{pm}	10^{01}_{pm}	11^{01}_{pm}	12^{01}_{am}	1^{01}_{am}	2^{01}_{am}	3^{01}_{am}	4^{01}_{am}	5^{01}_{am}	6^{01}_{am}	7^{01}_{am}	8^{01}_{am}	9^{01}_{am}	10^{01}_{am}	11^{01}_{am}	12^{01}_{pm}	1^{01}_{pm}
Sun	Sun	Sun	Sun	Sun	Sun	Sun	Sun	Sun	Sun	Mon	Mon	Mon	Mon	Mon	Mon	Mon	Mon	Mon	Mon	Mon	Mon	Mon	Mon

Advanced Time
Period: *May 15 to September 30 (Approximate)*
Time Zone: *15:00 (+3hrs UTC)*

[a]	[b]	[c]	[d]	[e]	[f]	[g]	[h]	[i]	[j]	[k]	[l]	[m]	[n]	[o]	[p]	[q]	[r]	[s]	[t]	[u]	[v]	[w]	[x]
15:01	16:01	17:01	18:01	19:01	20:01	21:01	22:01	23:01	00:01	01:01	02:01	03:01	04:01	05:01	06:01	07:01	08:01	09:01	10:01	11:01	12:01	13:01	14:01
3^{01}_{pm}	4^{01}_{pm}	5^{01}_{pm}	6^{01}_{pm}	7^{01}_{pm}	8^{01}_{pm}	9^{01}_{pm}	10^{01}_{pm}	11^{01}_{pm}	12^{01}_{am}	1^{01}_{am}	2^{01}_{am}	3^{01}_{am}	4^{01}_{am}	5^{01}_{am}	6^{01}_{am}	7^{01}_{am}	8^{01}_{am}	9^{01}_{am}	10^{01}_{am}	11^{01}_{am}	12^{01}_{pm}	1^{01}_{pm}	2^{01}_{pm}
Sun	Sun	Sun	Sun	Sun	Sun	Sun	Sun	Sun	Mon	Mon	Mon	Mon	Mon	Mon	Mon	Mon	Mon	Mon	Mon	Mon	Mon	Mon	Mon

EL SALVADOR
Number of Time Zones: *1*
Standard Time: *Applicable for the entire year*
Advanced Time: *Not observed*
Time Zone: *06:00 (-6hrs UTC)*

[a]	[b]	[c]	[d]	[e]	[f]	[g]	[h]	[i]	[j]	[k]	[l]	[m]	[n]	[o]	[p]	[q]	[r]	[s]	[t]	[u]	[v]	[w]	[x]
06:01	07:01	08:01	09:01	10:01	11:01	12:01	13:01	14:01	15:01	16:01	17:01	18:01	19:01	20:01	21:01	22:01	23:01	00:01	01:01	02:01	03:01	04:01	05:01
6^{01}_{am}	7^{01}_{am}	8^{01}_{am}	9^{01}_{am}	10^{01}_{am}	11^{01}_{am}	12^{01}_{pm}	1^{01}_{pm}	2^{01}_{pm}	3^{01}_{pm}	4^{01}_{pm}	5^{01}_{pm}	6^{01}_{pm}	7^{01}_{pm}	8^{01}_{pm}	9^{01}_{pm}	10^{01}_{pm}	11^{01}_{pm}	12^{01}_{am}	1^{01}_{am}	2^{01}_{am}	3^{01}_{am}	4^{01}_{am}	5^{01}_{am}
Sun	Sun	Sun	Sun	Sun	Sun	Sun	Sun	Sun	Sun	Sun	Sun	Sun	Sun	Sun	Sun	Sun	Sun	Mon	Mon	Mon	Mon	Mon	Mon

EQUATORIAL GUINEA
Number of Time Zones: *1*
Standard Time: *Applicable for the entire year*
Advanced Time: *Not observed*
Time Zone: *13:00 (+1hr UTC)*

[a]	[b]	[c]	[d]	[e]	[f]	[g]	[h]	[i]	[j]	[k]	[l]	[m]	[n]	[o]	[p]	[q]	[r]	[s]	[t]	[u]	[v]	[w]	[x]
13:01	14:01	15:01	16:01	17:01	18:01	19:01	20:01	21:01	22:01	23:01	00:01	01:01	02:01	03:01	04:01	05:01	06:01	07:01	08:01	09:01	10:01	11:01	12:01
1^{01}_{pm}	2^{01}_{pm}	3^{01}_{pm}	4^{01}_{pm}	5^{01}_{pm}	6^{01}_{pm}	7^{01}_{pm}	8^{01}_{pm}	9^{01}_{pm}	10^{01}_{pm}	11^{01}_{pm}	12^{01}_{am}	1^{01}_{am}	2^{01}_{am}	3^{01}_{am}	4^{01}_{am}	5^{01}_{am}	6^{01}_{am}	7^{01}_{am}	8^{01}_{am}	9^{01}_{am}	10^{01}_{am}	11^{01}_{am}	12^{01}_{pm}
Sun	Sun	Sun	Sun	Sun	Sun	Sun	Sun	Sun	Sun	Sun	Mon	Mon	Mon	Mon	Mon	Mon	Mon	Mon	Mon	Mon	Mon	Mon	Mon

Note: Advanced Time = Daylight Saving Time = Summer Time

ETHIOPIA

Number of Time Zones: *1*
Standard Time: *Applicable for the entire year*
Advanced Time: *Not observed*
Time Zone: *15:00 (+3hrs UTC)*

[a]	[b]	[c]	[d]	[e]	[f]	[g]	[h]	[i]	[j]	[k]	[l]	[m]	[n]	[o]	[p]	[q]	[r]	[s]	[t]	[u]	[v]	[w]	[x
15:01	16:01	17:01	18:01	19:01	20:01	21:01	22:01	23:01	00:01	01:01	02:01	03:01	04:01	05:01	06:01	07:01	08:01	09:01	10:01	11:01	12:01	13:01	14:0(
3^{01}_{pm}	4^{01}_{pm}	5^{01}_{pm}	6^{01}_{pm}	7^{01}_{pm}	8^{01}_{pm}	9^{01}_{pm}	10^{01}_{pm}	11^{01}_{pm}	12^{01}_{am}	1^{01}_{am}	2^{01}_{am}	3^{01}_{am}	4^{01}_{am}	5^{01}_{am}	6^{01}_{am}	7^{01}_{am}	8^{01}_{am}	9^{01}_{am}	10^{01}_{am}	11^{01}_{am}	12^{01}_{pm}	1^{01}_{pm}	2^{0}_{p}
Sun	Sun	Sun	Sun	Sun	Sun	Sun	Sun	Sun	Mon	Mon	Mon	Mon	Mon	Mon	Mon	Mon	Mon	Mon	Mon	Mon	Mon	Mon	Mo

FALKLAND ISLANDS

Number of Time Zones: *1*

Standard Time

Period: *Third Sunday in April to Second Sunday in September*
Time Zone: *08:00 (-4hrs UTC)*

[a]	[b]	[c]	[d]	[e]	[f]	[g]	[h]	[i]	[j]	[k]	[l]	[m]	[n]	[o]	[p]	[q]	[r]	[s]	[t]	[u]	[v]	[w]	[x
08:01	09:01	10:01	11:01	12:01	13:01	14:01	15:01	16:01	17:01	18:01	19:01	20:01	21:01	22:01	23:01	00:01	01:01	02:01	03:01	04:01	05:01	06:01	07:0
8^{01}_{am}	9^{01}_{am}	10^{01}_{am}	11^{01}_{am}	12^{01}_{pm}	1^{01}_{pm}	2^{01}_{pm}	3^{01}_{pm}	4^{01}_{pm}	5^{01}_{pm}	6^{01}_{pm}	7^{01}_{pm}	8^{01}_{pm}	9^{01}_{pm}	10^{01}_{pm}	11^{01}_{pm}	12^{01}_{am}	1^{01}_{am}	2^{01}_{am}	3^{01}_{am}	4^{01}_{am}	5^{01}_{am}	6^{01}_{am}	7^{01}_{a}
Sun	Sun	Sun	Sun	Sun	Sun	Sun	Sun	Sun	Sun	Sun	Sun	Sun	Sun	Sun	Sun	Mon	Mon	Mon	Mon	Mon	Mon	Mon	Mon

Advanced Time

Period: *Second Sunday in September to Third Sunday in April*
Time Zone: *09:00 (-3hrs UTC)*

[a]	[b]	[c]	[d]	[e]	[f]	[g]	[h]	[i]	[j]	[k]	[l]	[m]	[n]	[o]	[p]	[q]	[r]	[s]	[t]	[u]	[v]	[w]	[x]
09:01	10:01	11:01	12:01	13:01	14:01	15:01	16:01	17:01	18:01	19:01	20:01	21:01	22:01	23:01	00:01	01:01	02:01	03:01	04:01	05:01	06:01	07:01	08:01
9^{01}_{am}	10^{01}_{am}	11^{01}_{am}	12^{01}_{pm}	1^{01}_{pm}	2^{01}_{pm}	3^{01}_{pm}	4^{01}_{pm}	5^{01}_{pm}	6^{01}_{pm}	7^{01}_{pm}	8^{01}_{pm}	9^{01}_{pm}	10^{01}_{pm}	11^{01}_{pm}	12^{01}_{am}	1^{01}_{am}	2^{01}_{am}	3^{01}_{am}	4^{01}_{am}	5^{01}_{am}	6^{01}_{am}	7^{01}_{am}	8^{01}_{am}
Sun	Sun	Sun	Sun	Sun	Sun	Sun	Sun	Sun	Sun	Sun	Sun	Sun	Sun	Sun	Mon	Mon	Mon	Mon	Mon	Mon	Mon	Mon	Mon

Note: Advanced Time = Daylight Saving Time = Summer Time

FAROE ISLANDS
Number of Time Zones: *1*

Standard Time
Period: *Last Sunday in September to Last Sunday in March*
Time Zone: *12:00 (UTC)*

[a]	[b]	[c]	[d]	[e]	[f]	[g]	[h]	[i]	[j]	[k]	[l]	[m]	[n]	[o]	[p]	[q]	[r]	[s]	[t]	[u]	[v]	[w]	[x]
12:01	13:01	14:01	15:01	16:01	17:01	18:01	19:01	20:01	21:01	22:01	23:01	00:01	01:01	02:01	03:01	04:01	05:01	06:01	07:01	08:01	09:01	10:01	11:01
12^{01}_{pm}	1^{01}_{pm}	2^{01}_{pm}	3^{01}_{pm}	4^{01}_{pm}	5^{01}_{pm}	6^{01}_{pm}	7^{01}_{pm}	8^{01}_{pm}	9^{01}_{pm}	10^{01}_{pm}	11^{01}_{pm}	12^{01}_{am}	1^{01}_{am}	2^{01}_{am}	3^{01}_{am}	4^{01}_{am}	5^{01}_{am}	6^{01}_{am}	7^{01}_{am}	8^{01}_{am}	9^{01}_{am}	10^{01}_{am}	11^{01}_{am}
Sun	Sun	Sun	Sun	Sun	Sun	Sun	Sun	Sun	Sun	Sun	Sun	Mon	Mon	Mon	Mon	Mon	Mon	Mon	Mon	Mon	Mon	Mon	Mon

Advanced Time
Period: *Last Sunday in March to Last Sunday in September*
Time Zone: *13:00 (+1hr UTC)*

[a]	[b]	[c]	[d]	[e]	[f]	[g]	[h]	[i]	[j]	[k]	[l]	[m]	[n]	[o]	[p]	[q]	[r]	[s]	[t]	[u]	[v]	[w]	[x]
13:01	14:01	15:01	16:01	17:01	18:01	19:01	20:01	21:01	22:01	23:01	00:01	01:01	02:01	03:01	04:01	05:01	06:01	07:01	08:01	09:01	10:01	11:01	12:01
1^{01}_{pm}	2^{01}_{pm}	3^{01}_{pm}	4^{01}_{pm}	5^{01}_{pm}	6^{01}_{pm}	7^{01}_{pm}	8^{01}_{pm}	9^{01}_{pm}	10^{01}_{pm}	11^{01}_{pm}	12^{01}_{am}	1^{01}_{am}	2^{01}_{am}	3^{01}_{am}	4^{01}_{am}	5^{01}_{am}	6^{01}_{am}	7^{01}_{am}	8^{01}_{am}	9^{01}_{am}	10^{01}_{am}	11^{01}_{am}	12^{01}_{pm}
Sun	Sun	Sun	Sun	Sun	Sun	Sun	Sun	Sun	Sun	Sun	Mon	Mon	Mon	Mon	Mon	Mon	Mon	Mon	Mon	Mon	Mon	Mon	Mon

FERNANDO DE NORONHA ISLAND
Number of Time Zones: *1*

Standard Time
Period: *Varies: March/April to Mid-October*
Time Zone: *10:00 (-2hrs UTC)*

[a]	[b]	[c]	[d]	[e]	[f]	[g]	[h]	[i]	[j]	[k]	[l]	[m]	[n]	[o]	[p]	[q]	[r]	[s]	[t]	[u]	[v]	[w]	[x]
10:01	11:01	12:01	13:01	14:01	15:01	16:01	17:01	18:01	19:01	20:01	21:01	22:01	23:01	00:01	01:01	02:01	03:01	04:01	05:01	06:01	07:01	08:01	09:01
10^{01}_{am}	11^{01}_{am}	12^{01}_{pm}	1^{01}_{pm}	2^{01}_{pm}	3^{01}_{pm}	4^{01}_{pm}	5^{01}_{pm}	6^{01}_{pm}	7^{01}_{pm}	8^{01}_{pm}	9^{01}_{pm}	10^{01}_{pm}	11^{01}_{pm}	12^{01}_{am}	1^{01}_{am}	2^{01}_{am}	3^{01}_{am}	4^{01}_{am}	5^{01}_{am}	6^{01}_{am}	7^{01}_{am}	8^{01}_{am}	9^{01}_{am}
Sun	Sun	Sun	Sun	Sun	Sun	Sun	Sun	Sun	Sun	Sun	Sun	Sun	Sun	Mon	Mon	Mon	Mon	Mon	Mon	Mon	Mon	Mon	Mon

Advanced Time
Period: *Varies: Mid-October to March/April*
Time Zone: *11:00 (-1hr UTC)*

[a]	[b]	[c]	[d]	[e]	[f]	[g]	[h]	[i]	[j]	[k]	[l]	[m]	[n]	[o]	[p]	[q]	[r]	[s]	[t]	[u]	[v]	[w]	[x]
11:01	12:01	13:01	14:01	15:01	16:01	17:01	18:01	19:01	20:01	21:01	22:01	23:01	00:01	01:01	02:01	03:01	04:01	05:01	06:01	07:01	08:01	09:01	10:01
11^{01}_{am}	12^{01}_{pm}	1^{01}_{pm}	2^{01}_{pm}	3^{01}_{pm}	4^{01}_{pm}	5^{01}_{pm}	6^{01}_{pm}	7^{01}_{pm}	8^{01}_{pm}	9^{01}_{pm}	10^{01}_{pm}	11^{01}_{pm}	12^{01}_{am}	1^{01}_{am}	2^{01}_{am}	3^{01}_{am}	4^{01}_{am}	5^{01}_{am}	6^{01}_{am}	7^{01}_{am}	8^{01}_{am}	9^{01}_{am}	10^{01}_{am}
Sun	Sun	Sun	Sun	Sun	Sun	Sun	Sun	Sun	Sun	Sun	Sun	Sun	Mon	Mon	Mon	Mon	Mon	Mon	Mon	Mon	Mon	Mon	Mon

Note: Advanced Time = Daylight Saving Time = Summer Time

FIJI

Number of Time Zones: *1*
Standard Time: *Applicable for the entire year*
Advanced Time: *Not observed*
Time Zone: *24:00 (+12hrs UTC)*

[a]	[b]	[c]	[d]	[e]	[f]	[g]	[h]	[i]	[j]	[k]	[l]	[m]	[n]	[o]	[p]	[q]	[r]	[s]	[t]	[u]	[v]	[w]	[x]
00:01	01:01	02:01	03:01	04:01	05:01	06:01	07:01	08:01	09:01	10:01	11:01	12:01	13:01	14:01	15:01	16:01	17:01	18:01	19:01	20:01	21:01	22:01	23:0
12^{01}_{am}	1^{01}_{am}	2^{01}_{am}	3^{01}_{am}	4^{01}_{am}	5^{01}_{am}	6^{01}_{am}	7^{01}_{am}	8^{01}_{am}	9^{01}_{am}	10^{01}_{am}	11^{01}_{am}	12^{01}_{pm}	1^{01}_{pm}	2^{01}_{pm}	3^{01}_{pm}	4^{01}_{pm}	5^{01}_{pm}	6^{01}_{pm}	7^{01}_{pm}	8^{01}_{pm}	9^{01}_{pm}	10^{01}_{pm}	11^{0}_{p}
Mon	Mon	Mon	Mon	Mon	Mon	Mon	Mon	Mon	Mon	Mon	Mon	Mon	Mon	Mon	Mon	Mon	Mon	Mon	Mon	Mon	Mon	Mon	Mo

FINLAND

Number of Time Zones: *1*

Standard Time

Period: *Last Sunday in September to Last Sunday in March*
Time Zone: *14:00 (+2hrs UTC)*

[a]	[b]	[c]	[d]	[e]	[f]	[g]	[h]	[i]	[j]	[k]	[l]	[m]	[n]	[o]	[p]	[q]	[r]	[s]	[t]	[u]	[v]	[w]	[x]
14:01	15:01	16:01	17:01	18:01	19:01	20:01	21:01	22:01	23:01	00:01	01:01	02:01	03:01	04:01	05:01	06:01	07:01	08:01	09:01	10:01	11:01	12:01	13:0
2^{01}_{pm}	3^{01}_{pm}	4^{01}_{pm}	5^{01}_{pm}	6^{01}_{pm}	7^{01}_{pm}	8^{01}_{pm}	9^{01}_{pm}	10^{01}_{pm}	11^{01}_{pm}	12^{01}_{am}	1^{01}_{am}	2^{01}_{am}	3^{01}_{am}	4^{01}_{am}	5^{01}_{am}	6^{01}_{am}	7^{01}_{am}	8^{01}_{am}	9^{01}_{am}	10^{01}_{am}	11^{01}_{am}	12^{01}_{pm}	1_{p}
Sun	Sun	Sun	Sun	Sun	Sun	Sun	Sun	Sun	Sun	Mon	Mon	Mon	Mon	Mon	Mon	Mon	Mon	Mon	Mon	Mon	Mon	Mon	Mo

Advanced Time

Period: *Last Sunday in March to Last Sunday in September*
Time Zone: *15:00 (+3hrs UTC)*

[a]	[b]	[c]	[d]	[e]	[f]	[g]	[h]	[i]	[j]	[k]	[l]	[m]	[n]	[o]	[p]	[q]	[r]	[s]	[t]	[u]	[v]	[w]	[x]
15:01	16:01	17:01	18:01	19:01	20:01	21:01	22:01	23:01	00:01	01:01	02:01	03:01	04:01	05:01	06:01	07:01	08:01	09:01	10:01	11:01	12:01	13:01	14:0
3^{01}_{pm}	4^{01}_{pm}	5^{01}_{pm}	6^{01}_{pm}	7^{01}_{pm}	8^{01}_{pm}	9^{01}_{pm}	10^{01}_{pm}	11^{01}_{pm}	12^{01}_{am}	1^{01}_{am}	2^{01}_{am}	3^{01}_{am}	4^{01}_{am}	5^{01}_{am}	6^{01}_{am}	7^{01}_{am}	8^{01}_{am}	9^{01}_{am}	10^{01}_{am}	11^{01}_{am}	12^{01}_{pm}	1^{01}_{pm}	2^{0}_{p}
Sun	Sun	Sun	Sun	Sun	Sun	Sun	Sun	Sun	Mon	Mon	Mon	Mon	Mon	Mon	Mon	Mon	Mon	Mon	Mon	Mon	Mon	Mon	Mo

Note: Advanced Time = Daylight Saving Time = Summer Time

FRANCE
Number of Time Zones: *1*

Standard Time
Period: *Last Sunday in September to Last Sunday in March*
Time Zone: *13:00 (+1hr UTC)*

[a]	[b]	[c]	[d]	[e]	[f]	[g]	[h]	[i]	[j]	[k]	[l]	[m]	[n]	[o]	[p]	[q]	[r]	[s]	[t]	[u]	[v]	[w]	[x]
13:01	14:01	15:01	16:01	17:01	18:01	19:01	20:01	21:01	22:01	23:01	00:01	01:01	02:01	03:01	04:01	05:01	06:01	07:01	08:01	09:01	10:01	11:01	12:01
1:01pm	2:01pm	3:01pm	4:01pm	5:01pm	6:01pm	7:01pm	8:01pm	9:01pm	10:01pm	11:01pm	12:01am	1:01am	2:01am	3:01am	4:01am	5:01am	6:01am	7:01am	8:01am	9:01am	10:01am	11:01am	12:01pm
Sun	Sun	Sun	Sun	Sun	Sun	Sun	Sun	Sun	Sun	Sun	Mon	Mon	Mon	Mon	Mon	Mon	Mon	Mon	Mon	Mon	Mon	Mon	Mon

Advanced Time
Period: *Last Sunday in March to Last Sunday in September*
Time Zone: *14:00 (+2hrs UTC)*

[a]	[b]	[c]	[d]	[e]	[f]	[g]	[h]	[i]	[j]	[k]	[l]	[m]	[n]	[o]	[p]	[q]	[r]	[s]	[t]	[u]	[v]	[w]	[x]
14:01	15:01	16:01	17:01	18:01	19:01	20:01	21:01	22:01	23:01	00:01	01:01	02:01	03:01	04:01	05:01	06:01	07:01	08:01	09:01	10:01	11:01	12:01	13:01
2:01pm	3:01pm	4:01pm	5:01pm	6:01pm	7:01pm	8:01pm	9:01pm	10:01pm	11:01pm	12:01am	1:01am	2:01am	3:01am	4:01am	5:01am	6:01am	7:01am	8:01am	9:01am	10:01am	11:01am	12:01pm	1:01pm
Sun	Sun	Sun	Sun	Sun	Sun	Sun	Sun	Sun	Sun	Mon	Mon	Mon	Mon	Mon	Mon	Mon	Mon	Mon	Mon	Mon	Mon	Mon	Mon

FRENCH GUIANA
Number of Time Zones: *1*
Standard Time: *Applicable for the entire year*
Advanced Time: *Not observed*
Time Zone: *09:00 (-3hrs UTC)*

[a]	[b]	[c]	[d]	[e]	[f]	[g]	[h]	[i]	[j]	[k]	[l]	[m]	[n]	[o]	[p]	[q]	[r]	[s]	[t]	[u]	[v]	[w]	[x]
09:01	10:01	11:01	12:01	13:01	14:01	15:01	16:01	17:01	18:01	19:01	20:01	21:01	22:01	23:01	00:01	01:01	02:01	03:01	04:01	05:01	06:01	07:01	08:01
9:01am	10:01am	11:01am	12:01pm	1:01pm	2:01pm	3:01pm	4:01pm	5:01pm	6:01pm	7:01pm	8:01pm	9:01pm	10:01pm	11:01pm	12:01am	1:01am	2:01am	3:01am	4:01am	5:01am	6:01am	7:01am	8:01am
Sun	Sun	Sun	Sun	Sun	Sun	Sun	Sun	Sun	Sun	Sun	Sun	Sun	Sun	Sun	Sun	Mon	Mon	Mon	Mon	Mon	Mon	Mon	Mon

Note: Advanced Time = Daylight Saving Time = Summer Time

FRENCH POLYNESIA
Number of Time Zones: *3*
Notes: *Advanced Time not observed;*
See Reference Map I for graphic depiction of time zones

EASTERN TIME ZONE
Note: *Comprises the Gambier Islands*

Standard Time: *Applicable for the entire year*
Time Zone: *03:00 (-9hrs UTC)*

[a]	[b]	[c]	[d]	[e]	[f]	[g]	[h]	[i]	[j]	[k]	[l]	[m]	[n]	[o]	[p]	[q]	[r]	[s]	[t]	[u]	[v]	[w]	[
03:01	04:01	05:01	06:01	07:01	08:01	09:01	10:01	11:01	12:01	13:01	14:01	15:01	16:01	17:01	18:01	19:01	20:01	21:01	22:01	23:01	00:01	01:01	02:
3^{01}_{am}	4^{01}_{am}	5^{01}_{am}	6^{01}_{am}	7^{01}_{am}	8^{01}_{am}	9^{01}_{am}	10^{01}_{am}	11^{01}_{am}	12^{01}_{pm}	1^{01}_{pm}	2^{01}_{pm}	3^{01}_{pm}	4^{01}_{pm}	5^{01}_{pm}	6^{01}_{pm}	7^{01}_{pm}	8^{01}_{pm}	9^{01}_{pm}	10^{01}_{pm}	11^{01}_{pm}	12^{01}_{am}	1^{01}_{am}	2
Sun	Sun	Sun	Sun	Sun	Sun	Sun	Sun	Sun	Sun	Sun	Sun	Sun	Sun	Sun	Sun	Sun	Sun	Sun	Sun	Sun	Mon	Mon	M

CENTRAL TIME ZONE
Note: *Comprises the Marquesas Islands*

Standard Time: *Applicable for the entire year*
Time Zone: *02:30 (-9hrs 30mins UTC)*

[a]	[b]	[c]	[d]	[e]	[f]	[g]	[h]	[i]	[j]	[k]	[l]	[m]	[n]	[o]	[p]	[q]	[r]	[s]	[t]	[u]	[v]	[w]	[
02:31	03:31	04:31	05:31	06:31	07:31	08:31	09:31	10:31	11:31	12:31	13:31	14:31	15:31	16:31	17:31	18:31	19:31	20:31	21:31	22:31	23:31	00:31	01:
2^{31}_{am}	3^{31}_{am}	4^{31}_{am}	5^{31}_{am}	6^{31}_{am}	7^{31}_{am}	8^{31}_{am}	9^{31}_{am}	10^{31}_{am}	11^{31}_{am}	12^{31}_{pm}	1^{31}_{pm}	2^{31}_{pm}	3^{31}_{pm}	4^{31}_{pm}	5^{31}_{pm}	6^{31}_{pm}	7^{31}_{pm}	8^{31}_{pm}	9^{31}_{pm}	10^{31}_{pm}	11^{31}_{pm}	12^{31}_{am}	1
Sun	Sun	Sun	Sun	Sun	Sun	Sun	Sun	Sun	Sun	Sun	Sun	Sun	Sun	Sun	Sun	Sun	Sun	Sun	Sun	Sun	Sun	Mon	M

WESTERN TIME ZONE
Note: *Comprises the Society Islands, the Tuamotus, and Tubuai*

Standard Time: *Applicable for the entire year*
Time Zone: *02:00 (-10hrs UTC)*

[a]	[b]	[c]	[d]	[e]	[f]	[g]	[h]	[i]	[j]	[k]	[l]	[m]	[n]	[o]	[p]	[q]	[r]	[s]	[t]	[u]	[v]	[w]	[×
02:01	03:01	04:01	05:01	06:01	07:01	08:01	09:01	10:01	11:01	12:01	13:01	14:01	15:01	16:01	17:01	18:01	19:01	20:01	21:01	22:01	23:01	00:01	01:0
2^{01}_{am}	3^{01}_{am}	4^{01}_{am}	5^{01}_{am}	6^{01}_{am}	7^{01}_{am}	8^{01}_{am}	9^{01}_{am}	10^{01}_{am}	11^{01}_{am}	12^{01}_{pm}	1^{01}_{pm}	2^{01}_{pm}	3^{01}_{pm}	4^{01}_{pm}	5^{01}_{pm}	6^{01}_{pm}	7^{01}_{pm}	8^{01}_{pm}	9^{01}_{pm}	10^{01}_{pm}	11^{01}_{pm}	12^{01}_{am}	1
Sun	Sun	Sun	Sun	Sun	Sun	Sun	Sun	Sun	Sun	Sun	Sun	Sun	Sun	Sun	Sun	Sun	Sun	Sun	Sun	Sun	Sun	Mon	Mo

Note: Advanced Time = Daylight Saving Time = Summer Time

GABON

Number of Time Zones: *1*
Standard Time: *Applicable for the entire year*
Advanced Time: *Not observed*
Time Zone: *13:00 (+1hr UTC)*

[a]	[b]	[c]	[d]	[e]	[f]	[g]	[h]	[i]	[j]	[k]	[l]	[m]	[n]	[o]	[p]	[q]	[r]	[s]	[t]	[u]	[v]	[w]	[x]
13:01	14:01	15:01	16:01	17:01	18:01	19:01	20:01	21:01	22:01	23:01	00:01	01:01	02:01	03:01	04:01	05:01	06:01	07:01	08:01	09:01	10:01	11:01	12:01
1^{01}_{pm}	2^{01}_{pm}	3^{01}_{pm}	4^{01}_{pm}	5^{01}_{pm}	6^{01}_{pm}	7^{01}_{pm}	8^{01}_{pm}	9^{01}_{pm}	10^{01}_{pm}	11^{01}_{pm}	12^{01}_{am}	1^{01}_{am}	2^{01}_{am}	3^{01}_{am}	4^{01}_{am}	5^{01}_{am}	6^{01}_{am}	7^{01}_{am}	8^{01}_{am}	9^{01}_{am}	10^{01}_{am}	11^{01}_{am}	12^{01}_{pm}
Sun	Sun	Sun	Sun	Sun	Sun	Sun	Sun	Sun	Sun	Sun	Mon	Mon	Mon	Mon	Mon	Mon	Mon	Mon	Mon	Mon	Mon	Mon	Mon

GALAPAGOS ISLANDS

Number of Time Zones: *1*
Standard Time: *Applicable for the entire year*
Advanced Time: *Not observed*
Time Zone: *06:00 (-6hrs UTC)*

[a]	[b]	[c]	[d]	[e]	[f]	[g]	[h]	[i]	[j]	[k]	[l]	[m]	[n]	[o]	[p]	[q]	[r]	[s]	[t]	[u]	[v]	[w]	[x]
06:01	07:01	08:01	09:01	10:01	11:01	12:01	13:01	14:01	15:01	16:01	17:01	18:01	19:01	20:01	21:01	22:01	23:01	00:01	01:01	02:01	03:01	04:01	05:01
6^{01}_{am}	7^{01}_{am}	8^{01}_{am}	9^{01}_{am}	10^{01}_{am}	11^{01}_{am}	12^{01}_{pm}	1^{01}_{pm}	2^{01}_{pm}	3^{01}_{pm}	4^{01}_{pm}	5^{01}_{pm}	6^{01}_{pm}	7^{01}_{pm}	8^{01}_{pm}	9^{01}_{pm}	10^{01}_{pm}	11^{01}_{pm}	12^{01}_{am}	1^{01}_{am}	2^{01}_{am}	3^{01}_{am}	4^{01}_{am}	5^{01}_{am}
Sun	Sun	Sun	Sun	Sun	Sun	Sun	Sun	Sun	Sun	Sun	Sun	Sun	Sun	Sun	Sun	Sun	Sun	Mon	Mon	Mon	Mon	Mon	Mon

THE GAMBIA

Number of Time Zones: *1*
Standard Time: *Applicable for the entire year*
Advanced Time: *Not observed*
Time Zone: *12:00 (UTC)*

[a]	[b]	[c]	[d]	[e]	[f]	[g]	[h]	[i]	[j]	[k]	[l]	[m]	[n]	[o]	[p]	[q]	[r]	[s]	[t]	[u]	[v]	[w]	[x]
12:01	13:01	14:01	15:01	16:01	17:01	18:01	19:01	20:01	21:01	22:01	23:01	00:01	01:01	02:01	03:01	04:01	05:01	06:01	07:01	08:01	09:01	10:01	11:01
12^{01}_{pm}	1^{01}_{pm}	2^{01}_{pm}	3^{01}_{pm}	4^{01}_{pm}	5^{01}_{pm}	6^{01}_{pm}	7^{01}_{pm}	8^{01}_{pm}	9^{01}_{pm}	10^{01}_{pm}	11^{01}_{pm}	12^{01}_{am}	1^{01}_{am}	2^{01}_{am}	3^{01}_{am}	4^{01}_{am}	5^{01}_{am}	6^{01}_{am}	7^{01}_{am}	8^{01}_{am}	9^{01}_{am}	10^{01}_{am}	11^{01}_{am}
Sun	Sun	Sun	Sun	Sun	Sun	Sun	Sun	Sun	Sun	Sun	Sun	Mon	Mon	Mon	Mon	Mon	Mon	Mon	Mon	Mon	Mon	Mon	Mon

Note: Advanced Time = Daylight Saving Time = Summer Time

GERMANY, EAST
Number of Time Zones: *1*

Standard Time
Period: *Last Sunday in September to Last Sunday in March*
Time Zone: *13:00 (+1hr UTC)*

[a]	[b]	[c]	[d]	[e]	[f]	[g]	[h]	[i]	[j]	[k]	[l]	[m]	[n]	[o]	[p]	[q]	[r]	[s]	[t]	[u]	[v]	[w]	[x]
13:01	14:01	15:01	16:01	17:01	18:01	19:01	20:01	21:01	22:01	23:01	00:01	01:01	02:01	03:01	04:01	05:01	06:01	07:01	08:01	09:01	10:01	11:01	12:01
1^{01}_{pm}	2^{01}_{pm}	3^{01}_{pm}	4^{01}_{pm}	5^{01}_{pm}	6^{01}_{pm}	7^{01}_{pm}	8^{01}_{pm}	9^{01}_{pm}	10^{01}_{pm}	11^{01}_{pm}	12^{01}_{am}	1^{01}_{am}	2^{01}_{am}	3^{01}_{am}	4^{01}_{am}	5^{01}_{am}	6^{01}_{am}	7^{01}_{am}	8^{01}_{am}	9^{01}_{am}	10^{01}_{am}	11^{01}_{am}	12^{01}_{pm}
Sun	Sun	Sun	Sun	Sun	Sun	Sun	Sun	Sun	Sun	Sun	Mon	Mon	Mon	Mon	Mon	Mon	Mon	Mon	Mon	Mon	Mon	Mon	Mon

Advanced Time
Period: *Last Sunday in March to Last Sunday in September*
Time Zone: *14:00 (+2hrs UTC)*

[a]	[b]	[c]	[d]	[e]	[f]	[g]	[h]	[i]	[j]	[k]	[l]	[m]	[n]	[o]	[p]	[q]	[r]	[s]	[t]	[u]	[v]	[w]	[x]
14:01	15:01	16:01	17:01	18:01	19:01	20:01	21:01	22:01	23:01	00:01	01:01	02:01	03:01	04:01	05:01	06:01	07:01	08:01	09:01	10:01	11:01	12:01	13:01
2^{01}_{pm}	3^{01}_{pm}	4^{01}_{pm}	5^{01}_{pm}	6^{01}_{pm}	7^{01}_{pm}	8^{01}_{pm}	9^{01}_{pm}	10^{01}_{pm}	11^{01}_{pm}	12^{01}_{am}	1^{01}_{am}	2^{01}_{am}	3^{01}_{am}	4^{01}_{am}	5^{01}_{am}	6^{01}_{am}	7^{01}_{am}	8^{01}_{am}	9^{01}_{am}	10^{01}_{am}	11^{01}_{am}	12^{01}_{pm}	1^{01}_{pm}
Sun	Sun	Sun	Sun	Sun	Sun	Sun	Sun	Sun	Sun	Mon	Mon	Mon	Mon	Mon	Mon	Mon	Mon	Mon	Mon	Mon	Mon	Mon	Mon

GERMANY, WEST
Number of Time Zones: *1*

Standard Time
Period: *Last Sunday in September to Last Sunday in March*
Time Zone: *13:00 (+1hr UTC)*

[a]	[b]	[c]	[d]	[e]	[f]	[g]	[h]	[i]	[j]	[k]	[l]	[m]	[n]	[o]	[p]	[q]	[r]	[s]	[t]	[u]	[v]	[w]	[x]
13:01	14:01	15:01	16:01	17:01	18:01	19:01	20:01	21:01	22:01	23:01	00:01	01:01	02:01	03:01	04:01	05:01	06:01	07:01	08:01	09:01	10:01	11:01	12:01
1^{01}_{pm}	2^{01}_{pm}	3^{01}_{pm}	4^{01}_{pm}	5^{01}_{pm}	6^{01}_{pm}	7^{01}_{pm}	8^{01}_{pm}	9^{01}_{pm}	10^{01}_{pm}	11^{01}_{pm}	12^{01}_{am}	1^{01}_{am}	2^{01}_{am}	3^{01}_{am}	4^{01}_{am}	5^{01}_{am}	6^{01}_{am}	7^{01}_{am}	8^{01}_{am}	9^{01}_{am}	10^{01}_{am}	11^{01}_{am}	12^{01}_{pm}
Sun	Sun	Sun	Sun	Sun	Sun	Sun	Sun	Sun	Sun	Sun	Mon	Mon	Mon	Mon	Mon	Mon	Mon	Mon	Mon	Mon	Mon	Mon	Mon

Advanced Time
Period: *Last Sunday in March to Last Sunday in September*
Time Zone: *14:00 (+2hrs UTC)*

[a]	[b]	[c]	[d]	[e]	[f]	[g]	[h]	[i]	[j]	[k]	[l]	[m]	[n]	[o]	[p]	[q]	[r]	[s]	[t]	[u]	[v]	[w]	[x]
14:01	15:01	16:01	17:01	18:01	19:01	20:01	21:01	22:01	23:01	00:01	01:01	02:01	03:01	04:01	05:01	06:01	07:01	08:01	09:01	10:01	11:01	12:01	13:01
2^{01}_{pm}	3^{01}_{pm}	4^{01}_{pm}	5^{01}_{pm}	6^{01}_{pm}	7^{01}_{pm}	8^{01}_{pm}	9^{01}_{pm}	10^{01}_{pm}	11^{01}_{pm}	12^{01}_{am}	1^{01}_{am}	2^{01}_{am}	3^{01}_{am}	4^{01}_{am}	5^{01}_{am}	6^{01}_{am}	7^{01}_{am}	8^{01}_{am}	9^{01}_{am}	10^{01}_{am}	11^{01}_{am}	12^{01}_{pm}	1^{01}_{pm}
Sun	Sun	Sun	Sun	Sun	Sun	Sun	Sun	Sun	Sun	Mon	Mon	Mon	Mon	Mon	Mon	Mon	Mon	Mon	Mon	Mon	Mon	Mon	Mon

Note: Advanced Time = Daylight Saving Time = Summer Time

GHANA

Number of Time Zones: *1*
Standard Time: *Applicable for the entire year*
Advanced Time: *Not observed*
Time Zone: *12:00 (UTC)*

[a]	[b]	[c]	[d]	[e]	[f]	[g]	[h]	[i]	[j]	[k]	[l]	[m]	[n]	[o]	[p]	[q]	[r]	[s]	[t]	[u]	[v]	[w]	[x]
:01	13:01	14:01	15:01	16:01	17:01	18:01	19:01	20:01	21:01	22:01	23:01	00:01	01:01	02:01	03:01	04:01	05:01	06:01	07:01	08:01	09:01	10:01	11:01
12^{01}_{pm}	1^{01}_{pm}	2^{01}_{pm}	3^{01}_{pm}	4^{01}_{pm}	5^{01}_{pm}	6^{01}_{pm}	7^{01}_{pm}	8^{01}_{pm}	9^{01}_{pm}	10^{01}_{pm}	11^{01}_{pm}	12^{01}_{am}	1^{01}_{am}	2^{01}_{am}	3^{01}_{am}	4^{01}_{am}	5^{01}_{am}	6^{01}_{am}	7^{01}_{am}	8^{01}_{am}	9^{01}_{am}	10^{01}_{am}	11^{01}_{am}
Sun	Sun	Sun	Sun	Sun	Sun	Sun	Sun	Sun	Sun	Sun	Sun	Mon	Mon	Mon	Mon	Mon	Mon	Mon	Mon	Mon	Mon	Mon	Mon

GIBRALTAR

Number of Time Zones: *1*

Standard Time

Period: *Last Sunday in September to Last Sunday in March*
Time Zone: *13:00 (+1hr UTC)*

[a]	[b]	[c]	[d]	[e]	[f]	[g]	[h]	[i]	[j]	[k]	[l]	[m]	[n]	[o]	[p]	[q]	[r]	[s]	[t]	[u]	[v]	[w]	[x]
:01	14:01	15:01	16:01	17:01	18:01	19:01	20:01	21:01	22:01	23:01	00:01	01:01	02:01	03:01	04:01	05:01	06:01	07:01	08:01	09:01	10:01	11:01	12:01
1^{01}_{pm}	2^{01}_{pm}	3^{01}_{pm}	4^{01}_{pm}	5^{01}_{pm}	6^{01}_{pm}	7^{01}_{pm}	8^{01}_{pm}	9^{01}_{pm}	10^{01}_{pm}	11^{01}_{pm}	12^{01}_{am}	1^{01}_{am}	2^{01}_{am}	3^{01}_{am}	4^{01}_{am}	5^{01}_{am}	6^{01}_{am}	7^{01}_{am}	8^{01}_{am}	9^{01}_{am}	10^{01}_{am}	11^{01}_{am}	12^{01}_{pm}
Sun	Sun	Sun	Sun	Sun	Sun	Sun	Sun	Sun	Sun	Sun	Mon	Mon	Mon	Mon	Mon	Mon	Mon	Mon	Mon	Mon	Mon	Mon	Mon

Advanced Time

Period: *Last Sunday in March to Last Sunday in September*
Time Zone: *14:00 (+2hrs UTC)*

[a]	[b]	[c]	[d]	[e]	[f]	[g]	[h]	[i]	[j]	[k]	[l]	[m]	[n]	[o]	[p]	[q]	[r]	[s]	[t]	[u]	[v]	[w]	[x]
:01	15:01	16:01	17:01	18:01	19:01	20:01	21:01	22:01	23:01	00:01	01:01	02:01	03:01	04:01	05:01	06:01	07:01	08:01	09:01	10:01	11:01	12:01	13:01
2^{01}_{pm}	3^{01}_{pm}	4^{01}_{pm}	5^{01}_{pm}	6^{01}_{pm}	7^{01}_{pm}	8^{01}_{pm}	9^{01}_{pm}	10^{01}_{pm}	11^{01}_{pm}	12^{01}_{am}	1^{01}_{am}	2^{01}_{am}	3^{01}_{am}	4^{01}_{am}	5^{01}_{am}	6^{01}_{am}	7^{01}_{am}	8^{01}_{am}	9^{01}_{am}	10^{01}_{am}	11^{01}_{am}	12^{01}_{pm}	1^{01}_{pm}
Sun	Sun	Sun	Sun	Sun	Sun	Sun	Sun	Sun	Sun	Mon	Mon	Mon	Mon	Mon	Mon	Mon	Mon	Mon	Mon	Mon	Mon	Mon	Mon

Note: Advanced Time = Daylight Saving Time = Summer Time

GREECE
Number of Time Zones: *1*

Standard Time
Period: *Last Sunday in September to Last Sunday in March*
Time Zone: *14:00 (+2hrs UTC)*

[a]	[b]	[c]	[d]	[e]	[f]	[g]	[h]	[i]	[j]	[k]	[l]	[m]	[n]	[o]	[p]	[q]	[r]	[s]	[t]	[u]	[v]	[w]	
14:01	15:01	16:01	17:01	18:01	19:01	20:01	21:01	22:01	23:01	00:01	01:01	02:01	03:01	04:01	05:01	06:01	07:01	08:01	09:01	10:01	11:01	12:01	13:
2^{01}_{pm}	3^{01}_{pm}	4^{01}_{pm}	5^{01}_{pm}	6^{01}_{pm}	7^{01}_{pm}	8^{01}_{pm}	9^{01}_{pm}	10^{01}_{pm}	11^{01}_{pm}	12^{01}_{am}	1^{01}_{am}	2^{01}_{am}	3^{01}_{am}	4^{01}_{am}	5^{01}_{am}	6^{01}_{am}	7^{01}_{am}	8^{01}_{am}	9^{01}_{am}	10^{01}_{am}	11^{01}_{am}	12^{01}_{pm}	
Sun	Sun	Sun	Sun	Sun	Sun	Sun	Sun	Sun	Sun	Mon	Mon	Mon	Mon	Mon	Mon	Mon	Mon	Mon	Mon	Mon	Mon	Mon	M

Advanced Time
Period: *Last Sunday in March to Last Sunday in September*
Time Zone: *15:00 (+3hrs UTC)*

[a]	[b]	[c]	[d]	[e]	[f]	[g]	[h]	[i]	[j]	[k]	[l]	[m]	[n]	[o]	[p]	[q]	[r]	[s]	[t]	[u]	[v]	[w]	
15:01	16:01	17:01	18:01	19:01	20:01	21:01	22:01	23:01	00:01	01:01	02:01	03:01	04:01	05:01	06:01	07:01	08:01	09:01	10:01	11:01	12:01	13:01	14:
3^{01}_{pm}	4^{01}_{pm}	5^{01}_{pm}	6^{01}_{pm}	7^{01}_{pm}	8^{01}_{pm}	9^{01}_{pm}	10^{01}_{pm}	11^{01}_{pm}	12^{01}_{am}	1^{01}_{am}	2^{01}_{am}	3^{01}_{am}	4^{01}_{am}	5^{01}_{am}	6^{01}_{am}	7^{01}_{am}	8^{01}_{am}	9^{01}_{am}	10^{01}_{am}	11^{01}_{am}	12^{01}_{pm}	1^{01}_{pm}	2
Sun	Sun	Sun	Sun	Sun	Sun	Sun	Sun	Sun	Mon	Mon	Mon	Mon	Mon	Mon	Mon	Mon	Mon	Mon	Mon	Mon	Mon	Mon	M

GREENLAND
Number of Time Zones: *3*
Notes: *Advanced Time observed irregularly;*
See Reference Map I for graphic depiction of time zones

EASTERN TIME ZONE
Note: *Comprises the area of Scoresbysund and the northeast coast*

Standard Time
Period: *Last Sunday in September to Last Sunday in March*
Time Zone: *11:00 (-1hr UTC)*

[a]	[b]	[c]	[d]	[e]	[f]	[g]	[h]	[i]	[j]	[k]	[l]	[m]	[n]	[o]	[p]	[q]	[r]	[s]	[t]	[u]	[v]	[w]	[x
11:01	12:01	13:01	14:01	15:01	16:01	17:01	18:01	19:01	20:01	21:01	22:01	23:01	00:01	01:01	02:01	03:01	04:01	05:01	06:01	07:01	08:01	09:01	10:0
11^{01}_{am}	12^{01}_{pm}	1^{01}_{pm}	2^{01}_{pm}	3^{01}_{pm}	4^{01}_{pm}	5^{01}_{pm}	6^{01}_{pm}	7^{01}_{pm}	8^{01}_{pm}	9^{01}_{pm}	10^{01}_{pm}	11^{01}_{pm}	12^{01}_{am}	1^{01}_{am}	2^{01}_{am}	3^{01}_{am}	4^{01}_{am}	5^{01}_{am}	6^{01}_{am}	7^{01}_{am}	8^{01}_{am}	9^{01}_{am}	10^{0}_{a}
Sun	Sun	Sun	Sun	Sun	Sun	Sun	Sun	Sun	Sun	Sun	Sun	Sun	Mon	Mon	Mon	Mon	Mon	Mon	Mon	Mon	Mon	Mon	Mo

Advanced Time
Period: *Last Sunday in March to Last Sunday in September*
Time Zone: *12:00 (UTC)*

[a]	[b]	[c]	[d]	[e]	[f]	[g]	[h]	[i]	[j]	[k]	[l]	[m]	[n]	[o]	[p]	[q]	[r]	[s]	[t]	[u]	[v]	[w]	[x
12:01	13:01	14:01	15:01	16:01	17:01	18:01	19:01	20:01	21:01	22:01	23:01	00:01	01:01	02:01	03:01	04:01	05:01	06:01	07:01	08:01	09:01	10:01	11:0
12^{01}_{pm}	1^{01}_{pm}	2^{01}_{pm}	3^{01}_{pm}	4^{01}_{pm}	5^{01}_{pm}	6^{01}_{pm}	7^{01}_{pm}	8^{01}_{pm}	9^{01}_{pm}	10^{01}_{pm}	11^{01}_{pm}	12^{01}_{am}	1^{01}_{am}	2^{01}_{am}	3^{01}_{am}	4^{01}_{am}	5^{01}_{am}	6^{01}_{am}	7^{01}_{am}	8^{01}_{am}	9^{01}_{am}	10^{01}_{am}	11
Sun	Sun	Sun	Sun	Sun	Sun	Sun	Sun	Sun	Sun	Sun	Sun	Mon	Mon	Mon	Mon	Mon	Mon	Mon	Mon	Mon	Mon	Mon	Mo

Note: Advanced Time = Daylight Saving Time = Summer Time

GREENLAND *(Continued)*

CENTRAL TIME ZONE
Note: *Comprises the area of Angmagssalik and the west coast*

Standard Time
Period: *Last Sunday in September to Last Sunday in March*
Time Zone: *09:00 (-3hrs UTC)*

[a]	[b]	[c]	[d]	[e]	[f]	[g]	[h]	[i]	[j]	[k]	[l]	[m]	[n]	[o]	[p]	[q]	[r]	[s]	[t]	[u]	[v]	[w]	[x]
:01	10:01	11:01	12:01	13:01	14:01	15:01	16:01	17:01	18:01	19:01	20:01	21:01	22:01	23:01	00:01	01:01	02:01	03:01	04:01	05:01	06:01	07:01	08:01
9^{01}am	10^{01}am	11^{01}am	12^{01}pm	1^{01}pm	2^{01}pm	3^{01}pm	4^{01}pm	5^{01}pm	6^{01}pm	7^{01}pm	8^{01}pm	9^{01}pm	10^{01}pm	11^{01}pm	12^{01}am	1^{01}am	2^{01}am	3^{01}am	4^{01}am	5^{01}am	6^{01}am	7^{01}am	8^{01}am
Sun	Sun	Sun	Sun	Sun	Sun	Sun	Sun	Sun	Sun	Sun	Sun	Sun	Sun	Sun	Mon	Mon	Mon	Mon	Mon	Mon	Mon	Mon	Mon

Advanced Time
Period: *Last Sunday in March to Last Sunday in September*
Time Zone: *10:00 (-2hrs UTC)*

[a]	[b]	[c]	[d]	[e]	[f]	[g]	[h]	[i]	[j]	[k]	[l]	[m]	[n]	[o]	[p]	[q]	[r]	[s]	[t]	[u]	[v]	[w]	[x]
:01	11:01	12:01	13:01	14:01	15:01	16:01	17:01	18:01	19:01	20:01	21:01	22:01	23:01	00:01	01:01	02:01	03:01	04:01	05:01	06:01	07:01	08:01	09:01
9^{01}am	11^{01}am	12^{01}pm	1^{01}pm	2^{01}pm	3^{01}pm	4^{01}pm	5^{01}pm	6^{01}pm	7^{01}pm	8^{01}pm	9^{01}pm	10^{01}pm	11^{01}pm	12^{01}am	1^{01}am	2^{01}am	3^{01}am	4^{01}am	5^{01}am	6^{01}am	7^{01}am	8^{01}am	9^{01}am
Sun	Sun	Sun	Sun	Sun	Sun	Sun	Sun	Sun	Sun	Sun	Sun	Sun	Sun	Mon	Mon	Mon	Mon	Mon	Mon	Mon	Mon	Mon	Mon

WESTERN TIME ZONE
Note: *Comprises the area of Thule*

Standard Time: *Applicable for the entire year*
Time Zone: *08:00 (-4hrs UTC)*

[a]	[b]	[c]	[d]	[e]	[f]	[g]	[h]	[i]	[j]	[k]	[l]	[m]	[n]	[o]	[p]	[q]	[r]	[s]	[t]	[u]	[v]	[w]	[x]
:01	09:01	10:01	11:01	12:01	13:01	14:01	15:01	16:01	17:01	18:01	19:01	20:01	21:01	22:01	23:01	00:01	01:01	02:01	03:01	04:01	05:01	06:01	07:01
8^{01}am	9^{01}am	10^{01}am	11^{01}am	12^{01}pm	1^{01}pm	2^{01}pm	3^{01}pm	4^{01}pm	5^{01}pm	6^{01}pm	7^{01}pm	8^{01}pm	9^{01}pm	10^{01}pm	11^{01}pm	12^{01}am	1^{01}am	2^{01}am	3^{01}am	4^{01}am	5^{01}am	6^{01}am	7^{01}am
Sun	Sun	Sun	Sun	Sun	Sun	Sun	Sun	Sun	Sun	Sun	Sun	Sun	Sun	Sun	Sun	Mon	Mon	Mon	Mon	Mon	Mon	Mon	Mon

GRENADA
Number of Time Zones: *1*
Standard Time: *Applicable for the entire year*
Advanced Time: *Not observed*
Time Zone: *08:00 (-4hrs UTC)*

[a]	[b]	[c]	[d]	[e]	[f]	[g]	[h]	[i]	[j]	[k]	[l]	[m]	[n]	[o]	[p]	[q]	[r]	[s]	[t]	[u]	[v]	[w]	[x]
:01	09:01	10:01	11:01	12:01	13:01	14:01	15:01	16:01	17:01	18:01	19:01	20:01	21:01	22:01	23:01	00:01	01:01	02:01	03:01	04:01	05:01	06:01	07:01
8^{01}am	9^{01}am	10^{01}am	11^{01}am	12^{01}pm	1^{01}pm	2^{01}pm	3^{01}pm	4^{01}pm	5^{01}pm	6^{01}pm	7^{01}pm	8^{01}pm	9^{01}pm	10^{01}pm	11^{01}pm	12^{01}am	1^{01}am	2^{01}am	3^{01}am	4^{01}am	5^{01}am	6^{01}am	7^{01}am
Sun	Sun	Sun	Sun	Sun	Sun	Sun	Sun	Sun	Sun	Sun	Sun	Sun	Sun	Sun	Sun	Mon	Mon	Mon	Mon	Mon	Mon	Mon	Mon

Note: Advanced Time = Daylight Saving Time = Summer Time

GRENADINES
Number of Time Zones: *1*
Standard Time: *Applicable for the entire year*
Advanced Time: *Not observed*
Time Zone: *08:00 (-4hrs UTC)*

[a]	[b]	[c]	[d]	[e]	[f]	[g]	[h]	[i]	[j]	[k]	[l]	[m]	[n]	[o]	[p]	[q]	[r]	[s]	[t]	[u]	[v]	[w]	
08:01	09:01	10:01	11:01	12:01	13:01	14:01	15:01	16:01	17:01	18:01	19:01	20:01	21:01	22:01	23:01	00:01	01:01	02:01	03:01	04:01	05:01	06:01	07
8^{01}_{am}	9^{01}_{am}	10^{01}_{am}	11^{01}_{am}	12^{01}_{pm}	1^{01}_{pm}	2^{01}_{pm}	3^{01}_{pm}	4^{01}_{pm}	5^{01}_{pm}	6^{01}_{pm}	7^{01}_{pm}	8^{01}_{pm}	9^{01}_{pm}	10^{01}_{pm}	11^{01}_{pm}	12^{01}_{am}	1^{01}_{am}	2^{01}_{am}	3^{01}_{am}	4^{01}_{am}	5^{01}_{am}	6^{01}_{am}	
Sun	Sun	Sun	Sun	Sun	Sun	Sun	Sun	Sun	Sun	Sun	Sun	Sun	Sun	Sun	Sun	Mon	Mon	Mon	Mon	Mon	Mon	Mon	

GUADELOUPE
Number of Time Zones: *1*
Standard Time: *Applicable for the entire year*
Advanced Time: *Not observed*
Time Zone: *08:00 (-4hrs UTC)*

[a]	[b]	[c]	[d]	[e]	[f]	[g]	[h]	[i]	[j]	[k]	[l]	[m]	[n]	[o]	[p]	[q]	[r]	[s]	[t]	[u]	[v]	[w]	
08:01	09:01	10:01	11:01	12:01	13:01	14:01	15:01	16:01	17:01	18:01	19:01	20:01	21:01	22:01	23:01	00:01	01:01	02:01	03:01	04:01	05:01	06:01	07
8^{01}_{am}	9^{01}_{am}	10^{01}_{am}	11^{01}_{am}	12^{01}_{pm}	1^{01}_{pm}	2^{01}_{pm}	3^{01}_{pm}	4^{01}_{pm}	5^{01}_{pm}	6^{01}_{pm}	7^{01}_{pm}	8^{01}_{pm}	9^{01}_{pm}	10^{01}_{pm}	11^{01}_{pm}	12^{01}_{am}	1^{01}_{am}	2^{01}_{am}	3^{01}_{am}	4^{01}_{am}	5^{01}_{am}	6^{01}_{am}	
Sun	Sun	Sun	Sun	Sun	Sun	Sun	Sun	Sun	Sun	Sun	Sun	Sun	Sun	Sun	Sun	Mon	Mon	Mon	Mon	Mon	Mon	Mon	

GUAM
Number of Time Zones: *1*
Standard Time: *Applicable for the entire year*
Advanced Time: *Not observed*
Time Zone: *22:00 (+10hrs UTC)*

[a]	[b]	[c]	[d]	[e]	[f]	[g]	[h]	[i]	[j]	[k]	[l]	[m]	[n]	[o]	[p]	[q]	[r]	[s]	[t]	[u]	[v]	[w]	
22:01	23:01	00:01	01:01	02:01	03:01	04:01	05:01	06:01	07:01	08:01	09:01	10:01	11:01	12:01	13:01	14:01	15:01	16:01	17:01	18:01	19:01	20:01	21
10^{01}_{pm}	11^{01}_{pm}	12^{01}_{am}	1^{01}_{am}	2^{01}_{am}	3^{01}_{am}	4^{01}_{am}	5^{01}_{am}	6^{01}_{am}	7^{01}_{am}	8^{01}_{am}	9^{01}_{am}	10^{01}_{am}	11^{01}_{am}	12^{01}_{pm}	1^{01}_{pm}	2^{01}_{pm}	3^{01}_{pm}	4^{01}_{pm}	5^{01}_{pm}	6^{01}_{pm}	7^{01}_{pm}	8^{01}_{pm}	
Sun	Sun	Mon	Mon	Mon	Mon	Mon	Mon	Mon	Mon	Mon	Mon	Mon	Mon	Mon	Mon	Mon	Mon	Mon	Mon	Mon	Mon	Mon	M

GUATEMALA
Number of Time Zones: *1*
Standard Time: *Applicable for the entire year*
Advanced Time: *Not observed*
Time Zone: *06:00 (-6hrs UTC)*

[a]	[b]	[c]	[d]	[e]	[f]	[g]	[h]	[i]	[j]	[k]	[l]	[m]	[n]	[o]	[p]	[q]	[r]	[s]	[t]	[u]	[v]	[w]	
06:01	07:01	08:01	09:01	10:01	11:01	12:01	13:01	14:01	15:01	16:01	17:01	18:01	19:01	20:01	21:01	22:01	23:01	00:01	01:01	02:01	03:01	04:01	05
6^{01}_{am}	7^{01}_{am}	8^{01}_{am}	9^{01}_{am}	10^{01}_{am}	11^{01}_{am}	12^{01}_{pm}	1^{01}_{pm}	2^{01}_{pm}	3^{01}_{pm}	4^{01}_{pm}	5^{01}_{pm}	6^{01}_{pm}	7^{01}_{pm}	8^{01}_{pm}	9^{01}_{pm}	10^{01}_{pm}	11^{01}_{pm}	12^{01}_{am}	1^{01}_{am}	2^{01}_{am}	3^{01}_{am}	4^{01}_{am}	5
Sun	Sun	Sun	Sun	Sun	Sun	Sun	Sun	Sun	Sun	Sun	Sun	Sun	Sun	Sun	Sun	Sun	Sun	Mon	Mon	Mon	Mon	Mon	M

Note: Advanced Time = Daylight Saving Time = Summer Time

GUINEA

Number of Time Zones: *1*
Standard Time: *Applicable for the entire year*
Advanced Time: *Not observed*
Time Zone: *12:00 (UTC)*

[a]	[b]	[c]	[d]	[e]	[f]	[g]	[h]	[i]	[j]	[k]	[l]	[m]	[n]	[o]	[p]	[q]	[r]	[s]	[t]	[u]	[v]	[w]	[x]
12:01	13:01	14:01	15:01	16:01	17:01	18:01	19:01	20:01	21:01	22:01	23:01	00:01	01:01	02:01	03:01	04:01	05:01	06:01	07:01	08:01	09:01	10:01	11:01
12_{pm}^{01}	1_{pm}^{01}	2_{pm}^{01}	3_{pm}^{01}	4_{pm}^{01}	5_{pm}^{01}	6_{pm}^{01}	7_{pm}^{01}	8_{pm}^{01}	9_{pm}^{01}	10_{pm}^{01}	11_{pm}^{01}	12_{am}^{01}	1_{am}^{01}	2_{am}^{01}	3_{am}^{01}	4_{am}^{01}	5_{am}^{01}	6_{am}^{01}	7_{am}^{01}	8_{am}^{01}	9_{am}^{01}	10_{am}^{01}	11_{am}^{01}
Sun	Sun	Sun	Sun	Sun	Sun	Sun	Sun	Sun	Sun	Sun	Sun	Mon	Mon	Mon	Mon	Mon	Mon	Mon	Mon	Mon	Mon	Mon	Mon

GUINEA-BISSAU

Number of Time Zones: *1*
Standard Time: *Applicable for the entire year*
Advanced Time: *Not observed*
Time Zone: *12:00 (UTC)*

[a]	[b]	[c]	[d]	[e]	[f]	[g]	[h]	[i]	[j]	[k]	[l]	[m]	[n]	[o]	[p]	[q]	[r]	[s]	[t]	[u]	[v]	[w]	[x]
12:01	13:01	14:01	15:01	16:01	17:01	18:01	19:01	20:01	21:01	22:01	23:01	00:01	01:01	02:01	03:01	04:01	05:01	06:01	07:01	08:01	09:01	10:01	11:01
12_{pm}^{01}	1_{pm}^{01}	2_{pm}^{01}	3_{pm}^{01}	4_{pm}^{01}	5_{pm}^{01}	6_{pm}^{01}	7_{pm}^{01}	8_{pm}^{01}	9_{pm}^{01}	10_{pm}^{01}	11_{pm}^{01}	12_{am}^{01}	1_{am}^{01}	2_{am}^{01}	3_{am}^{01}	4_{am}^{01}	5_{am}^{01}	6_{am}^{01}	7_{am}^{01}	8_{am}^{01}	9_{am}^{01}	10_{am}^{01}	11_{am}^{01}
Sun	Sun	Sun	Sun	Sun	Sun	Sun	Sun	Sun	Sun	Sun	Sun	Mon	Mon	Mon	Mon	Mon	Mon	Mon	Mon	Mon	Mon	Mon	Mon

GUYANA

Number of Time Zones: *1*
Standard Time: *Applicable for the entire year*
Advanced Time: *Not observed*
Time Zone: *09:00 (-3hrs UTC)*

[a]	[b]	[c]	[d]	[e]	[f]	[g]	[h]	[i]	[j]	[k]	[l]	[m]	[n]	[o]	[p]	[q]	[r]	[s]	[t]	[u]	[v]	[w]	[x]
09:01	10:01	11:01	12:01	13:01	14:01	15:01	16:01	17:01	18:01	19:01	20:01	21:01	22:01	23:01	00:01	01:01	02:01	03:01	04:01	05:01	06:01	07:01	08:01
9_{am}^{01}	10_{am}^{01}	11_{am}^{01}	12_{pm}^{01}	1_{pm}^{01}	2_{pm}^{01}	3_{pm}^{01}	4_{pm}^{01}	5_{pm}^{01}	6_{pm}^{01}	7_{pm}^{01}	8_{pm}^{01}	9_{pm}^{01}	10_{pm}^{01}	11_{pm}^{01}	12_{am}^{01}	1_{am}^{01}	2_{am}^{01}	3_{am}^{01}	4_{am}^{01}	5_{am}^{01}	6_{am}^{01}	7_{am}^{01}	8_{am}^{01}
Sun	Sun	Sun	Sun	Sun	Sun	Sun	Sun	Sun	Sun	Sun	Sun	Sun	Sun	Sun	Mon	Mon	Mon	Mon	Mon	Mon	Mon	Mon	Mon

Note: Advanced Time = Daylight Saving Time = Summer Time

HAITI

Number of Time Zones: *1*

Standard Time

Period: *Last Sunday in October to First Sunday in April*
Time Zone: *07:00 (-5hrs UTC)*

[a]	[b]	[c]	[d]	[e]	[f]	[g]	[h]	[i]	[j]	[k]	[l]	[m]	[n]	[o]	[p]	[q]	[r]	[s]	[t]	[u]	[v]	[w]	[x]
07:01	08:01	09:01	10:01	11:01	12:01	13:01	14:01	15:01	16:01	17:01	18:01	19:01	20:01	21:01	22:01	23:01	00:01	01:01	02:01	03:01	04:01	05:01	06:0
7_{am}^{01}	8_{am}^{01}	9_{am}^{01}	10_{am}^{01}	11_{am}^{01}	12_{pm}^{01}	1_{pm}^{01}	2_{pm}^{01}	3_{pm}^{01}	4_{pm}^{01}	5_{pm}^{01}	6_{pm}^{01}	7_{pm}^{01}	8_{pm}^{01}	9_{pm}^{01}	10_{pm}^{01}	11_{pm}^{01}	12_{am}^{01}	1_{am}^{01}	2_{am}^{01}	3_{am}^{01}	4_{am}^{01}	5_{am}^{01}	6_{a}
Sun	Sun	Sun	Sun	Sun	Sun	Sun	Sun	Sun	Sun	Sun	Sun	Sun	Sun	Sun	Sun	Sun	Sun	Mon	Mon	Mon	Mon	Mon	Mo

Advanced Time

Period: *First Sunday in April to Last Sunday in October*
Time Zone: *08:00 (-4hrs UTC)*

[a]	[b]	[c]	[d]	[e]	[f]	[g]	[h]	[i]	[j]	[k]	[l]	[m]	[n]	[o]	[p]	[q]	[r]	[s]	[t]	[u]	[v]	[w]	[x]
08:01	09:01	10:01	11:01	12:01	13:01	14:01	15:01	16:01	17:01	18:01	19:01	20:01	21:01	22:01	23:01	00:01	01:01	02:01	03:01	04:01	05:01	06:01	07:0
8_{am}^{01}	9_{am}^{01}	10_{am}^{01}	11_{am}^{01}	12_{pm}^{01}	1_{pm}^{01}	2_{pm}^{01}	3_{pm}^{01}	4_{pm}^{01}	5_{pm}^{01}	6_{pm}^{01}	7_{pm}^{01}	8_{pm}^{01}	9_{pm}^{01}	10_{pm}^{01}	11_{pm}^{01}	12_{am}^{01}	1_{am}^{01}	2_{am}^{01}	3_{am}^{01}	4_{am}^{01}	5_{am}^{01}	6_{am}^{01}	7_{a}
Sun	Sun	Sun	Sun	Sun	Sun	Sun	Sun	Sun	Sun	Sun	Sun	Sun	Sun	Sun	Sun	Mon	Mon	Mon	Mon	Mon	Mon	Mon	

HONDURAS

Number of Time Zones: *1*
Standard Time: *Applicable for the entire year*
Advanced Time: *Not observed*
Time Zone: *06:00 (-6hrs UTC)*

[a]	[b]	[c]	[d]	[e]	[f]	[g]	[h]	[i]	[j]	[k]	[l]	[m]	[n]	[o]	[p]	[q]	[r]	[s]	[t]	[u]	[v]	[w]	[x]
06:01	07:01	08:01	09:01	10:01	11:01	12:01	13:01	14:01	15:01	16:01	17:01	18:01	19:01	20:01	21:01	22:01	23:01	00:01	01:01	02:01	03:01	04:01	05:01
6_{am}^{01}	7_{am}^{01}	8_{am}^{01}	9_{am}^{01}	10_{am}^{01}	11_{am}^{01}	12_{pm}^{01}	1_{pm}^{01}	2_{pm}^{01}	3_{pm}^{01}	4_{pm}^{01}	5_{pm}^{01}	6_{pm}^{01}	7_{pm}^{01}	8_{pm}^{01}	9_{pm}^{01}	10_{pm}^{01}	11_{pm}^{01}	12_{am}^{01}	1_{am}^{01}	2_{am}^{01}	3_{am}^{01}	4_{am}^{01}	5_{a}
Sun	Sun	Sun	Sun	Sun	Sun	Sun	Sun	Sun	Sun	Sun	Sun	Sun	Sun	Sun	Sun	Sun	Sun	Mon	Mon	Mon	Mon	Mon	Mon

HONG KONG

Number of Time Zones: *1*
Standard Time: *Applicable for the entire year*
Advanced Time: *Not observed*
Time Zone: *20:00 (+8hrs UTC)*

[a]	[b]	[c]	[d]	[e]	[f]	[g]	[h]	[i]	[j]	[k]	[l]	[m]	[n]	[o]	[p]	[q]	[r]	[s]	[t]	[u]	[v]	[w]	[x]
20:01	21:01	22:01	23:01	00:01	01:01	02:01	03:01	04:01	05:01	06:01	07:01	08:01	09:01	10:01	11:01	12:01	13:01	14:01	15:01	16:01	17:01	18:01	19:01
8_{pm}^{01}	9_{pm}^{01}	10_{pm}^{01}	11_{pm}^{01}	12_{am}^{01}	1_{am}^{01}	2_{am}^{01}	3_{am}^{01}	4_{am}^{01}	5_{am}^{01}	6_{am}^{01}	7_{am}^{01}	8_{am}^{01}	9_{am}^{01}	10_{am}^{01}	11_{am}^{01}	12_{pm}^{01}	1_{pm}^{01}	2_{pm}^{01}	3_{pm}^{01}	4_{pm}^{01}	5_{pm}^{01}	6_{pm}^{01}	7_{pm}^{01}
Sun	Sun	Sun	Sun	Mon	Mon	Mon	Mon	Mon	Mon	Mon	Mon	Mon	Mon	Mon	Mon	Mon	Mon	Mon	Mon	Mon	Mon	Mon	Mon

Note: Advanced Time = Daylight Saving Time = Summer Time

HUNGARY
Number of Time Zones: *1*

Standard Time
Period: *Last Sunday in September to Last Sunday in March*
Time Zone: *13:00 (+1hr UTC)*

[a]	[b]	[c]	[d]	[e]	[f]	[g]	[h]	[i]	[j]	[k]	[l]	[m]	[n]	[o]	[p]	[q]	[r]	[s]	[t]	[u]	[v]	[w]	[x]
13:01	14:01	15:01	16:01	17:01	18:01	19:01	20:01	21:01	22:01	23:01	00:01	01:01	02:01	03:01	04:01	05:01	06:01	07:01	08:01	09:01	10:01	11:01	12:01
1^{01}_{pm}	2^{01}_{pm}	3^{01}_{pm}	4^{01}_{pm}	5^{01}_{pm}	6^{01}_{pm}	7^{01}_{pm}	8^{01}_{pm}	9^{01}_{pm}	10^{01}_{pm}	11^{01}_{pm}	12^{01}_{am}	1^{01}_{am}	2^{01}_{am}	3^{01}_{am}	4^{01}_{am}	5^{01}_{am}	6^{01}_{am}	7^{01}_{am}	8^{01}_{am}	9^{01}_{am}	10^{01}_{am}	11^{01}_{am}	12^{01}_{pm}
Sun	Sun	Sun	Sun	Sun	Sun	Sun	Sun	Sun	Sun	Sun	Mon	Mon	Mon	Mon	Mon	Mon	Mon	Mon	Mon	Mon	Mon	Mon	Mon

Advanced Time
Period: *Last Sunday in March to Last Sunday in September*
Time Zone: *14:00 (+2hrs UTC)*

[a]	[b]	[c]	[d]	[e]	[f]	[g]	[h]	[i]	[j]	[k]	[l]	[m]	[n]	[o]	[p]	[q]	[r]	[s]	[t]	[u]	[v]	[w]	[x]
14:01	15:01	16:01	17:01	18:01	19:01	20:01	21:01	22:01	23:01	00:01	01:01	02:01	03:01	04:01	05:01	06:01	07:01	08:01	09:01	10:01	11:01	12:01	13:01
2^{01}_{pm}	3^{01}_{pm}	4^{01}_{pm}	5^{01}_{pm}	6^{01}_{pm}	7^{01}_{pm}	8^{01}_{pm}	9^{01}_{pm}	10^{01}_{pm}	11^{01}_{pm}	12^{01}_{am}	1^{01}_{am}	2^{01}_{am}	3^{01}_{am}	4^{01}_{am}	5^{01}_{am}	6^{01}_{am}	7^{01}_{am}	8^{01}_{am}	9^{01}_{am}	10^{01}_{am}	11^{01}_{am}	12^{01}_{pm}	1^{01}_{pm}
Sun	Sun	Sun	Sun	Sun	Sun	Sun	Sun	Sun	Sun	Mon	Mon	Mon	Mon	Mon	Mon	Mon	Mon	Mon	Mon	Mon	Mon	Mon	Mon

ICELAND
Number of Time Zones: *1*
Standard Time: *Applicable for the entire year*
Advanced Time: *Not observed*
Time Zone: *12:00 (UTC)*

[a]	[b]	[c]	[d]	[e]	[f]	[g]	[h]	[i]	[j]	[k]	[l]	[m]	[n]	[o]	[p]	[q]	[r]	[s]	[t]	[u]	[v]	[w]	[x]
12:01	13:01	14:01	15:01	16:01	17:01	18:01	19:01	20:01	21:01	22:01	23:01	00:01	01:01	02:01	03:01	04:01	05:01	06:01	07:01	08:01	09:01	10:01	11:01
12^{01}_{pm}	1^{01}_{pm}	2^{01}_{pm}	3^{01}_{pm}	4^{01}_{pm}	5^{01}_{pm}	6^{01}_{pm}	7^{01}_{pm}	8^{01}_{pm}	9^{01}_{pm}	10^{01}_{pm}	11^{01}_{pm}	12^{01}_{am}	1^{01}_{am}	2^{01}_{am}	3^{01}_{am}	4^{01}_{am}	5^{01}_{am}	6^{01}_{am}	7^{01}_{am}	8^{01}_{am}	9^{01}_{am}	10^{01}_{am}	11^{01}_{am}
Sun	Sun	Sun	Sun	Sun	Sun	Sun	Sun	Sun	Sun	Sun	Sun	Mon	Mon	Mon	Mon	Mon	Mon	Mon	Mon	Mon	Mon	Mon	Mon

INDIA
Number of Time Zones: *1*
Standard Time: *Applicable for the entire year*
Advanced Time: *Not observed*
Time Zone: *17:30 (+5hrs 30mins UTC)*

[a]	[b]	[c]	[d]	[e]	[f]	[g]	[h]	[i]	[j]	[k]	[l]	[m]	[n]	[o]	[p]	[q]	[r]	[s]	[t]	[u]	[v]	[w]	[x]
17:31	18:31	19:31	20:31	21:31	22:31	23:31	00:31	01:31	02:31	03:31	04:31	05:31	06:31	07:31	08:31	09:31	10:31	11:31	12:31	13:31	14:31	15:31	16:31
5^{31}_{pm}	6^{31}_{pm}	7^{31}_{pm}	8^{31}_{pm}	9^{31}_{pm}	10^{31}_{pm}	11^{31}_{pm}	12^{31}_{am}	1^{31}_{am}	2^{31}_{am}	3^{31}_{am}	4^{31}_{am}	5^{31}_{am}	6^{31}_{am}	7^{31}_{am}	8^{31}_{am}	9^{31}_{am}	10^{31}_{am}	11^{31}_{am}	12^{31}_{pm}	1^{31}_{pm}	2^{31}_{pm}	3^{31}_{pm}	4^{31}_{pm}
Sun	Sun	Sun	Sun	Sun	Sun	Sun	Mon	Mon	Mon	Mon	Mon	Mon	Mon	Mon	Mon	Mon	Mon	Mon	Mon	Mon	Mon	Mon	Mon

Note: Advanced Time = Daylight Saving Time = Summer Time

INDONESIA
Number of Time Zones: *3*
Note: *Advanced Time not observed;*
See Reference Map I for graphic depiction of time zones

EASTERN TIME ZONE
Note: *Comprises Irian Barat*
Standard Time: *Applicable for the entire year*
Time Zone: *21:00 (+9hrs UTC)*

[a]	[b]	[c]	[d]	[e]	[f]	[g]	[h]	[i]	[j]	[k]	[l]	[m]	[n]	[o]	[p]	[q]	[r]	[s]	[t]	[u]	[v]	[w]	[·]
21:01	22:01	23:01	00:01	01:01	02:01	03:01	04:01	05:01	06:01	07:01	08:01	09:01	10:01	11:01	12:01	13:01	14:01	15:01	16:01	17:01	18:01	19:01	20:·
9^{01}pm	10^{01}pm	11^{01}pm	12^{01}am	1^{01}am	2^{01}am	3^{01}am	4^{01}am	5^{01}am	6^{01}am	7^{01}am	8^{01}am	9^{01}am	10^{01}am	11^{01}am	12^{01}pm	1^{01}pm	2^{01}pm	3^{01}pm	4^{01}pm	5^{01}pm	6^{01}pm	7^{01}pm	8
Sun	Sun	Sun	Mon	Mon	Mon	Mon	Mon	Mon	Mon	Mon	Mon	Mon	Mon	Mon	Mon	Mon	Mon	Mon	Mon	Mon	Mon	Mon	M

CENTRAL TIME ZONE
Note: *Comprises Kalimantan, Sulawesi, Lesser Sunda Islands, and Moluccas*
Standard Time: *Applicable for the entire year*
Time Zone: *20:00 (+8hrs UTC)*

[a]	[b]	[c]	[d]	[e]	[f]	[g]	[h]	[i]	[j]	[k]	[l]	[m]	[n]	[o]	[p]	[q]	[r]	[s]	[t]	[u]	[v]	[w]	[x]
20:01	21:01	22:01	23:01	00:01	01:01	02:01	03:01	04:01	05:01	06:01	07:01	08:01	09:01	10:01	11:01	12:01	13:01	14:01	15:01	16:01	17:01	18:01	19:0
8^{01}pm	9^{01}pm	10^{01}pm	11^{01}pm	12^{01}am	1^{01}am	2^{01}am	3^{01}am	4^{01}am	5^{01}am	6^{01}am	7^{01}am	8^{01}am	9^{01}am	10^{01}am	11^{01}am	12^{01}pm	1^{01}pm	2^{01}pm	3^{01}pm	4^{01}pm	5^{01}pm	6^{01}pm	$7^{}$p
Sun	Sun	Sun	Sun	Mon	Mon	Mon	Mon	Mon	Mon	Mon	Mon	Mon	Mon	Mon	Mon	Mon	Mon	Mon	Mon	Mon	Mon	Mon	Mo

WESTERN TIME ZONE
Note: *Comprises Sumatra, Java, and Bali*
Standard Time: *Applicable for the entire year*
Time Zone: *19:00 (+7hrs UTC)*

[a]	[b]	[c]	[d]	[e]	[f]	[g]	[h]	[i]	[j]	[k]	[l]	[m]	[n]	[o]	[p]	[q]	[r]	[s]	[t]	[u]	[v]	[w]	[x]
19:01	20:01	21:01	22:01	23:01	00:01	01:01	02:01	03:01	04:01	05:01	06:01	07:01	08:01	09:01	10:01	11:01	12:01	13:01	14:01	15:01	16:01	17:01	18:0
7^{01}pm	8^{01}pm	9^{01}pm	10^{01}pm	11^{01}pm	12^{01}am	1^{01}am	2^{01}am	3^{01}am	4^{01}am	5^{01}am	6^{01}am	7^{01}am	8^{01}am	9^{01}am	10^{01}am	11^{01}am	12^{01}pm	1^{01}pm	2^{01}pm	3^{01}pm	4^{01}pm	5^{01}pm	$6^{}$p
Sun	Sun	Sun	Sun	Sun	Mon	Mon	Mon	Mon	Mon	Mon	Mon	Mon	Mon	Mon	Mon	Mon	Mon	Mon	Mon	Mon	Mon	Mon	Mo

IRAN
Number of Time Zones: *1*
Standard Time: *Applicable for the entire year*
Advanced Time: *Not observed*
Time Zone: *15:30 (+3hrs 30mins UTC)*

[a]	[b]	[c]	[d]	[e]	[f]	[g]	[h]	[i]	[j]	[k]	[l]	[m]	[n]	[o]	[p]	[q]	[r]	[s]	[t]	[u]	[v]	[w]	[x]
15:31	16:31	17:31	18:31	19:31	20:31	21:31	22:31	23:31	00:31	01:31	02:31	03:31	04:31	05:31	06:31	07:31	08:31	09:31	10:31	11:31	12:31	13:31	14:3
3^{31}pm	4^{31}pm	5^{31}pm	6^{31}pm	7^{31}pm	8^{31}pm	9^{31}pm	10^{31}pm	11^{31}pm	12^{31}am	1^{31}am	2^{31}am	3^{31}am	4^{31}am	5^{31}am	6^{31}am	7^{31}am	8^{31}am	9^{31}am	10^{31}am	11^{31}am	12^{31}pm	1^{31}pm	2^{3}p
Sun	Sun	Sun	Sun	Sun	Sun	Sun	Sun	Sun	Mon	Mon	Mon	Mon	Mon	Mon	Mon	Mon	Mon	Mon	Mon	Mon	Mon	Mon	Mon

Note: Advanced Time = Daylight Saving Time = Summer Time

IRAQ

Number of Time Zones: *1*

Standard Time

Period: *September 30 to April 1*
Time Zone: *15:00 (+3hrs UTC)*

[a]	[b]	[c]	[d]	[e]	[f]	[g]	[h]	[i]	[j]	[k]	[l]	[m]	[n]	[o]	[p]	[q]	[r]	[s]	[t]	[u]	[v]	[w]	[x]
15:01	16:01	17:01	18:01	19:01	20:01	21:01	22:01	23:01	00:01	01:01	02:01	03:01	04:01	05:01	06:01	07:01	08:01	09:01	10:01	11:01	12:01	13:01	14:01
3:01 pm	4:01 pm	5:01 pm	6:01 pm	7:01 pm	8:01 pm	9:01 pm	10:01 pm	11:01 pm	12:01 am	1:01 am	2:01 am	3:01 am	4:01 am	5:01 am	6:01 am	7:01 am	8:01 am	9:01 am	10:01 am	11:01 am	12:01 pm	1:01 pm	2:01 pm
Sun	Sun	Sun	Sun	Sun	Sun	Sun	Sun	Sun	Mon	Mon	Mon	Mon	Mon	Mon	Mon	Mon	Mon	Mon	Mon	Mon	Mon	Mon	Mon

Advanced Time

Period: *April 1 to September 30*
Time Zone: *16:00 (+4hrs UTC)*

[a]	[b]	[c]	[d]	[e]	[f]	[g]	[h]	[i]	[j]	[k]	[l]	[m]	[n]	[o]	[p]	[q]	[r]	[s]	[t]	[u]	[v]	[w]	[x]
16:01	17:01	18:01	19:01	20:01	21:01	22:01	23:01	00:01	01:01	02:01	03:01	04:01	05:01	06:01	07:01	08:01	09:01	10:01	11:01	12:01	13:01	14:01	15:01
4:01 pm	5:01 pm	6:01 pm	7:01 pm	8:01 pm	9:01 pm	10:01 pm	11:01 pm	12:01 am	1:01 am	2:01 am	3:01 am	4:01 am	5:01 am	6:01 am	7:01 am	8:01 am	9:01 am	10:01 am	11:01 am	12:01 pm	1:01 pm	2:01 pm	3:01 pm
Sun	Sun	Sun	Sun	Sun	Sun	Sun	Sun	Mon	Mon	Mon	Mon	Mon	Mon	Mon	Mon	Mon	Mon	Mon	Mon	Mon	Mon	Mon	Mon

IRELAND

Number of Time Zones: *1*

Standard Time

Period: *Fourth Sunday in October to Last Sunday in March*
Time Zone: *12:00 (UTC)*

[a]	[b]	[c]	[d]	[e]	[f]	[g]	[h]	[i]	[j]	[k]	[l]	[m]	[n]	[o]	[p]	[q]	[r]	[s]	[t]	[u]	[v]	[w]	[x]
12:01	13:01	14:01	15:01	16:01	17:01	18:01	19:01	20:01	21:01	22:01	23:01	00:01	01:01	02:01	03:01	04:01	05:01	06:01	07:01	08:01	09:01	10:01	11:01
12:01 pm	1:01 pm	2:01 pm	3:01 pm	4:01 pm	5:01 pm	6:01 pm	7:01 pm	8:01 pm	9:01 pm	10:01 pm	11:01 pm	12:01 am	1:01 am	2:01 am	3:01 am	4:01 am	5:01 am	6:01 am	7:01 am	8:01 am	9:01 am	10:01 am	11:01 am
Sun	Sun	Sun	Sun	Sun	Sun	Sun	Sun	Sun	Sun	Sun	Sun	Mon	Mon	Mon	Mon	Mon	Mon	Mon	Mon	Mon	Mon	Mon	Mon

Advanced Time

Period: *Last Sunday in March to Fourth Sunday in September*
Time Zone: *13:00 (+1hr UTC)*

[a]	[b]	[c]	[d]	[e]	[f]	[g]	[h]	[i]	[j]	[k]	[l]	[m]	[n]	[o]	[p]	[q]	[r]	[s]	[t]	[u]	[v]	[w]	[x]
13:01	14:01	15:01	16:01	17:01	18:01	19:01	20:01	21:01	22:01	23:01	00:01	01:01	02:01	03:01	04:01	05:01	06:01	07:01	08:01	09:01	10:01	11:01	12:01
1:01 pm	2:01 pm	3:01 pm	4:01 pm	5:01 pm	6:01 pm	7:01 pm	8:01 pm	9:01 pm	10:01 pm	11:01 pm	12:01 am	1:01 am	2:01 am	3:01 am	4:01 am	5:01 am	6:01 am	7:01 am	8:01 am	9:01 am	10:01 am	11:01 am	12:01 pm
Sun	Sun	Sun	Sun	Sun	Sun	Sun	Sun	Sun	Sun	Sun	Mon	Mon	Mon	Mon	Mon	Mon	Mon	Mon	Mon	Mon	Mon	Mon	Mon

Note: Advanced Time = Daylight Saving Time = Summer Time

ISRAEL
Number of Time Zones: *1*

Standard Time
Period: *Varies: October to April*
Time Zone: *14:00 (+2hrs UTC)*

[a]	[b]	[c]	[d]	[e]	[f]	[g]	[h]	[i]	[j]	[k]	[l]	[m]	[n]	[o]	[p]	[q]	[r]	[s]	[t]	[u]	[v]	[w]	[x]
14:01	15:01	16:01	17:01	18:01	19:01	20:01	21:01	22:01	23:01	00:01	01:01	02:01	03:01	04:01	05:01	06:01	07:01	08:01	09:01	10:01	11:01	12:01	13:0
2^{01}_{pm}	3^{01}_{pm}	4^{01}_{pm}	5^{01}_{pm}	6^{01}_{pm}	7^{01}_{pm}	8^{01}_{pm}	9^{01}_{pm}	10^{01}_{pm}	11^{01}_{pm}	12^{01}_{am}	1^{01}_{am}	2^{01}_{am}	3^{01}_{am}	4^{01}_{am}	5^{01}_{am}	6^{01}_{am}	7^{01}_{am}	8^{01}_{am}	9^{01}_{am}	10^{01}_{am}	11^{01}_{am}	12^{01}_{pm}	1^{0}_{p}
Sun	Sun	Sun	Sun	Sun	Sun	Sun	Sun	Sun	Sun	Mon	Mon	Mon	Mon	Mon	Mon	Mon	Mon	Mon	Mon	Mon	Mon	Mon	Mo

Advanced Time
Period: *Varies: April to October*
Time Zone: *15:00 (+3hrs UTC)*

[a]	[b]	[c]	[d]	[e]	[f]	[g]	[h]	[i]	[j]	[k]	[l]	[m]	[n]	[o]	[p]	[q]	[r]	[s]	[t]	[u]	[v]	[w]	[x]
15:01	16:01	17:01	18:01	19:01	20:01	21:01	22:01	23:01	00:01	01:01	02:01	03:01	04:01	05:01	06:01	07:01	08:01	09:01	10:01	11:01	12:01	13:01	14:0
3^{01}_{pm}	4^{01}_{pm}	5^{01}_{pm}	6^{01}_{pm}	7^{01}_{pm}	8^{01}_{pm}	9^{01}_{pm}	10^{01}_{pm}	11^{01}_{pm}	12^{01}_{am}	1^{01}_{am}	2^{01}_{am}	3^{01}_{am}	4^{01}_{am}	5^{01}_{am}	6^{01}_{am}	7^{01}_{am}	8^{01}_{am}	9^{01}_{am}	10^{01}_{am}	11^{01}_{am}	12^{01}_{pm}	1^{01}_{pm}	2^{0}_{pr}
Sun	Sun	Sun	Sun	Sun	Sun	Sun	Sun	Sun	Mon	Mon	Mon	Mon	Mon	Mon	Mon	Mon	Mon	Mon	Mon	Mon	Mon	Mon	Mo

ITALY
Number of Time Zones: *1*

Standard Time
Period: *Last Sunday in September to Last Sunday in March*
Time Zone: *13:00 (+1hr UTC)*

[a]	[b]	[c]	[d]	[e]	[f]	[g]	[h]	[i]	[j]	[k]	[l]	[m]	[n]	[o]	[p]	[q]	[r]	[s]	[t]	[u]	[v]	[w]	[x]
13:01	14:01	15:01	16:01	17:01	18:01	19:01	20:01	21:01	22:01	23:01	00:01	01:01	02:01	03:01	04:01	05:01	06:01	07:01	08:01	09:01	10:01	11:01	12:0
1^{01}_{pm}	2^{01}_{pm}	3^{01}_{pm}	4^{01}_{pm}	5^{01}_{pm}	6^{01}_{pm}	7^{01}_{pm}	8^{01}_{pm}	9^{01}_{pm}	10^{01}_{pm}	11^{01}_{pm}	12^{01}_{am}	1^{01}_{am}	2^{01}_{am}	3^{01}_{am}	4^{01}_{am}	5^{01}_{am}	6^{01}_{am}	7^{01}_{am}	8^{01}_{am}	9^{01}_{am}	10^{01}_{am}	11^{01}_{am}	12^{01}_{pm}
Sun	Sun	Sun	Sun	Sun	Sun	Sun	Sun	Sun	Sun	Sun	Mon	Mon	Mon	Mon	Mon	Mon	Mon	Mon	Mon	Mon	Mon	Mon	Mon

Advanced Time
Period: *Last Sunday in March to Last Sunday in September*
Time Zone: *14:00 (+2hrs UTC)*

[a]	[b]	[c]	[d]	[e]	[f]	[g]	[h]	[i]	[j]	[k]	[l]	[m]	[n]	[o]	[p]	[q]	[r]	[s]	[t]	[u]	[v]	[w]	[x]
14:01	15:01	16:01	17:01	18:01	19:01	20:01	21:01	22:01	23:01	00:01	01:01	02:01	03:01	04:01	05:01	06:01	07:01	08:01	09:01	10:01	11:01	12:01	13:01
2^{01}_{pm}	3^{01}_{pm}	4^{01}_{pm}	5^{01}_{pm}	6^{01}_{pm}	7^{01}_{pm}	8^{01}_{pm}	9^{01}_{pm}	10^{01}_{pm}	11^{01}_{pm}	12^{01}_{am}	1^{01}_{am}	2^{01}_{am}	3^{01}_{am}	4^{01}_{am}	5^{01}_{am}	6^{01}_{am}	7^{01}_{am}	8^{01}_{am}	9^{01}_{am}	10^{01}_{am}	11^{01}_{am}	12^{01}_{pm}	1^{01}_{pm}
Sun	Sun	Sun	Sun	Sun	Sun	Sun	Sun	Sun	Sun	Mon	Mon	Mon	Mon	Mon	Mon	Mon	Mon	Mon	Mon	Mon	Mon	Mon	Mon

Note: Advanced Time = Daylight Saving Time = Summer Time

IVORY COAST

Number of Time Zones: *1*
Standard Time: *Applicable for the entire year*
Advanced Time: *Not observed*
Time Zone: *12:00 (UTC)*

[a]	[b]	[c]	[d]	[e]	[f]	[g]	[h]	[i]	[j]	[k]	[l]	[m]	[n]	[o]	[p]	[q]	[r]	[s]	[t]	[u]	[v]	[w]	[x]
12:01	13:01	14:01	15:01	16:01	17:01	18:01	19:01	20:01	21:01	22:01	23:01	00:01	01:01	02:01	03:01	04:01	05:01	06:01	07:01	08:01	09:01	10:01	11:01
12^{01}_{pm}	1^{01}_{pm}	2^{01}_{pm}	3^{01}_{pm}	4^{01}_{pm}	5^{01}_{pm}	6^{01}_{pm}	7^{01}_{pm}	8^{01}_{pm}	9^{01}_{pm}	10^{01}_{pm}	11^{01}_{pm}	12^{01}_{am}	1^{01}_{am}	2^{01}_{am}	3^{01}_{am}	4^{01}_{am}	5^{01}_{am}	6^{01}_{am}	7^{01}_{am}	8^{01}_{am}	9^{01}_{am}	10^{01}_{am}	11^{01}_{am}
Sun	Sun	Sun	Sun	Sun	Sun	Sun	Sun	Sun	Sun	Sun	Sun	Mon	Mon	Mon	Mon	Mon	Mon	Mon	Mon	Mon	Mon	Mon	Mon

JAMAICA

Number of Time Zones: *1*
Standard Time: *Applicable for the entire year*
Advanced Time: *Not observed*
Time Zone: *07:00 (-5hrs UTC)*

[a]	[b]	[c]	[d]	[e]	[f]	[g]	[h]	[i]	[j]	[k]	[l]	[m]	[n]	[o]	[p]	[q]	[r]	[s]	[t]	[u]	[v]	[w]	[x]
07:01	08:01	09:01	10:01	11:01	12:01	13:01	14:01	15:01	16:01	17:01	18:01	19:01	20:01	21:01	22:01	23:01	00:01	01:01	02:01	03:01	04:01	05:01	06:01
7^{01}_{am}	8^{01}_{am}	9^{01}_{am}	10^{01}_{am}	11^{01}_{am}	12^{01}_{pm}	1^{01}_{pm}	2^{01}_{pm}	3^{01}_{pm}	4^{01}_{pm}	5^{01}_{pm}	6^{01}_{pm}	7^{01}_{pm}	8^{01}_{pm}	9^{01}_{pm}	10^{01}_{pm}	11^{01}_{pm}	12^{01}_{am}	1^{01}_{am}	2^{01}_{am}	3^{01}_{am}	4^{01}_{am}	5^{01}_{am}	6^{01}_{am}
Sun	Sun	Sun	Sun	Sun	Sun	Sun	Sun	Sun	Sun	Sun	Sun	Sun	Sun	Sun	Sun	Sun	Mon	Mon	Mon	Mon	Mon	Mon	Mon

JAPAN

Number of Time Zones: *1*
Standard Time: *Applicable for the entire year*
Advanced Time: *Not observed*
Time Zone: *21:00 (+9hrs UTC)*

[a]	[b]	[c]	[d]	[e]	[f]	[g]	[h]	[i]	[j]	[k]	[l]	[m]	[n]	[o]	[p]	[q]	[r]	[s]	[t]	[u]	[v]	[w]	[x]
21:01	22:01	23:01	00:01	01:01	02:01	03:01	04:01	05:01	06:01	07:01	08:01	09:01	10:01	11:01	12:01	13:01	14:01	15:01	16:01	17:01	18:01	19:01	20:01
9^{01}_{pm}	10^{01}_{pm}	11^{01}_{pm}	12^{01}_{am}	1^{01}_{am}	2^{01}_{am}	3^{01}_{am}	4^{01}_{am}	5^{01}_{am}	6^{01}_{am}	7^{01}_{am}	8^{01}_{am}	9^{01}_{am}	10^{01}_{am}	11^{01}_{am}	12^{01}_{pm}	1^{01}_{pm}	2^{01}_{pm}	3^{01}_{pm}	4^{01}_{pm}	5^{01}_{pm}	6^{01}_{pm}	7^{01}_{pm}	8^{01}_{pm}
Sun	Sun	Sun	Mon	Mon	Mon	Mon	Mon	Mon	Mon	Mon	Mon	Mon	Mon	Mon	Mon	Mon	Mon	Mon	Mon	Mon	Mon	Mon	Mon

JOHNSTON ATOLL

Number of Time Zones: *1*
Standard Time: *Applicable for the entire year*
Advanced Time: *Not observed*
Time Zone: *02:00 (-10hrs UTC)*

[a]	[b]	[c]	[d]	[e]	[f]	[g]	[h]	[i]	[j]	[k]	[l]	[m]	[n]	[o]	[p]	[q]	[r]	[s]	[t]	[u]	[v]	[w]	[x]
02:01	03:01	04:01	05:01	06:01	07:01	08:01	09:01	10:01	11:01	12:01	13:01	14:01	15:01	16:01	17:01	18:01	19:01	20:01	21:01	22:01	23:01	00:01	01:01
2^{01}_{am}	3^{01}_{am}	4^{01}_{am}	5^{01}_{am}	6^{01}_{am}	7^{01}_{am}	8^{01}_{am}	9^{01}_{am}	10^{01}_{am}	11^{01}_{am}	12^{01}_{pm}	1^{01}_{pm}	2^{01}_{pm}	3^{01}_{pm}	4^{01}_{pm}	5^{01}_{pm}	6^{01}_{pm}	7^{01}_{pm}	8^{01}_{pm}	9^{01}_{pm}	10^{01}_{pm}	11^{01}_{pm}	12^{01}_{am}	1^{01}_{am}
Sun	Sun	Sun	Sun	Sun	Sun	Sun	Sun	Sun	Sun	Sun	Sun	Sun	Sun	Sun	Sun	Sun	Sun	Sun	Sun	Sun	Sun	Mon	Mon

Note: Advanced Time = Daylight Saving Time = Summer Time

JORDAN
Number of Time Zones: *1*

Standard Time
Period: *First Friday in October to First Saturday in April*
Time Zone: *14:00 (+2hrs UTC)*

[a]	[b]	[c]	[d]	[e]	[f]	[g]	[h]	[i]	[j]	[k]	[l]	[m]	[n]	[o]	[p]	[q]	[r]	[s]	[t]	[u]	[v]	[w]	[x]
14:01	15:01	16:01	17:01	18:01	19:01	20:01	21:01	22:01	23:01	00:01	01:01	02:01	03:01	04:01	05:01	06:01	07:01	08:01	09:01	10:01	11:01	12:01	13:01
2^{01}_{pm}	3^{01}_{pm}	4^{01}_{pm}	5^{01}_{pm}	6^{01}_{pm}	7^{01}_{pm}	8^{01}_{pm}	9^{01}_{pm}	10^{01}_{pm}	11^{01}_{pm}	12^{01}_{am}	1^{01}_{am}	2^{01}_{am}	3^{01}_{am}	4^{01}_{am}	5^{01}_{am}	6^{01}_{am}	7^{01}_{am}	8^{01}_{am}	9^{01}_{am}	10^{01}_{am}	11^{01}_{am}	12^{01}_{pm}	1^{01}_{pm}
Sun	Sun	Sun	Sun	Sun	Sun	Sun	Sun	Sun	Sun	Mon	Mon	Mon	Mon	Mon	Mon	Mon	Mon	Mon	Mon	Mon	Mon	Mon	Mon

Advanced Time
Period: *First Saturday in April to First Friday in October*
Time Zone: *15:00 (+3hrs UTC)*

[a]	[b]	[c]	[d]	[e]	[f]	[g]	[h]	[i]	[j]	[k]	[l]	[m]	[n]	[o]	[p]	[q]	[r]	[s]	[t]	[u]	[v]	[w]	[x]
15:01	16:01	17:01	18:01	19:01	20:01	21:01	22:01	23:01	00:01	01:01	02:01	03:01	04:01	05:01	06:01	07:01	08:01	09:01	10:01	11:01	12:01	13:01	14:01
3^{01}_{pm}	4^{01}_{pm}	5^{01}_{pm}	6^{01}_{pm}	7^{01}_{pm}	8^{01}_{pm}	9^{01}_{pm}	10^{01}_{pm}	11^{01}_{pm}	12^{01}_{am}	1^{01}_{am}	2^{01}_{am}	3^{01}_{am}	4^{01}_{am}	5^{01}_{am}	6^{01}_{am}	7^{01}_{am}	8^{01}_{am}	9^{01}_{am}	10^{01}_{am}	11^{01}_{am}	12^{01}_{pm}	1^{01}_{pm}	2^{01}_{pm}
Sun	Sun	Sun	Sun	Sun	Sun	Sun	Sun	Sun	Mon	Mon	Mon	Mon	Mon	Mon	Mon	Mon	Mon	Mon	Mon	Mon	Mon	Mon	Mon

KENYA
Number of Time Zones: *1*
Standard Time: *Applicable for the entire year*
Advanced Time: *Not observed*
Time Zone: *15:00 (+3hrs UTC)*

[a]	[b]	[c]	[d]	[e]	[f]	[g]	[h]	[i]	[j]	[k]	[l]	[m]	[n]	[o]	[p]	[q]	[r]	[s]	[t]	[u]	[v]	[w]	[x]
15:01	16:01	17:01	18:01	19:01	20:01	21:01	22:01	23:01	00:01	01:01	02:01	03:01	04:01	05:01	06:01	07:01	08:01	09:01	10:01	11:01	12:01	13:01	14:01
3^{01}_{pm}	4^{01}_{pm}	5^{01}_{pm}	6^{01}_{pm}	7^{01}_{pm}	8^{01}_{pm}	9^{01}_{pm}	10^{01}_{pm}	11^{01}_{pm}	12^{01}_{am}	1^{01}_{am}	2^{01}_{am}	3^{01}_{am}	4^{01}_{am}	5^{01}_{am}	6^{01}_{am}	7^{01}_{am}	8^{01}_{am}	9^{01}_{am}	10^{01}_{am}	11^{01}_{am}	12^{01}_{pm}	1^{01}_{pm}	2^{01}_{pm}
Sun	Sun	Sun	Sun	Sun	Sun	Sun	Sun	Sun	Mon	Mon	Mon	Mon	Mon	Mon	Mon	Mon	Mon	Mon	Mon	Mon	Mon	Mon	Mon

Note: Advanced Time = Daylight Saving Time = Summer Time

KIRIBATI

Number of Time Zones: *2*
Note: *Advanced Time not observed;*
    See Reference Map I for graphic depiction of time zones

EASTERN TIME ZONE

Note: *Comprises Canton and Enderbury Islands*
Standard Time: *Applicable for the entire year*
Time Zone: *24:00 (+12hrs UTC)*

[a]	[b]	[c]	[d]	[e]	[f]	[g]	[h]	[i]	[j]	[k]	[l]	[m]	[n]	[o]	[p]	[q]	[r]	[s]	[t]	[u]	[v]	[w]	[x]
:01	01:01	02:01	03:01	04:01	05:01	06:01	07:01	08:01	09:01	10:01	11:01	12:01	13:01	14:01	15:01	16:01	17:01	18:01	19:01	20:01	21:01	22:01	23:01
12^{01}_{am}	1^{01}_{am}	2^{01}_{am}	3^{01}_{am}	4^{01}_{am}	5^{01}_{am}	6^{01}_{am}	7^{01}_{am}	8^{01}_{am}	9^{01}_{am}	10^{01}_{am}	11^{01}_{am}	12^{01}_{pm}	1^{01}_{pm}	2^{01}_{pm}	3^{01}_{pm}	4^{01}_{pm}	5^{01}_{pm}	6^{01}_{pm}	7^{01}_{pm}	8^{01}_{pm}	9^{01}_{pm}	10^{01}_{pm}	11^{01}_{pm}
Mon	Mon	Mon	Mon	Mon	Mon	Mon	Mon	Mon	Mon	Mon	Mon	Mon	Mon	Mon	Mon	Mon	Mon	Mon	Mon	Mon	Mon	Mon	Mon

WESTERN TIME ZONE

Note: *Comprises Christmas Island*
Standard Time: *Applicable for the entire year*
Time Zone: *23:00 (+11hrs UTC)*

[a]	[b]	[c]	[d]	[e]	[f]	[g]	[h]	[i]	[j]	[k]	[l]	[m]	[n]	[o]	[p]	[q]	[r]	[s]	[t]	[u]	[v]	[w]	[x]
:01	00:01	01:01	02:01	03:01	04:01	05:01	06:01	07:01	08:01	09:01	10:01	11:01	12:01	13:01	14:01	15:01	16:01	17:01	18:01	19:01	20:01	21:01	22:01
1^{01}_{pm}	12^{01}_{am}	1^{01}_{am}	2^{01}_{am}	3^{01}_{am}	4^{01}_{am}	5^{01}_{am}	6^{01}_{am}	7^{01}_{am}	8^{01}_{am}	9^{01}_{am}	10^{01}_{am}	11^{01}_{am}	12^{01}_{pm}	1^{01}_{pm}	2^{01}_{pm}	3^{01}_{pm}	4^{01}_{pm}	5^{01}_{pm}	6^{01}_{pm}	7^{01}_{pm}	8^{01}_{pm}	9^{01}_{pm}	10^{01}_{pm}
Sun	Mon	Mon	Mon	Mon	Mon	Mon	Mon	Mon	Mon	Mon	Mon	Mon	Mon	Mon	Mon	Mon	Mon	Mon	Mon	Mon	Mon	Mon	Mon

KOREA, NORTH

Number of Time Zones: *1*
Standard Time: *Applicable for the entire year*
Advanced Time: *Not observed*
Time Zone: *21:00 (+9hrs UTC)*

[a]	[b]	[c]	[d]	[e]	[f]	[g]	[h]	[i]	[j]	[k]	[l]	[m]	[n]	[o]	[p]	[q]	[r]	[s]	[t]	[u]	[v]	[w]	[x]
:01	22:01	23:01	00:01	01:01	02:01	03:01	04:01	05:01	06:01	07:01	08:01	09:01	10:01	11:01	12:01	13:01	14:01	15:01	16:01	17:01	18:01	19:01	20:01
9^{01}_{pm}	10^{01}_{pm}	11^{01}_{pm}	12^{01}_{am}	1^{01}_{am}	2^{01}_{am}	3^{01}_{am}	4^{01}_{am}	5^{01}_{am}	6^{01}_{am}	7^{01}_{am}	8^{01}_{am}	9^{01}_{am}	10^{01}_{am}	11^{01}_{am}	12^{01}_{pm}	1^{01}_{pm}	2^{01}_{pm}	3^{01}_{pm}	4^{01}_{pm}	5^{01}_{pm}	6^{01}_{pm}	7^{01}_{pm}	8^{01}_{pm}
Sun	Sun	Sun	Mon	Mon	Mon	Mon	Mon	Mon	Mon	Mon	Mon	Mon	Mon	Mon	Mon	Mon	Mon	Mon	Mon	Mon	Mon	Mon	Mon

Note: Advanced Time = Daylight Saving Time = Summer Time

KOREA, SOUTH
Number of Time Zones: *1*

Standard Time
Period: *Second Sunday in October to Second Sunday in May*
Time Zone: *21:00 (+9hrS UTC)*

[a]	[b]	[c]	[d]	[e]	[f]	[g]	[h]	[i]	[j]	[k]	[l]	[m]	[n]	[o]	[p]	[q]	[r]	[s]	[t]	[u]	[v]	[w]	
21:01	22:01	23:01	00:01	01:01	02:01	03:01	04:01	05:01	06:01	07:01	08:01	09:01	10:01	11:01	12:01	13:01	14:01	15:01	16:01	17:01	18:01	19:01	20
9^{01}_{pm}	10^{01}_{pm}	11^{01}_{pm}	12^{01}_{am}	1^{01}_{am}	2^{01}_{am}	3^{01}_{am}	4^{01}_{am}	5^{01}_{am}	6^{01}_{am}	7^{01}_{am}	8^{01}_{am}	9^{01}_{am}	10^{01}_{am}	11^{01}_{am}	12^{01}_{pm}	1^{01}_{pm}	2^{01}_{pm}	3^{01}_{pm}	4^{01}_{pm}	5^{01}_{pm}	6^{01}_{pm}	7^{01}_{pm}	
Sun	Sun	Sun	Mon	Mon	Mon	Mon	Mon	Mon	Mon	Mon	Mon	Mon	Mon	Mon	Mon	Mon	Mon	Mon	Mon	Mon	Mon	Mon	M

Advanced Time
Period: *Second Sunday in May to Second Sunday in October*
Time Zone: *22:00 (+10hrs UTC)*

[a]	[b]	[c]	[d]	[e]	[f]	[g]	[h]	[i]	[j]	[k]	[l]	[m]	[n]	[o]	[p]	[q]	[r]	[s]	[t]	[u]	[v]	[w]	
22:01	23:01	00:01	01:01	02:01	03:01	04:01	05:01	06:01	07:01	08:01	09:01	10:01	11:01	12:01	13:01	14:01	15:01	16:01	17:01	18:01	19:01	20:01	21
10^{01}_{pm}	11^{01}_{pm}	12^{01}_{am}	1^{01}_{am}	2^{01}_{am}	3^{01}_{am}	4^{01}_{am}	5^{01}_{am}	6^{01}_{am}	7^{01}_{am}	8^{01}_{am}	9^{01}_{am}	10^{01}_{am}	11^{01}_{am}	12^{01}_{pm}	1^{01}_{pm}	2^{01}_{pm}	3^{01}_{pm}	4^{01}_{pm}	5^{01}_{pm}	6^{01}_{pm}	7^{01}_{pm}	8^{01}_{pm}	9
Sun	Sun	Mon	Mon	Mon	Mon	Mon	Mon	Mon	Mon	Mon	Mon	Mon	Mon	Mon	Mon	Mon	Mon	Mon	Mon	Mon	Mon	Mon	M

KUWAIT
Number of Time Zones: *1*
Standard Time: *Applicable for the entire year*
Advanced Time: *Not observed*
Time Zone: *15:00 (+3hrs UTC)*

[a]	[b]	[c]	[d]	[e]	[f]	[g]	[h]	[i]	[j]	[k]	[l]	[m]	[n]	[o]	[p]	[q]	[r]	[s]	[t]	[u]	[v]	[w]	
15:01	16:01	17:01	18:01	19:01	20:01	21:01	22:01	23:01	00:01	01:01	02:01	03:01	04:01	05:01	06:01	07:01	08:01	09:01	10:01	11:01	12:01	13:01	14
3^{01}_{pm}	4^{01}_{pm}	5^{01}_{pm}	6^{01}_{pm}	7^{01}_{pm}	8^{01}_{pm}	9^{01}_{pm}	10^{01}_{pm}	11^{01}_{pm}	12^{01}_{am}	1^{01}_{am}	2^{01}_{am}	3^{01}_{am}	4^{01}_{am}	5^{01}_{am}	6^{01}_{am}	7^{01}_{am}	8^{01}_{am}	9^{01}_{am}	10^{01}_{am}	11^{01}_{am}	12^{01}_{pm}	1^{01}_{pm}	2
Sun	Sun	Sun	Sun	Sun	Sun	Sun	Sun	Sun	Mon	Mon	Mon	Mon	Mon	Mon	Mon	Mon	Mon	Mon	Mon	Mon	Mon	Mon	M

LAOS
Number of Time Zones: *1*
Standard Time: *Applicable for the entire year*
Advanced Time: *Not observed*
Time Zone: *19:00 (+7hrs UTC)*

[a]	[b]	[c]	[d]	[e]	[f]	[g]	[h]	[i]	[j]	[k]	[l]	[m]	[n]	[o]	[p]	[q]	[r]	[s]	[t]	[u]	[v]	[w]	
19:01	20:01	21:01	22:01	23:01	00:01	01:01	02:01	03:01	04:01	05:01	06:01	07:01	08:01	09:01	10:01	11:01	12:01	13:01	14:01	15:01	16:01	17:01	18
7^{01}_{pm}	8^{01}_{pm}	9^{01}_{pm}	10^{01}_{pm}	11^{01}_{pm}	12^{01}_{am}	1^{01}_{am}	2^{01}_{am}	3^{01}_{am}	4^{01}_{am}	5^{01}_{am}	6^{01}_{am}	7^{01}_{am}	8^{01}_{am}	9^{01}_{am}	10^{01}_{am}	11^{01}_{am}	12^{01}_{pm}	1^{01}_{pm}	2^{01}_{pm}	3^{01}_{pm}	4^{01}_{pm}	5^{01}_{pm}	6
Sun	Sun	Sun	Sun	Sun	Mon	Mon	Mon	Mon	Mon	Mon	Mon	Mon	Mon	Mon	Mon	Mon	Mon	Mon	Mon	Mon	Mon	Mon	M

Note: Advanced Time = Daylight Saving Time = Summer Time

LEBANON
Number of Time Zones: *1*

Standard Time
Period: *Varies: October to May*
Time Zone: *14:00 (+2hrs UTC)*

[a]	[b]	[c]	[d]	[e]	[f]	[g]	[h]	[i]	[j]	[k]	[l]	[m]	[n]	[o]	[p]	[q]	[r]	[s]	[t]	[u]	[v]	[w]	[x]
14:01	15:01	16:01	17:01	18:01	19:01	20:01	21:01	22:01	23:01	00:01	01:01	02:01	03:01	04:01	05:01	06:01	07:01	08:01	09:01	10:01	11:01	12:01	13:01
2^{01}_{pm}	3^{01}_{pm}	4^{01}_{pm}	5^{01}_{pm}	6^{01}_{pm}	7^{01}_{pm}	8^{01}_{pm}	9^{01}_{pm}	10^{01}_{pm}	11^{01}_{pm}	12^{01}_{am}	1^{01}_{am}	2^{01}_{am}	3^{01}_{am}	4^{01}_{am}	5^{01}_{am}	6^{01}_{am}	7^{01}_{am}	8^{01}_{am}	9^{01}_{am}	10^{01}_{am}	11^{01}_{am}	12^{01}_{pm}	1^{01}_{pm}
Sun	Sun	Sun	Sun	Sun	Sun	Sun	Sun	Sun	Sun	Mon	Mon	Mon	Mon	Mon	Mon	Mon	Mon	Mon	Mon	Mon	Mon	Mon	Mon

Advanced Time
Period: *Varies: May to October*
Time Zone: *15:00 (+3hrs UTC)*

[a]	[b]	[c]	[d]	[e]	[f]	[g]	[h]	[i]	[j]	[k]	[l]	[m]	[n]	[o]	[p]	[q]	[r]	[s]	[t]	[u]	[v]	[w]	[x]
15:01	16:01	17:01	18:01	19:01	20:01	21:01	22:01	23:01	00:01	01:01	02:01	03:01	04:01	05:01	06:01	07:01	08:01	09:01	10:01	11:01	12:01	13:01	14:01
3^{01}_{pm}	4^{01}_{pm}	5^{01}_{pm}	6^{01}_{pm}	7^{01}_{pm}	8^{01}_{pm}	9^{01}_{pm}	10^{01}_{pm}	11^{01}_{pm}	12^{01}_{am}	1^{01}_{am}	2^{01}_{am}	3^{01}_{am}	4^{01}_{am}	5^{01}_{am}	6^{01}_{am}	7^{01}_{am}	8^{01}_{am}	9^{01}_{am}	10^{01}_{am}	11^{01}_{am}	12^{01}_{pm}	1^{01}_{pm}	2^{01}_{pm}
Sun	Sun	Sun	Sun	Sun	Sun	Sun	Sun	Sun	Mon	Mon	Mon	Mon	Mon	Mon	Mon	Mon	Mon	Mon	Mon	Mon	Mon	Mon	Mon

LESOTHO
Number of Time Zones: *1*
Standard Time: *Applicable for the entire year*
Advanced Time: *Not observed*
Time Zone: *14:00 (+2hrs UTC)*

[a]	[b]	[c]	[d]	[e]	[f]	[g]	[h]	[i]	[j]	[k]	[l]	[m]	[n]	[o]	[p]	[q]	[r]	[s]	[t]	[u]	[v]	[w]	[x]
14:01	15:01	16:01	17:01	18:01	19:01	20:01	21:01	22:01	23:01	00:01	01:01	02:01	03:01	04:01	05:01	06:01	07:01	08:01	09:01	10:01	11:01	12:01	13:01
2^{01}_{pm}	3^{01}_{pm}	4^{01}_{pm}	5^{01}_{pm}	6^{01}_{pm}	7^{01}_{pm}	8^{01}_{pm}	9^{01}_{pm}	10^{01}_{pm}	11^{01}_{pm}	12^{01}_{am}	1^{01}_{am}	2^{01}_{am}	3^{01}_{am}	4^{01}_{am}	5^{01}_{am}	6^{01}_{am}	7^{01}_{am}	8^{01}_{am}	9^{01}_{am}	10^{01}_{am}	11^{01}_{am}	12^{01}_{pm}	1^{01}_{pm}
Sun	Sun	Sun	Sun	Sun	Sun	Sun	Sun	Sun	Sun	Mon	Mon	Mon	Mon	Mon	Mon	Mon	Mon	Mon	Mon	Mon	Mon	Mon	Mon

LIBERIA
Number of Time Zones: *1*
Standard Time: *Applicable for the entire year*
Advanced Time: *Not observed*
Time Zone: *12:00 (UTC)*

[a]	[b]	[c]	[d]	[e]	[f]	[g]	[h]	[i]	[j]	[k]	[l]	[m]	[n]	[o]	[p]	[q]	[r]	[s]	[t]	[u]	[v]	[w]	[x]
12:01	13:01	14:01	15:01	16:01	17:01	18:01	19:01	20:01	21:01	22:01	23:01	00:01	01:01	02:01	03:01	04:01	05:01	06:01	07:01	08:01	09:01	10:01	11:01
12^{01}_{pm}	1^{01}_{pm}	2^{01}_{pm}	3^{01}_{pm}	4^{01}_{pm}	5^{01}_{pm}	6^{01}_{pm}	7^{01}_{pm}	8^{01}_{pm}	9^{01}_{pm}	10^{01}_{pm}	11^{01}_{pm}	12^{01}_{am}	1^{01}_{am}	2^{01}_{am}	3^{01}_{am}	4^{01}_{am}	5^{01}_{am}	6^{01}_{am}	7^{01}_{am}	8^{01}_{am}	9^{01}_{am}	10^{01}_{am}	11^{01}_{am}
Sun	Sun	Sun	Sun	Sun	Sun	Sun	Sun	Sun	Sun	Sun	Sun	Mon	Mon	Mon	Mon	Mon	Mon	Mon	Mon	Mon	Mon	Mon	Mon

Note: Advanced Time = Daylight Saving Time = Summer Time

LIBYA

Number of Time Zones: *1*
Standard Time: *Applicable for the entire year*
Advanced Time: *Not observed*
Time Zone: *13:00 (+1hr UTC)*

[a]	[b]	[c]	[d]	[e]	[f]	[g]	[h]	[i]	[j]	[k]	[l]	[m]	[n]	[o]	[p]	[q]	[r]	[s]	[t]	[u]	[v]	[w]	[x]
13:01	14:01	15:01	16:01	17:01	18:01	19:01	20:01	21:01	22:01	23:01	00:01	01:01	02:01	03:01	04:01	05:01	06:01	07:01	08:01	09:01	10:01	11:01	12:01
1:01pm	2:01pm	3:01pm	4:01pm	5:01pm	6:01pm	7:01pm	8:01pm	9:01pm	10:01pm	11:01pm	12:01am	1:01am	2:01am	3:01am	4:01am	5:01am	6:01am	7:01am	8:01am	9:01am	10:01am	11:01am	12:01pm
Sun	Sun	Sun	Sun	Sun	Sun	Sun	Sun	Sun	Sun	Sun	Mon	Mon	Mon	Mon	Mon	Mon	Mon	Mon	Mon	Mon	Mon	Mon	Mon

LIECHTENSTEIN

Number of Time Zones: *1*

Standard Time

Period: *Last Sunday in September to Last Sunday in March*
Time Zone: *13:00 (+1hr UTC)*

[a]	[b]	[c]	[d]	[e]	[f]	[g]	[h]	[i]	[j]	[k]	[l]	[m]	[n]	[o]	[p]	[q]	[r]	[s]	[t]	[u]	[v]	[w]	[x]
13:01	14:01	15:01	16:01	17:01	18:01	19:01	20:01	21:01	22:01	23:01	00:01	01:01	02:01	03:01	04:01	05:01	06:01	07:01	08:01	09:01	10:01	11:01	12:01
1:01pm	2:01pm	3:01pm	4:01pm	5:01pm	6:01pm	7:01pm	8:01pm	9:01pm	10:01pm	11:01pm	12:01am	1:01am	2:01am	3:01am	4:01am	5:01am	6:01am	7:01am	8:01am	9:01am	10:01am	11:01am	12:01pm
Sun	Sun	Sun	Sun	Sun	Sun	Sun	Sun	Sun	Sun	Sun	Mon	Mon	Mon	Mon	Mon	Mon	Mon	Mon	Mon	Mon	Mon	Mon	Mon

Advanced Time

Period: *Last Sunday in March to Last Sunday in September*
Time Zone: *14:00 (+2hrs UTC)*

[a]	[b]	[c]	[d]	[e]	[f]	[g]	[h]	[i]	[j]	[k]	[l]	[m]	[n]	[o]	[p]	[q]	[r]	[s]	[t]	[u]	[v]	[w]	[x]
14:01	15:01	16:01	17:01	18:01	19:01	20:01	21:01	22:01	23:01	00:01	01:01	02:01	03:01	04:01	05:01	06:01	07:01	08:01	09:01	10:01	11:01	12:01	13:01
2:01pm	3:01pm	4:01pm	5:01pm	6:01pm	7:01pm	8:01pm	9:01pm	10:01pm	11:01pm	12:01am	1:01am	2:01am	3:01am	4:01am	5:01am	6:01am	7:01am	8:01am	9:01am	10:01am	11:01am	12:01pm	1:01pm
Sun	Sun	Sun	Sun	Sun	Sun	Sun	Sun	Sun	Sun	Mon	Mon	Mon	Mon	Mon	Mon	Mon	Mon	Mon	Mon	Mon	Mon	Mon	Mon

Note: Advanced Time = Daylight Saving Time = Summer Time

LORD HOWE ISLAND
Number of Time Zones: *1*

Standard Time
Period: *First Sunday in March to Last Sunday in October*
Time Zone: *22:30 (+10hrs 30mins UTC)*

[a]	[b]	[c]	[d]	[e]	[f]	[g]	[h]	[i]	[j]	[k]	[l]	[m]	[n]	[o]	[p]	[q]	[r]	[s]	[t]	[u]	[v]	[w]	[x]
:31	23:31	00:31	01:31	02:31	03:31	04:31	05:31	06:31	07:31	08:31	09:31	10:31	11:31	12:31	13:31	14:31	15:31	16:31	17:31	18:31	19:31	20:31	21:31
0^{31}_{pm}	11^{31}_{pm}	12^{31}_{am}	1^{31}_{am}	2^{31}_{am}	3^{31}_{am}	4^{31}_{am}	5^{31}_{am}	6^{31}_{am}	7^{31}_{am}	8^{31}_{am}	9^{31}_{am}	10^{31}_{am}	11^{31}_{am}	12^{31}_{pm}	1^{31}_{pm}	2^{31}_{pm}	3^{31}_{pm}	4^{31}_{pm}	5^{31}_{pm}	6^{31}_{pm}	7^{31}_{pm}	8^{31}_{pm}	9^{31}_{pm}
Sun	Sun	Mon	Mon	Mon	Mon	Mon	Mon	Mon	Mon	Mon	Mon	Mon	Mon	Mon	Mon	Mon	Mon	Mon	Mon	Mon	Mon	Mon	Mon

Advanced Time
Period: *Last Sunday in October to First Sunday in March*
Time Zone: *23:30 (+11hrs 30mins UTC)*

[a]	[b]	[c]	[d]	[e]	[f]	[g]	[h]	[i]	[j]	[k]	[l]	[m]	[n]	[o]	[p]	[q]	[r]	[s]	[t]	[u]	[v]	[w]	[x]
:31	00:31	01:31	02:31	03:31	04:31	05:31	06:31	07:31	08:31	09:31	10:31	11:31	12:31	13:31	14:31	15:31	16:31	17:31	18:31	19:31	20:31	21:31	22:31
1^{31}_{pm}	12^{31}_{am}	1^{31}_{am}	2^{31}_{am}	3^{31}_{am}	4^{31}_{am}	5^{31}_{am}	6^{31}_{am}	7^{31}_{am}	8^{31}_{am}	9^{31}_{am}	10^{31}_{am}	11^{31}_{am}	12^{31}_{pm}	1^{31}_{pm}	2^{31}_{pm}	3^{31}_{pm}	4^{31}_{pm}	5^{31}_{pm}	6^{31}_{pm}	7^{31}_{pm}	8^{31}_{pm}	9^{31}_{pm}	10^{31}_{pm}
Sun	Mon	Mon	Mon	Mon	Mon	Mon	Mon	Mon	Mon	Mon	Mon	Mon	Mon	Mon	Mon	Mon	Mon	Mon	Mon	Mon	Mon	Mon	Mon

LUXEMBOURG
Number of Time Zones: *1*

Standard Time
Period: *Last Sunday in September to Last Sunday in March*
Time Zone: *13:00 (+1hr UTC)*

[a]	[b]	[c]	[d]	[e]	[f]	[g]	[h]	[i]	[j]	[k]	[l]	[m]	[n]	[o]	[p]	[q]	[r]	[s]	[t]	[u]	[v]	[w]	[x]
:01	14:01	15:01	16:01	17:01	18:01	19:01	20:01	21:01	22:01	23:01	00:01	01:01	02:01	03:01	04:01	05:01	06:01	07:01	08:01	09:01	10:01	11:01	12:01
1^{01}_{pm}	2^{01}_{pm}	3^{01}_{pm}	4^{01}_{pm}	5^{01}_{pm}	6^{01}_{pm}	7^{01}_{pm}	8^{01}_{pm}	9^{01}_{pm}	10^{01}_{pm}	11^{01}_{pm}	12^{01}_{am}	1^{01}_{am}	2^{01}_{am}	3^{01}_{am}	4^{01}_{am}	5^{01}_{am}	6^{01}_{am}	7^{01}_{am}	8^{01}_{am}	9^{01}_{am}	10^{01}_{am}	11^{01}_{am}	12^{01}_{pm}
Sun	Sun	Sun	Sun	Sun	Sun	Sun	Sun	Sun	Sun	Sun	Mon	Mon	Mon	Mon	Mon	Mon	Mon	Mon	Mon	Mon	Mon	Mon	Mon

Advanced Time
Period: *Last Sunday in March to Last Sunday in September*
Time Zone: *14:00 (+2hrs UTC)*

[a]	[b]	[c]	[d]	[e]	[f]	[g]	[h]	[i]	[j]	[k]	[l]	[m]	[n]	[o]	[p]	[q]	[r]	[s]	[t]	[u]	[v]	[w]	[x]
:01	15:01	16:01	17:01	18:01	19:01	20:01	21:01	22:01	23:01	00:01	01:01	02:01	03:01	04:01	05:01	06:01	07:01	08:01	09:01	10:01	11:01	12:01	13:01
2^{01}_{pm}	3^{01}_{pm}	4^{01}_{pm}	5^{01}_{pm}	6^{01}_{pm}	7^{01}_{pm}	8^{01}_{pm}	9^{01}_{pm}	10^{01}_{pm}	11^{01}_{pm}	12^{01}_{am}	1^{01}_{am}	2^{01}_{am}	3^{01}_{am}	4^{01}_{am}	5^{01}_{am}	6^{01}_{am}	7^{01}_{am}	8^{01}_{am}	9^{01}_{am}	10^{01}_{am}	11^{01}_{am}	12^{01}_{pm}	1^{01}_{pm}
Sun	Sun	Sun	Sun	Sun	Sun	Sun	Sun	Sun	Sun	Mon	Mon	Mon	Mon	Mon	Mon	Mon	Mon	Mon	Mon	Mon	Mon	Mon	Mon

Note: Advanced Time = Daylight Saving Time = Summer Time

MACAU

Number of Time Zones: *1*
Standard Time: *Applicable for the entire year*
Advanced Time: *Not observed*
Time Zone: *20:00 (+8hrs UTC)*

[a]	[b]	[c]	[d]	[e]	[f]	[g]	[h]	[i]	[j]	[k]	[l]	[m]	[n]	[o]	[p]	[q]	[r]	[s]	[t]	[u]	[v]	[w]	[
20:01	21:01	22:01	23:01	00:01	01:01	02:01	03:01	04:01	05:01	06:01	07:01	08:01	09:01	10:01	11:01	12:01	13:01	14:01	15:01	16:01	17:01	18:01	19:
8:01pm	9:01pm	10:01pm	11:01pm	12:01am	1:01am	2:01am	3:01am	4:01am	5:01am	6:01am	7:01am	8:01am	9:01am	10:01am	11:01am	12:01pm	1:01pm	2:01pm	3:01pm	4:01pm	5:01pm	6:01pm	7:
Sun	Sun	Sun	Sun	Mon	Mon	Mon	Mon	Mon	Mon	Mon	Mon	Mon	Mon	Mon	Mon	Mon	Mon	Mon	Mon	Mon	Mon	Mon	M

MADAGASCAR

Number of Time Zones: *1*
Standard Time: *Applicable for the entire year*
Advanced Time: *Not observed*
Time Zone: *15:00 (+3hrs UTC)*

[a]	[b]	[c]	[d]	[e]	[f]	[g]	[h]	[i]	[j]	[k]	[l]	[m]	[n]	[o]	[p]	[q]	[r]	[s]	[t]	[u]	[v]	[w]	[x
15:01	16:01	17:01	18:01	19:01	20:01	21:01	22:01	23:01	00:01	01:01	02:01	03:01	04:01	05:01	06:01	07:01	08:01	09:01	10:01	11:01	12:01	13:01	14:
3:01pm	4:01pm	5:01pm	6:01pm	7:01pm	8:01pm	9:01pm	10:01pm	11:01pm	12:01am	1:01am	2:01am	3:01am	4:01am	5:01am	6:01am	7:01am	8:01am	9:01am	10:01am	11:01am	12:01pm	1:01pm	2:
Sun	Sun	Sun	Sun	Sun	Sun	Sun	Sun	Sun	Mon	Mon	Mon	Mon	Mon	Mon	Mon	Mon	Mon	Mon	Mon	Mon	Mon	Mon	Mo

MADEIRA ISLANDS

Number of Time Zones: *1*

Standard Time

Period: *Last Sunday in September to Last Sunday in March*
Time Zone: *12:00 (UTC)*

[a]	[b]	[c]	[d]	[e]	[f]	[g]	[h]	[i]	[j]	[k]	[l]	[m]	[n]	[o]	[p]	[q]	[r]	[s]	[t]	[u]	[v]	[w]	[x
12:01	13:01	14:01	15:01	16:01	17:01	18:01	19:01	20:01	21:01	22:01	23:01	00:01	01:01	02:01	03:01	04:01	05:01	06:01	07:01	08:01	09:01	10:01	11:
12:01pm	1:01pm	2:01pm	3:01pm	4:01pm	5:01pm	6:01pm	7:01pm	8:01pm	9:01pm	10:01pm	11:01pm	12:01am	1:01am	2:01am	3:01am	4:01am	5:01am	6:01am	7:01am	8:01am	9:01am	10:01am	11:
Sun	Sun	Sun	Sun	Sun	Sun	Sun	Sun	Sun	Sun	Sun	Sun	Mon	Mon	Mon	Mon	Mon	Mon	Mon	Mon	Mon	Mon	Mon	Mo

Advanced Time

Period: *Last Sunday in March to Last Sunday in September*
Time Zone: *13:00 (+1hr UTC)*

[a]	[b]	[c]	[d]	[e]	[f]	[g]	[h]	[i]	[j]	[k]	[l]	[m]	[n]	[o]	[p]	[q]	[r]	[s]	[t]	[u]	[v]	[w]	[x
13:01	14:01	15:01	16:01	17:01	18:01	19:01	20:01	21:01	22:01	23:01	00:01	01:01	02:01	03:01	04:01	05:01	06:01	07:01	08:01	09:01	10:01	11:01	12:0
1:01pm	2:01pm	3:01pm	4:01pm	5:01pm	6:01pm	7:01pm	8:01pm	9:01pm	10:01pm	11:01pm	12:01am	1:01am	2:01am	3:01am	4:01am	5:01am	6:01am	7:01am	8:01am	9:01am	10:01am	11:01am	12:pr
Sun	Sun	Sun	Sun	Sun	Sun	Sun	Sun	Sun	Sun	Sun	Mon	Mon	Mon	Mon	Mon	Mon	Mon	Mon	Mon	Mon	Mon	Mon	Mor

Note: Advanced Time = Daylight Saving Time = Summer Time

MALAWI

Number of Time Zones: *1*
Standard Time: *Applicable for the entire year*
Advanced Time: *Not observed*
Time Zone: *14:00 (+2hrs UTC)*

[a]	[b]	[c]	[d]	[e]	[f]	[g]	[h]	[i]	[j]	[k]	[l]	[m]	[n]	[o]	[p]	[q]	[r]	[s]	[t]	[u]	[v]	[w]	[x]
14:01	15:01	16:01	17:01	18:01	19:01	20:01	21:01	22:01	23:01	00:01	01:01	02:01	03:01	04:01	05:01	06:01	07:01	08:01	09:01	10:01	11:01	12:01	13:01
2^{01}_{pm}	3^{01}_{pm}	4^{01}_{pm}	5^{01}_{pm}	6^{01}_{pm}	7^{01}_{pm}	8^{01}_{pm}	9^{01}_{pm}	10^{01}_{pm}	11^{01}_{pm}	12^{01}_{am}	1^{01}_{am}	2^{01}_{am}	3^{01}_{am}	4^{01}_{am}	5^{01}_{am}	6^{01}_{am}	7^{01}_{am}	8^{01}_{am}	9^{01}_{am}	10^{01}_{am}	11^{01}_{am}	12^{01}_{pm}	1^{01}_{pm}
Sun	Sun	Sun	Sun	Sun	Sun	Sun	Sun	Sun	Sun	Mon	Mon	Mon	Mon	Mon	Mon	Mon	Mon	Mon	Mon	Mon	Mon	Mon	Mon

MALAYSIA

Number of Time Zones: *1*
Standard Time: *Applicable for the entire year*
Advanced Time: *Not observed*
Time Zone: *20:00 (+8hrs UTC)*

[a]	[b]	[c]	[d]	[e]	[f]	[g]	[h]	[i]	[j]	[k]	[l]	[m]	[n]	[o]	[p]	[q]	[r]	[s]	[t]	[u]	[v]	[w]	[x]
20:01	21:01	22:01	23:01	00:01	01:01	02:01	03:01	04:01	05:01	06:01	07:01	08:01	09:01	10:01	11:01	12:01	13:01	14:01	15:01	16:01	17:01	18:01	19:01
8^{01}_{pm}	9^{01}_{pm}	10^{01}_{pm}	11^{01}_{pm}	12^{01}_{am}	1^{01}_{am}	2^{01}_{am}	3^{01}_{am}	4^{01}_{am}	5^{01}_{am}	6^{01}_{am}	7^{01}_{am}	8^{01}_{am}	9^{01}_{am}	10^{01}_{am}	11^{01}_{am}	12^{01}_{pm}	1^{01}_{pm}	2^{01}_{pm}	3^{01}_{pm}	4^{01}_{pm}	5^{01}_{pm}	6^{01}_{pm}	7^{01}_{pm}
Sun	Sun	Sun	Sun	Mon	Mon	Mon	Mon	Mon	Mon	Mon	Mon	Mon	Mon	Mon	Mon	Mon	Mon	Mon	Mon	Mon	Mon	Mon	Mon

MALDIVES

Number of Time Zones: *1*
Standard Time: *Applicable for the entire year*
Advanced Time: *Not observed*
Time Zone: *17:00 (+5hrs UTC)*

[a]	[b]	[c]	[d]	[e]	[f]	[g]	[h]	[i]	[j]	[k]	[l]	[m]	[n]	[o]	[p]	[q]	[r]	[s]	[t]	[u]	[v]	[w]	[x]
17:01	18:01	19:01	20:01	21:01	22:01	23:01	00:01	01:01	02:01	03:01	04:01	05:01	06:01	07:01	08:01	09:01	10:01	11:01	12:01	13:01	14:01	15:01	16:01
5^{01}_{pm}	6^{01}_{pm}	7^{01}_{pm}	8^{01}_{pm}	9^{01}_{pm}	10^{01}_{pm}	11^{01}_{pm}	12^{01}_{am}	1^{01}_{am}	2^{01}_{am}	3^{01}_{am}	4^{01}_{am}	5^{01}_{am}	6^{01}_{am}	7^{01}_{am}	8^{01}_{am}	9^{01}_{am}	10^{01}_{am}	11^{01}_{am}	12^{01}_{pm}	1^{01}_{pm}	2^{01}_{pm}	3^{01}_{pm}	4^{01}_{pm}
Sun	Sun	Sun	Sun	Sun	Sun	Sun	Mon	Mon	Mon	Mon	Mon	Mon	Mon	Mon	Mon	Mon	Mon	Mon	Mon	Mon	Mon	Mon	Mon

MALI

Number of Time Zones: *1*
Standard Time: *Applicable for the entire year*
Advanced Time: *Not observed*
Time Zone: *12:00 (UTC)*

[a]	[b]	[c]	[d]	[e]	[f]	[g]	[h]	[i]	[j]	[k]	[l]	[m]	[n]	[o]	[p]	[q]	[r]	[s]	[t]	[u]	[v]	[w]	[x]
12:01	13:01	14:01	15:01	16:01	17:01	18:01	19:01	20:01	21:01	22:01	23:01	00:01	01:01	02:01	03:01	04:01	05:01	06:01	07:01	08:01	09:01	10:01	11:01
12^{01}_{pm}	1^{01}_{pm}	2^{01}_{pm}	3^{01}_{pm}	4^{01}_{pm}	5^{01}_{pm}	6^{01}_{pm}	7^{01}_{pm}	8^{01}_{pm}	9^{01}_{pm}	10^{01}_{pm}	11^{01}_{pm}	12^{01}_{am}	1^{01}_{am}	2^{01}_{am}	3^{01}_{am}	4^{01}_{am}	5^{01}_{am}	6^{01}_{am}	7^{01}_{am}	8^{01}_{am}	9^{01}_{am}	10^{01}_{am}	11^{01}_{am}
Sun	Sun	Sun	Sun	Sun	Sun	Sun	Sun	Sun	Sun	Sun	Sun	Mon	Mon	Mon	Mon	Mon	Mon	Mon	Mon	Mon	Mon	Mon	Mon

Note: Advanced Time = Daylight Saving Time = Summer Time

MALTA

Number of Time Zones: *1*

Standard Time

Period: *Last Sunday in September to Last Sunday in March*
Time Zone: *13:00 (+1hr UTC)*

[a]	[b]	[c]	[d]	[e]	[f]	[g]	[h]	[i]	[j]	[k]	[l]	[m]	[n]	[o]	[p]	[q]	[r]	[s]	[t]	[u]	[v]	[w]	
13:01	14:01	15:01	16:01	17:01	18:01	19:01	20:01	21:01	22:01	23:01	00:01	01:01	02:01	03:01	04:01	05:01	06:01	07:01	08:01	09:01	10:01	11:01	12:
1^{01}_{pm}	2^{01}_{pm}	3^{01}_{pm}	4^{01}_{pm}	5^{01}_{pm}	6^{01}_{pm}	7^{01}_{pm}	8^{01}_{pm}	9^{01}_{pm}	10^{01}_{pm}	11^{01}_{pm}	12^{01}_{am}	1^{01}_{am}	2^{01}_{am}	3^{01}_{am}	4^{01}_{am}	5^{01}_{am}	6^{01}_{am}	7^{01}_{am}	8^{01}_{am}	9^{01}_{am}	10^{01}_{am}	11^{01}_{am}	12
Sun	Sun	Sun	Sun	Sun	Sun	Sun	Sun	Sun	Sun	Sun	Mon	Mon	Mon	Mon	Mon	Mon	Mon	Mon	Mon	Mon	Mon	Mon	M

Advanced Time

Period: *Last Sunday in March to Last Sunday in September*
Time Zone: *14:00 (+2hrs UTC)*

[a]	[b]	[c]	[d]	[e]	[f]	[g]	[h]	[i]	[j]	[k]	[l]	[m]	[n]	[o]	[p]	[q]	[r]	[s]	[t]	[u]	[v]	[w]	
14:01	15:01	16:01	17:01	18:01	19:01	20:01	21:01	22:01	23:01	00:01	01:01	02:01	03:01	04:01	05:01	06:01	07:01	08:01	09:01	10:01	11:01	12:01	13:
2^{01}_{pm}	3^{01}_{pm}	4^{01}_{pm}	5^{01}_{pm}	6^{01}_{pm}	7^{01}_{pm}	8^{01}_{pm}	9^{01}_{pm}	10^{01}_{pm}	11^{01}_{pm}	12^{01}_{am}	1^{01}_{am}	2^{01}_{am}	3^{01}_{am}	4^{01}_{am}	5^{01}_{am}	6^{01}_{am}	7^{01}_{am}	8^{01}_{am}	9^{01}_{am}	10^{01}_{am}	11^{01}_{am}	12^{01}_{pm}	1
Sun	Sun	Sun	Sun	Sun	Sun	Sun	Sun	Sun	Sun	Mon	Mon	Mon	Mon	Mon	Mon	Mon	Mon	Mon	Mon	Mon	Mon	Mon	M

MARSHALL ISLANDS

Number of Time Zones: *1*
Standard Time: *Applicable for the entire year*
Advanced Time: *Not observed*
Time Zone: *24:00 (+12hrs UTC)*

[a]	[b]	[c]	[d]	[e]	[f]	[g]	[h]	[i]	[j]	[k]	[l]	[m]	[n]	[o]	[p]	[q]	[r]	[s]	[t]	[u]	[v]	[w]	
00:01	01:01	02:01	03:01	04:01	05:01	06:01	07:01	08:01	09:01	10:01	11:01	12:01	13:01	14:01	15:01	16:01	17:01	18:01	19:01	20:01	21:01	22:01	23:
12^{01}_{am}	1^{01}_{am}	2^{01}_{am}	3^{01}_{am}	4^{01}_{am}	5^{01}_{am}	6^{01}_{am}	7^{01}_{am}	8^{01}_{am}	9^{01}_{am}	10^{01}_{am}	11^{01}_{am}	12^{01}_{pm}	1^{01}_{pm}	2^{01}_{pm}	3^{01}_{pm}	4^{01}_{pm}	5^{01}_{pm}	6^{01}_{pm}	7^{01}_{pm}	8^{01}_{pm}	9^{01}_{pm}	10^{01}_{pm}	11
Mon	Mon	Mon	Mon	Mon	Mon	Mon	Mon	Mon	Mon	Mon	Mon	Mon	Mon	Mon	Mon	Mon	Mon	Mon	Mon	Mon	Mon	Mon	M

MARTINIQUE

Number of Time Zones: *1*
Standard Time: *Applicable for the entire year*
Advanced Time: *Not observed*
Time Zone: *08:00 (-4hrs UTC)*

[a]	[b]	[c]	[d]	[e]	[f]	[g]	[h]	[i]	[j]	[k]	[l]	[m]	[n]	[o]	[p]	[q]	[r]	[s]	[t]	[u]	[v]	[w]	
08:01	09:01	10:01	11:01	12:01	13:01	14:01	15:01	16:01	17:01	18:01	19:01	20:01	21:01	22:01	23:01	00:01	01:01	02:01	03:01	04:01	05:01	06:01	07:
8^{01}_{am}	9^{01}_{am}	10^{01}_{am}	11^{01}_{am}	12^{01}_{pm}	1^{01}_{pm}	2^{01}_{pm}	3^{01}_{pm}	4^{01}_{pm}	5^{01}_{pm}	6^{01}_{pm}	7^{01}_{pm}	8^{01}_{pm}	9^{01}_{pm}	10^{01}_{pm}	11^{01}_{pm}	12^{01}_{am}	1^{01}_{am}	2^{01}_{am}	3^{01}_{am}	4^{01}_{am}	5^{01}_{am}	6^{01}_{am}	7
Sun	Sun	Sun	Sun	Sun	Sun	Sun	Sun	Sun	Sun	Sun	Sun	Sun	Sun	Sun	Sun	Mon	Mon	Mon	Mon	Mon	Mon	Mon	Mo

Note: Advanced Time = Daylight Saving Time = Summer Time

MAURITANIA

Number of Time Zones: *1*
Standard Time: *Applicable for the entire year*
Advanced Time: *Not observed*
Time Zone: *12:00 (UTC)*

[a]	[b]	[c]	[d]	[e]	[f]	[g]	[h]	[i]	[j]	[k]	[l]	[m]	[n]	[o]	[p]	[q]	[r]	[s]	[t]	[u]	[v]	[w]	[x]
12:01	13:01	14:01	15:01	16:01	17:01	18:01	19:01	20:01	21:01	22:01	23:01	00:01	01:01	02:01	03:01	04:01	05:01	06:01	07:01	08:01	09:01	10:01	11:01
12^{01}_{pm}	1^{01}_{pm}	2^{01}_{pm}	3^{01}_{pm}	4^{01}_{pm}	5^{01}_{pm}	6^{01}_{pm}	7^{01}_{pm}	8^{01}_{pm}	9^{01}_{pm}	10^{01}_{pm}	11^{01}_{pm}	12^{01}_{am}	1^{01}_{am}	2^{01}_{am}	3^{01}_{am}	4^{01}_{am}	5^{01}_{am}	6^{01}_{am}	7^{01}_{am}	8^{01}_{am}	9^{01}_{am}	10^{01}_{am}	11^{01}_{am}
Sun	Sun	Sun	Sun	Sun	Sun	Sun	Sun	Sun	Sun	Sun	Sun	Mon	Mon	Mon	Mon	Mon	Mon	Mon	Mon	Mon	Mon	Mon	Mon

MAURITIUS

Number of Time Zones: *1*
Standard Time: *Applicable for the entire year*
Advanced Time: *Not observed*
Time Zone: *16:00 (+4hrs UTC)*

[a]	[b]	[c]	[d]	[e]	[f]	[g]	[h]	[i]	[j]	[k]	[l]	[m]	[n]	[o]	[p]	[q]	[r]	[s]	[t]	[u]	[v]	[w]	[x]
16:01	17:01	18:01	19:01	20:01	21:01	22:01	23:01	00:01	01:01	02:01	03:01	04:01	05:01	06:01	07:01	08:01	09:01	10:01	11:01	12:01	13:01	14:01	15:01
4^{01}_{pm}	5^{01}_{pm}	6^{01}_{pm}	7^{01}_{pm}	8^{01}_{pm}	9^{01}_{pm}	10^{01}_{pm}	11^{01}_{pm}	12^{01}_{am}	1^{01}_{am}	2^{01}_{am}	3^{01}_{am}	4^{01}_{am}	5^{01}_{am}	6^{01}_{am}	7^{01}_{am}	8^{01}_{am}	9^{01}_{am}	10^{01}_{am}	11^{01}_{am}	12^{01}_{pm}	1^{01}_{pm}	2^{01}_{pm}	3^{01}_{pm}
Sun	Sun	Sun	Sun	Sun	Sun	Sun	Sun	Mon	Mon	Mon	Mon	Mon	Mon	Mon	Mon	Mon	Mon	Mon	Mon	Mon	Mon	Mon	Mon

MAYOTTE

Number of Time Zones: *1*
Standard Time: *Applicable for the entire year*
Advanced Time: *Not observed*
Time Zone: *15:00 (+3hrs UTC)*

[a]	[b]	[c]	[d]	[e]	[f]	[g]	[h]	[i]	[j]	[k]	[l]	[m]	[n]	[o]	[p]	[q]	[r]	[s]	[t]	[u]	[v]	[w]	[x]
15:01	16:01	17:01	18:01	19:01	20:01	21:01	22:01	23:01	00:01	01:01	02:01	03:01	04:01	05:01	06:01	07:01	08:01	09:01	10:01	11:01	12:01	13:01	14:01
3^{01}_{pm}	4^{01}_{pm}	5^{01}_{pm}	6^{01}_{pm}	7^{01}_{pm}	8^{01}_{pm}	9^{01}_{pm}	10^{01}_{pm}	11^{01}_{pm}	12^{01}_{am}	1^{01}_{am}	2^{01}_{am}	3^{01}_{am}	4^{01}_{am}	5^{01}_{am}	6^{01}_{am}	7^{01}_{am}	8^{01}_{am}	9^{01}_{am}	10^{01}_{am}	11^{01}_{am}	12^{01}_{pm}	1^{01}_{pm}	2^{01}_{pm}
Sun	Sun	Sun	Sun	Sun	Sun	Sun	Sun	Sun	Mon	Mon	Mon	Mon	Mon	Mon	Mon	Mon	Mon	Mon	Mon	Mon	Mon	Mon	Mon

Note: Advanced Time = Daylight Saving Time = Summer Time

MEXICO

Number of Time Zones: *4*
Note: *Advanced Time observed irregularly*
See Reference Map I for graphic depiction of time zones

CENTRAL TIME ZONE

Note: *Comprises most of the country, including the southern and eastern portions*
Standard Time: *Applicable for the entire year*
Time Zone: *06:00 (-6hrs UTC)*

[a]	[b]	[c]	[d]	[e]	[f]	[g]	[h]	[i]	[j]	[k]	[l]	[m]	[n]	[o]	[p]	[q]	[r]	[s]	[t]	[u]	[v]	[w]	[x]
06:01	07:01	08:01	09:01	10:01	11:01	12:01	13:01	14:01	15:01	16:01	17:01	18:01	19:01	20:01	21:01	22:01	23:01	00:01	01:01	02:01	03:01	04:01	05:01
6^{01}_{am}	7^{01}_{am}	8^{01}_{am}	9^{01}_{am}	10^{01}_{am}	11^{01}_{am}	12^{01}_{pm}	1^{01}_{pm}	2^{01}_{pm}	3^{01}_{pm}	4^{01}_{pm}	5^{01}_{pm}	6^{01}_{pm}	7^{01}_{pm}	8^{01}_{pm}	9^{01}_{pm}	10^{01}_{pm}	11^{01}_{pm}	12^{01}_{am}	1^{01}_{am}	2^{01}_{am}	3^{01}_{am}	4^{01}_{am}	5^{01}_{am}
Sun	Sun	Sun	Sun	Sun	Sun	Sun	Sun	Sun	Sun	Sun	Sun	Sun	Sun	Sun	Sun	Sun	Sun	Mon	Mon	Mon	Mon	Mon	Mon

MOUNTAIN TIME ZONE

Note: *Comprises states of Durango, Coahuila, Nuevo Leon, and Tamaulipas*

Standard Time

Period: *Last Sunday in October to First Sunday in April*
Time Zone: *06:00 (-6hrs UTC)*

[a]	[b]	[c]	[d]	[e]	[f]	[g]	[h]	[i]	[j]	[k]	[l]	[m]	[n]	[o]	[p]	[q]	[r]	[s]	[t]	[u]	[v]	[w]	[x]
06:01	07:01	08:01	09:01	10:01	11:01	12:01	13:01	14:01	15:01	16:01	17:01	18:01	19:01	20:01	21:01	22:01	23:01	00:01	01:01	02:01	03:01	04:01	05:01
6^{01}_{am}	7^{01}_{am}	8^{01}_{am}	9^{01}_{am}	10^{01}_{am}	11^{01}_{am}	12^{01}_{pm}	1^{01}_{pm}	2^{01}_{pm}	3^{01}_{pm}	4^{01}_{pm}	5^{01}_{pm}	6^{01}_{pm}	7^{01}_{pm}	8^{01}_{pm}	9^{01}_{pm}	10^{01}_{pm}	11^{01}_{pm}	12^{01}_{am}	1^{01}_{am}	2^{01}_{am}	3^{01}_{am}	4^{01}_{am}	5^{01}_{am}
Sun	Sun	Sun	Sun	Sun	Sun	Sun	Sun	Sun	Sun	Sun	Sun	Sun	Sun	Sun	Sun	Sun	Sun	Mon	Mon	Mon	Mon	Mon	Mon

Advanced Time

Period: *First Sunday in April to Last Sunday in October*
Time Zone: *07:00 (-5hrs UTC)*

[a]	[b]	[c]	[d]	[e]	[f]	[g]	[h]	[i]	[j]	[k]	[l]	[m]	[n]	[o]	[p]	[q]	[r]	[s]	[t]	[u]	[v]	[w]	[x]
07:01	08:01	09:01	10:01	11:01	12:01	13:01	14:01	15:01	16:01	17:01	18:01	19:01	20:01	21:01	22:01	23:01	00:01	01:01	02:01	03:01	04:01	05:01	06:01
7^{01}_{am}	8^{01}_{am}	9^{01}_{am}	10^{01}_{am}	11^{01}_{am}	12^{01}_{pm}	1^{01}_{pm}	2^{01}_{pm}	3^{01}_{pm}	4^{01}_{pm}	5^{01}_{pm}	6^{01}_{pm}	7^{01}_{pm}	8^{01}_{pm}	9^{01}_{pm}	10^{01}_{pm}	11^{01}_{pm}	12^{01}_{am}	1^{01}_{am}	2^{01}_{am}	3^{01}_{am}	4^{01}_{am}	5^{01}_{am}	6^{01}_{am}
Sun	Sun	Sun	Sun	Sun	Sun	Sun	Sun	Sun	Sun	Sun	Sun	Sun	Sun	Sun	Sun	Sun	Sun	Mon	Mon	Mon	Mon	Mon	Mon

Note: Advanced Time = Daylight Saving Time = Summer Time

MEXICO *(Continued)*

PACIFIC TIME ZONE

Note: *Comprises Baja California Sur, Sinaloa, and Sonora*
Standard Time: *Applicable for the entire year*
Time Zone: *05:00 (-7hrs UTC)*

[a]	[b]	[c]	[d]	[e]	[f]	[g]	[h]	[i]	[j]	[k]	[l]	[m]	[n]	[o]	[p]	[q]	[r]	[s]	[t]	[u]	[v]	[w]	[x]
05:01	06:01	07:01	08:01	09:01	10:01	11:01	12:01	13:01	14:01	15:01	16:01	17:01	18:01	19:01	20:01	21:01	22:01	23:01	00:01	01:01	02:01	03:01	04:01
5^{01}_{am}	6^{01}_{am}	7^{01}_{am}	8^{01}_{am}	9^{01}_{am}	10^{01}_{am}	11^{01}_{am}	12^{01}_{pm}	1^{01}_{pm}	2^{01}_{pm}	3^{01}_{pm}	4^{01}_{pm}	5^{01}_{pm}	6^{01}_{pm}	7^{01}_{pm}	8^{01}_{pm}	9^{01}_{pm}	10^{01}_{pm}	11^{01}_{pm}	12^{01}_{am}	1^{01}_{am}	2^{01}_{am}	3^{01}_{am}	4^{01}_{am}
Sun	Sun	Sun	Sun	Sun	Sun	Sun	Sun	Sun	Sun	Sun	Sun	Sun	Sun	Sun	Sun	Sun	Sun	Sun	Mon	Mon	Mon	Mon	Mon

BAJA CALIFORNIA NORTE TIME ZONE

Note: *Comprises the state of Baja California Norte*

Standard Time

Period: *Last Sunday in October to First Sunday in April*
Time Zone: *04:00 (-8hrs UTC)*

[a]	[b]	[c]	[d]	[e]	[f]	[g]	[h]	[i]	[j]	[k]	[l]	[m]	[n]	[o]	[p]	[q]	[r]	[s]	[t]	[u]	[v]	[w]	[x]
04:01	05:01	06:01	07:01	08:01	09:01	10:01	11:01	12:01	13:01	14:01	15:01	16:01	17:01	18:01	19:01	20:01	21:01	22:01	23:01	00:01	01:01	02:01	03:01
4^{01}_{am}	5^{01}_{am}	6^{01}_{am}	7^{01}_{am}	8^{01}_{am}	9^{01}_{am}	10^{01}_{am}	11^{01}_{am}	12^{01}_{pm}	1^{01}_{pm}	2^{01}_{pm}	3^{01}_{pm}	4^{01}_{pm}	5^{01}_{pm}	6^{01}_{pm}	7^{01}_{pm}	8^{01}_{pm}	9^{01}_{pm}	10^{01}_{pm}	11^{01}_{pm}	12^{01}_{am}	1^{01}_{am}	2^{01}_{am}	3^{01}_{am}
Sun	Sun	Sun	Sun	Sun	Sun	Sun	Sun	Sun	Sun	Sun	Sun	Sun	Sun	Sun	Sun	Sun	Sun	Sun	Sun	Mon	Mon	Mon	Mon

Advanced Time

Period: *First Sunday in April to Last Sunday in October*
Time Zone: *05:00 (-7hrs UTC)*

[a]	[b]	[c]	[d]	[e]	[f]	[g]	[h]	[i]	[j]	[k]	[l]	[m]	[n]	[o]	[p]	[q]	[r]	[s]	[t]	[u]	[v]	[w]	[x]
05:01	06:01	07:01	08:01	09:01	10:01	11:01	12:01	13:01	14:01	15:01	16:01	17:01	18:01	19:01	20:01	21:01	22:01	23:01	00:01	01:01	02:01	03:01	04:01
5^{01}_{am}	6^{01}_{am}	7^{01}_{am}	8^{01}_{am}	9^{01}_{am}	10^{01}_{am}	11^{01}_{am}	12^{01}_{pm}	1^{01}_{pm}	2^{01}_{pm}	3^{01}_{pm}	4^{01}_{pm}	5^{01}_{pm}	6^{01}_{pm}	7^{01}_{pm}	8^{01}_{pm}	9^{01}_{pm}	10^{01}_{pm}	11^{01}_{pm}	12^{01}_{am}	1^{01}_{am}	2^{01}_{am}	3^{01}_{am}	4^{01}_{am}
Sun	Sun	Sun	Sun	Sun	Sun	Sun	Sun	Sun	Sun	Sun	Sun	Sun	Sun	Sun	Sun	Sun	Sun	Sun	Mon	Mon	Mon	Mon	Mon

Note: Advanced Time = Daylight Saving Time = Summer Time

MIDWAY ISLANDS
Number of Time Zones: *1*
Standard Time: *Applicable for the entire year*
Advanced Time: *Not observed*
Time Zone: *01:00 (-11hrs UTC)*

[a]	[b]	[c]	[d]	[e]	[f]	[g]	[h]	[i]	[j]	[k]	[l]	[m]	[n]	[o]	[p]	[q]	[r]	[s]	[t]	[u]	[v]	[w]	[x]
01:01	02:01	03:01	04:01	05:01	06:01	07:01	08:01	09:01	10:01	11:01	12:01	13:01	14:01	15:01	16:01	17:01	18:01	19:01	20:01	21:01	22:01	23:01	00:01
1^{01}_{am}	2^{01}_{am}	3^{01}_{am}	4^{01}_{am}	5^{01}_{am}	6^{01}_{am}	7^{01}_{am}	8^{01}_{am}	9^{01}_{am}	10^{01}_{am}	11^{01}_{am}	12^{01}_{pm}	1^{01}_{pm}	2^{01}_{pm}	3^{01}_{pm}	4^{01}_{pm}	5^{01}_{pm}	6^{01}_{pm}	7^{01}_{pm}	8^{01}_{pm}	9^{01}_{pm}	10^{01}_{pm}	11^{01}_{pm}	12^{01}_{am}
Sun	Sun	Sun	Sun	Sun	Sun	Sun	Sun	Sun	Sun	Sun	Sun	Sun	Sun	Sun	Sun	Sun	Sun	Sun	Sun	Sun	Sun	Sun	Mon

MONACO
Number of Time Zones: *1*

Standard Time
Period: *Last Sunday in September to Last Sunday in March*
Time Zone: *13:00 (+1hr UTC)*

[a]	[b]	[c]	[d]	[e]	[f]	[g]	[h]	[i]	[j]	[k]	[l]	[m]	[n]	[o]	[p]	[q]	[r]	[s]	[t]	[u]	[v]	[w]	[x]
13:01	14:01	15:01	16:01	17:01	18:01	19:01	20:01	21:01	22:01	23:01	00:01	01:01	02:01	03:01	04:01	05:01	06:01	07:01	08:01	09:01	10:01	11:01	12:01
1^{01}_{pm}	2^{01}_{pm}	3^{01}_{pm}	4^{01}_{pm}	5^{01}_{pm}	6^{01}_{pm}	7^{01}_{pm}	8^{01}_{pm}	9^{01}_{pm}	10^{01}_{pm}	11^{01}_{pm}	12^{01}_{am}	1^{01}_{am}	2^{01}_{am}	3^{01}_{am}	4^{01}_{am}	5^{01}_{am}	6^{01}_{am}	7^{01}_{am}	8^{01}_{am}	9^{01}_{am}	10^{01}_{am}	11^{01}_{am}	12^{01}_{pr}
Sun	Sun	Sun	Sun	Sun	Sun	Sun	Sun	Sun	Sun	Sun	Mon	Mon	Mon	Mon	Mon	Mon	Mon	Mon	Mon	Mon	Mon	Mon	Mon

Advanced Time
Period: *Last Sunday in March to Last Sunday in September*
Time Zone: *14:00 (+2hrs UTC)*

[a]	[b]	[c]	[d]	[e]	[f]	[g]	[h]	[i]	[j]	[k]	[l]	[m]	[n]	[o]	[p]	[q]	[r]	[s]	[t]	[u]	[v]	[w]	[x]
14:01	15:01	16:01	17:01	18:01	19:01	20:01	21:01	22:01	23:01	00:01	01:01	02:01	03:01	04:01	05:01	06:01	07:01	08:01	09:01	10:01	11:01	12:01	13:0
2^{01}_{pm}	3^{01}_{pm}	4^{01}_{pm}	5^{01}_{pm}	6^{01}_{pm}	7^{01}_{pm}	8^{01}_{pm}	9^{01}_{pm}	10^{01}_{pm}	11^{01}_{pm}	12^{01}_{am}	1^{01}_{am}	2^{01}_{am}	3^{01}_{am}	4^{01}_{am}	5^{01}_{am}	6^{01}_{am}	7^{01}_{am}	8^{01}_{am}	9^{01}_{am}	10^{01}_{am}	11^{01}_{am}	12^{01}_{pm}	1^{0}
Sun	Sun	Sun	Sun	Sun	Sun	Sun	Sun	Sun	Sun	Mon	Mon	Mon	Mon	Mon	Mon	Mon	Mon	Mon	Mon	Mon	Mon	Mon	Mo

Note: Advanced Time = Daylight Saving Time = Summer Time

MONGOLIA

Number of Time Zones: *3*
Note:*See Reference Map I for graphic depiction of time zones*

EASTERN TIME ZONE

Note: *Comprises eastern quarter of the country*

Standard Time

Period: *Last Sunday in September to Last Sunday in March*
Time Zone: *21:00 (+9hrs UTC)*

[a]	[b]	[c]	[d]	[e]	[f]	[g]	[h]	[i]	[j]	[k]	[l]	[m]	[n]	[o]	[p]	[q]	[r]	[s]	[t]	[u]	[v]	[w]	[x]
21:01	22:01	23:01	00:01	01:01	02:01	03:01	04:01	05:01	06:01	07:01	08:01	09:01	10:01	11:01	12:01	13:01	14:01	15:01	16:01	17:01	18:01	19:01	20:01
9^{01}_{pm}	10^{01}_{pm}	11^{01}_{pm}	12^{01}_{am}	1^{01}_{am}	2^{01}_{am}	3^{01}_{am}	4^{01}_{am}	5^{01}_{am}	6^{01}_{am}	7^{01}_{am}	8^{01}_{am}	9^{01}_{am}	10^{01}_{am}	11^{01}_{am}	12^{01}_{pm}	1^{01}_{pm}	2^{01}_{pm}	3^{01}_{pm}	4^{01}_{pm}	5^{01}_{pm}	6^{01}_{pm}	7^{01}_{pm}	8^{01}_{pm}
Sun	Sun	Sun	Mon	Mon	Mon	Mon	Mon	Mon	Mon	Mon	Mon	Mon	Mon	Mon	Mon	Mon	Mon	Mon	Mon	Mon	Mon	Mon	Mon

Advanced Time

Period: *Last Sunday in March to Last Sunday in September*
Time Zone: *22:00 (+10hrs UTC)*

[a]	[b]	[c]	[d]	[e]	[f]	[g]	[h]	[i]	[j]	[k]	[l]	[m]	[n]	[o]	[p]	[q]	[r]	[s]	[t]	[u]	[v]	[w]	[x]
22:01	23:01	00:01	01:01	02:01	03:01	04:01	05:01	06:01	07:01	08:01	09:01	10:01	11:01	12:01	13:01	14:01	15:01	16:01	17:01	18:01	19:01	20:01	21:01
10^{01}_{pm}	11^{01}_{pm}	12^{01}_{am}	1^{01}_{am}	2^{01}_{am}	3^{01}_{am}	4^{01}_{am}	5^{01}_{am}	6^{01}_{am}	7^{01}_{am}	8^{01}_{am}	9^{01}_{am}	10^{01}_{am}	11^{01}_{am}	12^{01}_{pm}	1^{01}_{pm}	2^{01}_{pm}	3^{01}_{pm}	4^{01}_{pm}	5^{01}_{pm}	6^{01}_{pm}	7^{01}_{pm}	8^{01}_{pm}	9^{01}_{pm}
Sun	Sun	Mon	Mon	Mon	Mon	Mon	Mon	Mon	Mon	Mon	Mon	Mon	Mon	Mon	Mon	Mon	Mon	Mon	Mon	Mon	Mon	Mon	Mon

CENTRAL TIME ZONE

Note: *Comprises middle half of the country*

Standard Time

Period: *Last Sunday in September to Last Sunday in March*
Time Zone: *20:00 (+8hrs UTC)*

[a]	[b]	[c]	[d]	[e]	[f]	[g]	[h]	[i]	[j]	[k]	[l]	[m]	[n]	[o]	[p]	[q]	[r]	[s]	[t]	[u]	[v]	[w]	[x]
20:01	21:01	22:01	23:01	00:01	01:01	02:01	03:01	04:01	05:01	06:01	07:01	08:01	09:01	10:01	11:01	12:01	13:01	14:01	15:01	16:01	17:01	18:01	19:01
8^{01}_{pm}	9^{01}_{pm}	10^{01}_{pm}	11^{01}_{pm}	12^{01}_{am}	1^{01}_{am}	2^{01}_{am}	3^{01}_{am}	4^{01}_{am}	5^{01}_{am}	6^{01}_{am}	7^{01}_{am}	8^{01}_{am}	9^{01}_{am}	10^{01}_{am}	11^{01}_{am}	12^{01}_{pm}	1^{01}_{pm}	2^{01}_{pm}	3^{01}_{pm}	4^{01}_{pm}	5^{01}_{pm}	6^{01}_{pm}	7^{01}_{pm}
Sun	Sun	Sun	Sun	Mon	Mon	Mon	Mon	Mon	Mon	Mon	Mon	Mon	Mon	Mon	Mon	Mon	Mon	Mon	Mon	Mon	Mon	Mon	Mon

Advanced Time

Period: *Last Sunday in March to Last Sunday in September*
Time Zone: *21:00 (+9hrs UTC)*

[a]	[b]	[c]	[d]	[e]	[f]	[g]	[h]	[i]	[j]	[k]	[l]	[m]	[n]	[o]	[p]	[q]	[r]	[s]	[t]	[u]	[v]	[w]	[x]
21:01	22:01	23:01	00:01	01:01	02:01	03:01	04:01	05:01	06:01	07:01	08:01	09:01	10:01	11:01	12:01	13:01	14:01	15:01	16:01	17:01	18:01	19:01	20:01
9^{01}_{pm}	10^{01}_{pm}	11^{01}_{pm}	12^{01}_{am}	1^{01}_{am}	2^{01}_{am}	3^{01}_{am}	4^{01}_{am}	5^{01}_{am}	6^{01}_{am}	7^{01}_{am}	8^{01}_{am}	9^{01}_{am}	10^{01}_{am}	11^{01}_{am}	12^{01}_{pm}	1^{01}_{pm}	2^{01}_{pm}	3^{01}_{pm}	4^{01}_{pm}	5^{01}_{pm}	6^{01}_{pm}	7^{01}_{pm}	8^{01}_{pm}
Sun	Sun	Sun	Mon	Mon	Mon	Mon	Mon	Mon	Mon	Mon	Mon	Mon	Mon	Mon	Mon	Mon	Mon	Mon	Mon	Mon	Mon	Mon	Mon

Note: Advanced Time = Daylight Saving Time = Summer Time

MONGOLIA *(Continued)*

WESTERN TIME ZONE
Note: *Comprises western quarter of the country*

Standard Time
Period: *Last Sunday in September to Last Sunday in March*
Time Zone: *19:00 (+7hrs UTC)*

[a]	[b]	[c]	[d]	[e]	[f]	[g]	[h]	[i]	[j]	[k]	[l]	[m]	[n]	[o]	[p]	[q]	[r]	[s]	[t]	[u]	[v]	[w]	[x]
19:01	20:01	21:01	22:01	23:01	00:01	01:01	02:01	03:01	04:01	05:01	06:01	07:01	08:01	09:01	10:01	11:01	12:01	13:01	14:01	15:01	16:01	17:01	18:0
7$^{01}_{pm}$	8$^{01}_{pm}$	9$^{01}_{pm}$	10$^{01}_{pm}$	11$^{01}_{pm}$	12$^{01}_{am}$	1$^{01}_{am}$	2$^{01}_{am}$	3$^{01}_{am}$	4$^{01}_{am}$	5$^{01}_{am}$	6$^{01}_{am}$	7$^{01}_{am}$	8$^{01}_{am}$	9$^{01}_{am}$	10$^{01}_{am}$	11$^{01}_{am}$	12$^{01}_{pm}$	1$^{01}_{pm}$	2$^{01}_{pm}$	3$^{01}_{pm}$	4$^{01}_{pm}$	5$^{01}_{pm}$	6$^{0}_{p}$
Sun	Sun	Sun	Sun	Sun	Mon	Mon	Mon	Mon	Mon	Mon	Mon	Mon	Mon	Mon	Mon	Mon	Mon	Mon	Mon	Mon	Mon	Mon	Mo

Advanced Time
Period: *Last Sunday in March to Last Sunday in September*
Time Zone: *20:00 (+8hrs UTC)*

[a]	[b]	[c]	[d]	[e]	[f]	[g]	[h]	[i]	[j]	[k]	[l]	[m]	[n]	[o]	[p]	[q]	[r]	[s]	[t]	[u]	[v]	[w]	[x]
20:01	21:01	22:01	23:01	00:01	01:01	02:01	03:01	04:01	05:01	06:01	07:01	08:01	09:01	10:01	11:01	12:01	13:01	14:01	15:01	16:01	17:01	18:01	19:0
8$^{01}_{pm}$	9$^{01}_{pm}$	10$^{01}_{pm}$	11$^{01}_{pm}$	12$^{01}_{am}$	1$^{01}_{am}$	2$^{01}_{am}$	3$^{01}_{am}$	4$^{01}_{am}$	5$^{01}_{am}$	6$^{01}_{am}$	7$^{01}_{am}$	8$^{01}_{am}$	9$^{01}_{am}$	10$^{01}_{am}$	11$^{01}_{am}$	12$^{01}_{pm}$	1$^{01}_{pm}$	2$^{01}_{pm}$	3$^{01}_{pm}$	4$^{01}_{pm}$	5$^{01}_{pm}$	6$^{01}_{pm}$	7$^{0}_{p}$
Sun	Sun	Sun	Sun	Mon	Mon	Mon	Mon	Mon	Mon	Mon	Mon	Mon	Mon	Mon	Mon	Mon	Mon	Mon	Mon	Mon	Mon	Mon	Mo

MONTSERRAT
Number of Time Zones: *1*
Standard Time: *Applicable for the entire year*
Advanced Time: *Not observed*
Time Zone: *08:00 (-4hrs UTC)*

[a]	[b]	[c]	[d]	[e]	[f]	[g]	[h]	[i]	[j]	[k]	[l]	[m]	[n]	[o]	[p]	[q]	[r]	[s]	[t]	[u]	[v]	[w]	[x]
08:01	09:01	10:01	11:01	12:01	13:01	14:01	15:01	16:01	17:01	18:01	19:01	20:01	21:01	22:01	23:01	00:01	01:01	02:01	03:01	04:01	05:01	06:01	07:0
8$^{01}_{am}$	9$^{01}_{am}$	10$^{01}_{am}$	11$^{01}_{am}$	12$^{01}_{pm}$	1$^{01}_{pm}$	2$^{01}_{pm}$	3$^{01}_{pm}$	4$^{01}_{pm}$	5$^{01}_{pm}$	6$^{01}_{pm}$	7$^{01}_{pm}$	8$^{01}_{pm}$	9$^{01}_{pm}$	10$^{01}_{pm}$	11$^{01}_{pm}$	12$^{01}_{am}$	1$^{01}_{am}$	2$^{01}_{am}$	3$^{01}_{am}$	4$^{01}_{am}$	5$^{01}_{am}$	6$^{01}_{am}$	7$^{0}_{am}$
Sun	Sun	Sun	Sun	Sun	Sun	Sun	Sun	Sun	Sun	Sun	Sun	Sun	Sun	Sun	Sun	Mon	Mon	Mon	Mon	Mon	Mon	Mon	Mon

MOROCCO
Number of Time Zones: *1*
Standard Time: *Applicable for the entire year*
Advanced Time: *Not observed*
Time Zone: *12:00 (UTC)*

[a]	[b]	[c]	[d]	[e]	[f]	[g]	[h]	[i]	[j]	[k]	[l]	[m]	[n]	[o]	[p]	[q]	[r]	[s]	[t]	[u]	[v]	[w]	[x]
12:01	13:01	14:01	15:01	16:01	17:01	18:01	19:01	20:01	21:01	22:01	23:01	00:01	01:01	02:01	03:01	04:01	05:01	06:01	07:01	08:01	09:01	10:01	11:01
12$^{01}_{pm}$	1$^{01}_{pm}$	2$^{01}_{pm}$	3$^{01}_{pm}$	4$^{01}_{pm}$	5$^{01}_{pm}$	6$^{01}_{pm}$	7$^{01}_{pm}$	8$^{01}_{pm}$	9$^{01}_{pm}$	10$^{01}_{pm}$	11$^{01}_{pm}$	12$^{01}_{am}$	1$^{01}_{am}$	2$^{01}_{am}$	3$^{01}_{am}$	4$^{01}_{am}$	5$^{01}_{am}$	6$^{01}_{am}$	7$^{01}_{am}$	8$^{01}_{am}$	9$^{01}_{am}$	10$^{01}_{am}$	11$^{01}_{am}$
Sun	Sun	Sun	Sun	Sun	Sun	Sun	Sun	Sun	Sun	Sun	Sun	Mon	Mon	Mon	Mon	Mon	Mon	Mon	Mon	Mon	Mon	Mon	Mon

Note: Advanced Time = Daylight Saving Time = Summer Time

MOZAMBIQUE

Number of Time Zones: *1*
Standard Time: *Applicable for the entire year*
Advanced Time: *Not observed*
Time Zone: *14:00 (+2hrs UTC)*

[a]	[b]	[c]	[d]	[e]	[f]	[g]	[h]	[i]	[j]	[k]	[l]	[m]	[n]	[o]	[p]	[q]	[r]	[s]	[t]	[u]	[v]	[w]	[x]
14:01	15:01	16:01	17:01	18:01	19:01	20:01	21:01	22:01	23:01	00:01	01:01	02:01	03:01	04:01	05:01	06:01	07:01	08:01	09:01	10:01	11:01	12:01	13:01
2^{01}_{pm}	3^{01}_{pm}	4^{01}_{pm}	5^{01}_{pm}	6^{01}_{pm}	7^{01}_{pm}	8^{01}_{pm}	9^{01}_{pm}	10^{01}_{pm}	11^{01}_{pm}	12^{01}_{am}	1^{01}_{am}	2^{01}_{am}	3^{01}_{am}	4^{01}_{am}	5^{01}_{am}	6^{01}_{am}	7^{01}_{am}	8^{01}_{am}	9^{01}_{am}	10^{01}_{am}	11^{01}_{am}	12^{01}_{pm}	1^{01}_{pm}
Sun	Sun	Sun	Sun	Sun	Sun	Sun	Sun	Sun	Sun	Mon	Mon	Mon	Mon	Mon	Mon	Mon	Mon	Mon	Mon	Mon	Mon	Mon	Mon

NAMIBIA

Number of Time Zones: *1*
Standard Time: *Applicable for the entire year*
Advanced Time: *Not observed*
Time Zone: *14:00 (+2hrs UTC)*

[a]	[b]	[c]	[d]	[e]	[f]	[g]	[h]	[i]	[j]	[k]	[l]	[m]	[n]	[o]	[p]	[q]	[r]	[s]	[t]	[u]	[v]	[w]	[x]
14:01	15:01	16:01	17:01	18:01	19:01	20:01	21:01	22:01	23:01	00:01	01:01	02:01	03:01	04:01	05:01	06:01	07:01	08:01	09:01	10:01	11:01	12:01	13:01
2^{01}_{pm}	3^{01}_{pm}	4^{01}_{pm}	5^{01}_{pm}	6^{01}_{pm}	7^{01}_{pm}	8^{01}_{pm}	9^{01}_{pm}	10^{01}_{pm}	11^{01}_{pm}	12^{01}_{am}	1^{01}_{am}	2^{01}_{am}	3^{01}_{am}	4^{01}_{am}	5^{01}_{am}	6^{01}_{am}	7^{01}_{am}	8^{01}_{am}	9^{01}_{am}	10^{01}_{am}	11^{01}_{am}	12^{01}_{pm}	1^{01}_{pm}
Sun	Sun	Sun	Sun	Sun	Sun	Sun	Sun	Sun	Sun	Mon	Mon	Mon	Mon	Mon	Mon	Mon	Mon	Mon	Mon	Mon	Mon	Mon	Mon

NAURU

Number of Time Zones: *1*
Standard Time: *Applicable for the entire year*
Advanced Time: *Not observed*
Time Zone: *24:00 (+12hrs UTC)*

[a]	[b]	[c]	[d]	[e]	[f]	[g]	[h]	[i]	[j]	[k]	[l]	[m]	[n]	[o]	[p]	[q]	[r]	[s]	[t]	[u]	[v]	[w]	[x]
00:01	01:01	02:01	03:01	04:01	05:01	06:01	07:01	08:01	09:01	10:01	11:01	12:01	13:01	14:01	15:01	16:01	17:01	18:01	19:01	20:01	21:01	22:01	23:01
12^{01}_{am}	1^{01}_{am}	2^{01}_{am}	3^{01}_{am}	4^{01}_{am}	5^{01}_{am}	6^{01}_{am}	7^{01}_{am}	8^{01}_{am}	9^{01}_{am}	10^{01}_{am}	11^{01}_{am}	12^{01}_{pm}	1^{01}_{pm}	2^{01}_{pm}	3^{01}_{pm}	4^{01}_{pm}	5^{01}_{pm}	6^{01}_{pm}	7^{01}_{pm}	8^{01}_{pm}	9^{01}_{pm}	10^{01}_{pm}	11^{01}_{pm}
Mon	Mon	Mon	Mon	Mon	Mon	Mon	Mon	Mon	Mon	Mon	Mon	Mon	Mon	Mon	Mon	Mon	Mon	Mon	Mon	Mon	Mon	Mon	Mon

NEPAL

Number of Time Zones: *1*
Standard Time: *Applicable for the entire year*
Advanced Time: *Not observed*
Time Zone: *17:45 (+5hrs 45mins UTC)*

[a]	[b]	[c]	[d]	[e]	[f]	[g]	[h]	[i]	[j]	[k]	[l]	[m]	[n]	[o]	[p]	[q]	[r]	[s]	[t]	[u]	[v]	[w]	[x]
7:46	18:46	19:46	20:46	21:46	22:46	23:46	00:46	01:46	02:46	03:46	04:46	05:46	06:46	07:46	08:46	09:46	10:46	11:46	12:46	13:46	14:46	15:46	16:46
5^{46}_{pm}	6^{46}_{pm}	7^{46}_{pm}	8^{46}_{pm}	9^{46}_{pm}	10^{46}_{pm}	11^{46}_{pm}	12^{46}_{am}	1^{46}_{am}	2^{46}_{am}	3^{46}_{am}	4^{46}_{am}	5^{46}_{am}	6^{46}_{am}	7^{46}_{am}	8^{46}_{am}	9^{46}_{am}	10^{46}_{am}	11^{46}_{am}	12^{46}_{pm}	1^{46}_{pm}	2^{46}_{pm}	3^{46}_{pm}	4^{46}_{pm}
Sun	Sun	Sun	Sun	Sun	Sun	Sun	Mon	Mon	Mon	Mon	Mon	Mon	Mon	Mon	Mon	Mon	Mon	Mon	Mon	Mon	Mon	Mon	Mon

Note: Advanced Time = Daylight Saving Time = Summer Time

NETHERLANDS
Number of Time Zones: *1*

Standard Time
Period: *Last Sunday in September to Last Sunday in March*
Time Zone: *13:00 (+ 1hr UTC)*

[a]	[b]	[c]	[d]	[e]	[f]	[g]	[h]	[i]	[j]	[k]	[l]	[m]	[n]	[o]	[p]	[q]	[r]	[s]	[t]	[u]	[v]	[w]	[x
13:01	14:01	15:01	16:01	17:01	18:01	19:01	20:01	21:01	22:01	23:01	00:01	01:01	02:01	03:01	04:01	05:01	06:01	07:01	08:01	09:01	10:01	11:01	12:
1^{01}_{pm}	2^{01}_{pm}	3^{01}_{pm}	4^{01}_{pm}	5^{01}_{pm}	6^{01}_{pm}	7^{01}_{pm}	8^{01}_{pm}	9^{01}_{pm}	10^{01}_{pm}	11^{01}_{pm}	12^{01}_{am}	1^{01}_{am}	2^{01}_{am}	3^{01}_{am}	4^{01}_{am}	5^{01}_{am}	6^{01}_{am}	7^{01}_{am}	8^{01}_{am}	9^{01}_{am}	10^{01}_{am}	11^{01}_{am}	12^{0}_{p}
Sun	Sun	Sun	Sun	Sun	Sun	Sun	Sun	Sun	Sun	Sun	Mon	Mon	Mon	Mon	Mon	Mon	Mon	Mon	Mon	Mon	Mon	Mon	Mo

Advanced Time
Period: *Last Sunday in March to Last Sunday in September*
Time Zone: *14:00 (+2hrs UTC)*

[a]	[b]	[c]	[d]	[e]	[f]	[g]	[h]	[i]	[j]	[k]	[l]	[m]	[n]	[o]	[p]	[q]	[r]	[s]	[t]	[u]	[v]	[w]	[x
14:01	15:01	16:01	17:01	18:01	19:01	20:01	21:01	22:01	23:01	00:01	01:01	02:01	03:01	04:01	05:01	06:01	07:01	08:01	09:01	10:01	11:01	12:01	13:0
2^{01}_{pm}	3^{01}_{pm}	4^{01}_{pm}	5^{01}_{pm}	6^{01}_{pm}	7^{01}_{pm}	8^{01}_{pm}	9^{01}_{pm}	10^{01}_{pm}	11^{01}_{pm}	12^{01}_{am}	1^{01}_{am}	2^{01}_{am}	3^{01}_{am}	4^{01}_{am}	5^{01}_{am}	6^{01}_{am}	7^{01}_{am}	8^{01}_{am}	9^{01}_{am}	10^{01}_{am}	11^{01}_{am}	12^{01}_{pm}	1^{0}_{p}
Sun	Sun	Sun	Sun	Sun	Sun	Sun	Sun	Sun	Sun	Mon	Mon	Mon	Mon	Mon	Mon	Mon	Mon	Mon	Mon	Mon	Mon	Mon	Mon

NETHERLANDS ANTILLES
Number of Time Zones: *1*
Standard Time: *Applicable for the entire year*
Advanced Time: *Not observed*
Time Zone: *08:00 (-4hrs UTC)*

[a]	[b]	[c]	[d]	[e]	[f]	[g]	[h]	[i]	[j]	[k]	[l]	[m]	[n]	[o]	[p]	[q]	[r]	[s]	[t]	[u]	[v]	[w]	[x
08:01	09:01	10:01	11:01	12:01	13:01	14:01	15:01	16:01	17:01	18:01	19:01	20:01	21:01	22:01	23:01	00:01	01:01	02:01	03:01	04:01	05:01	06:01	07:0
8^{01}_{am}	9^{01}_{am}	10^{01}_{am}	11^{01}_{am}	12^{01}_{pm}	1^{01}_{pm}	2^{01}_{pm}	3^{01}_{pm}	4^{01}_{pm}	5^{01}_{pm}	6^{01}_{pm}	7^{01}_{pm}	8^{01}_{pm}	9^{01}_{pm}	10^{01}_{pm}	11^{01}_{pm}	12^{01}_{am}	1^{01}_{am}	2^{01}_{am}	3^{01}_{am}	4^{01}_{am}	5^{01}_{am}	6^{01}_{am}	$7^{}_{a}$
Sun	Sun	Sun	Sun	Sun	Sun	Sun	Sun	Sun	Sun	Sun	Sun	Sun	Sun	Sun	Sun	Mon	Mon	Mon	Mon	Mon	Mon	Mon	Mon

NEVIS
Number of Time Zones: *1*
Standard Time: *Applicable for the entire year*
Advanced Time: *Not observed*
Time Zone: *08:00 (-4hrs UTC)*

[a]	[b]	[c]	[d]	[e]	[f]	[g]	[h]	[i]	[j]	[k]	[l]	[m]	[n]	[o]	[p]	[q]	[r]	[s]	[t]	[u]	[v]	[w]	[x
08:01	09:01	10:01	11:01	12:01	13:01	14:01	15:01	16:01	17:01	18:01	19:01	20:01	21:01	22:01	23:01	00:01	01:01	02:01	03:01	04:01	05:01	06:01	07:0
8^{01}_{am}	9^{01}_{am}	10^{01}_{am}	11^{01}_{am}	12^{01}_{pm}	1^{01}_{pm}	2^{01}_{pm}	3^{01}_{pm}	4^{01}_{pm}	5^{01}_{pm}	6^{01}_{pm}	7^{01}_{pm}	8^{01}_{pm}	9^{01}_{pm}	10^{01}_{pm}	11^{01}_{pm}	12^{01}_{am}	1^{01}_{am}	2^{01}_{am}	3^{01}_{am}	4^{01}_{am}	5^{01}_{am}	6^{01}_{am}	7^{0}_{a}
Sun	Sun	Sun	Sun	Sun	Sun	Sun	Sun	Sun	Sun	Sun	Sun	Sun	Sun	Sun	Sun	Mon	Mon	Mon	Mon	Mon	Mon	Mon	Mon

Note: Advanced Time = Daylight Saving Time = Summer Time

NEW CALEDONIA

Number of Time Zones: *1*
Standard Time: *Applicable for the entire year*
Advanced Time: *Not observed*
Time Zone: *23:00 (+11hrs UTC)*

[a]	[b]	[c]	[d]	[e]	[f]	[g]	[h]	[i]	[j]	[k]	[l]	[m]	[n]	[o]	[p]	[q]	[r]	[s]	[t]	[u]	[v]	[w]	[x]
...01	00:01	01:01	02:01	03:01	04:01	05:01	06:01	07:01	08:01	09:01	10:01	11:01	12:01	13:01	14:01	15:01	16:01	17:01	18:01	19:01	20:01	21:01	22:01
...01 pm	12:01 am	1:01 am	2:01 am	3:01 am	4:01 am	5:01 am	6:01 am	7:01 am	8:01 am	9:01 am	10:01 am	11:01 am	12:01 pm	1:01 pm	2:01 pm	3:01 pm	4:01 pm	5:01 pm	6:01 pm	7:01 pm	8:01 pm	9:01 pm	10:01 pm
...un	Mon	Mon	Mon	Mon	Mon	Mon	Mon	Mon	Mon	Mon	Mon	Mon	Mon	Mon	Mon	Mon	Mon	Mon	Mon	Mon	Mon	Mon	Mon

NEW ZEALAND

Number of Time Zones: *1*

Standard Time

Period: *First Sunday in March to Last Sunday in October*
Time Zone: *24:00 (+12hrs UTC)*

[a]	[b]	[c]	[d]	[e]	[f]	[g]	[h]	[i]	[j]	[k]	[l]	[m]	[n]	[o]	[p]	[q]	[r]	[s]	[t]	[u]	[v]	[w]	[x]
...01	01:01	02:01	03:01	04:01	05:01	06:01	07:01	08:01	09:01	10:01	11:01	12:01	13:01	14:01	15:01	16:01	17:01	18:01	19:01	20:01	21:01	22:01	23:01
...01 am	1:01 am	2:01 am	3:01 am	4:01 am	5:01 am	6:01 am	7:01 am	8:01 am	9:01 am	10:01 am	11:01 am	12:01 pm	1:01 pm	2:01 pm	3:01 pm	4:01 pm	5:01 pm	6:01 pm	7:01 pm	8:01 pm	9:01 pm	10:01 pm	11:01 pm
...on	Mon	Mon	Mon	Mon	Mon	Mon	Mon	Mon	Mon	Mon	Mon	Mon	Mon	Mon	Mon	Mon	Mon	Mon	Mon	Mon	Mon	Mon	Mon

Advanced Time

Period: *Last Sunday in October to First Sunday in March*
Time Zone: *25:00 (+13hrs UTC)*

[a]	[b]	[c]	[d]	[e]	[f]	[g]	[h]	[i]	[j]	[k]	[l]	[m]	[n]	[o]	[p]	[q]	[r]	[s]	[t]	[u]	[v]	[w]	[x]
...01	02:01	03:01	04:01	05:01	06:01	07:01	08:01	09:01	10:01	11:01	12:01	13:01	14:01	15:01	16:01	17:01	18:01	19:01	20:01	21:01	22:01	23:01	00:01
...01 am	2:01 am	3:01 am	4:01 am	5:01 am	6:01 am	7:01 am	8:01 am	9:01 am	10:01 am	11:01 am	12:01 pm	1:01 pm	2:01 pm	3:01 pm	4:01 pm	5:01 pm	6:01 pm	7:01 pm	8:01 pm	9:01 pm	10:01 pm	11:01 pm	12:01 am
...on	Mon	Mon	Mon	Mon	Mon	Mon	Mon	Mon	Mon	Mon	Mon	Mon	Mon	Mon	Mon	Mon	Mon	Mon	Mon	Mon	Mon	Mon	Tue

NICARAGUA

Number of Time Zones: *1*
Standard Time: *Applicable for the entire year*
Advanced Time: *Not observed*
Time Zone: *06:00 (-6hrs UTC)*

[a]	[b]	[c]	[d]	[e]	[f]	[g]	[h]	[i]	[j]	[k]	[l]	[m]	[n]	[o]	[p]	[q]	[r]	[s]	[t]	[u]	[v]	[w]	[x]
...01	07:01	08:01	09:01	10:01	11:01	12:01	13:01	14:01	15:01	16:01	17:01	18:01	19:01	20:01	21:01	22:01	23:01	00:01	01:01	02:01	03:01	04:01	05:01
...01 am	7:01 am	8:01 am	9:01 am	10:01 am	11:01 am	12:01 pm	1:01 pm	2:01 pm	3:01 pm	4:01 pm	5:01 pm	6:01 pm	7:01 pm	8:01 pm	9:01 pm	10:01 pm	11:01 pm	12:01 am	1:01 am	2:01 am	3:01 am	4:01 am	5:01 am
...un	Sun	Sun	Sun	Sun	Sun	Sun	Sun	Sun	Sun	Sun	Sun	Sun	Sun	Sun	Sun	Sun	Mon	Mon	Mon	Mon	Mon	Mon	Mon

Note: Advanced Time = Daylight Saving Time = Summer Time

NICOBAR ISLANDS

Number of Time Zones: *1*
Standard Time: *Applicable for the entire year*
Advanced Time: *Not observed*
Time Zone: *17:30 (+5hrs 30mins UTC)*

[a]	[b]	[c]	[d]	[e]	[f]	[g]	[h]	[i]	[j]	[k]	[l]	[m]	[n]	[o]	[p]	[q]	[r]	[s]	[t]	[u]	[v]	[w]	
17:31	18:31	19:31	20:31	21:31	22:31	23:31	00:31	01:31	02:31	03:31	04:31	05:31	06:31	07:31	08:31	09:31	10:31	11:31	12:31	13:31	14:31	15:31	16
5^{31}_{pm}	6^{31}_{pm}	7^{31}_{pm}	8^{31}_{pm}	9^{31}_{pm}	10^{31}_{pm}	11^{31}_{pm}	12^{31}_{am}	1^{31}_{am}	2^{31}_{am}	3^{31}_{am}	4^{31}_{am}	5^{31}_{am}	6^{31}_{am}	7^{31}_{am}	8^{31}_{am}	9^{31}_{am}	10^{31}_{am}	11^{31}_{am}	12^{31}_{pm}	1^{31}_{pm}	2^{31}_{pm}	3^{31}_{pm}	
Sun	Sun	Sun	Sun	Sun	Sun	Sun	Mon	Mon	Mon	Mon	Mon	Mon	Mon	Mon	Mon	Mon	Mon	Mon	Mon	Mon	Mon	Mon	

NIGER

Number of Time Zones: *1*
Standard Time: *Applicable for the entire year*
Advanced Time: *Not observed*
Time Zone: *13:00 (+1hrs UTC)*

[a]	[b]	[c]	[d]	[e]	[f]	[g]	[h]	[i]	[j]	[k]	[l]	[m]	[n]	[o]	[p]	[q]	[r]	[s]	[t]	[u]	[v]	[w]	
13:01	14:01	15:01	16:01	17:01	18:01	19:01	20:01	21:01	22:01	23:01	00:01	01:01	02:01	03:01	04:01	05:01	06:01	07:01	08:01	09:01	10:01	11:01	12
1^{01}_{pm}	2^{01}_{pm}	3^{01}_{pm}	4^{01}_{pm}	5^{01}_{pm}	6^{01}_{pm}	7^{01}_{pm}	8^{01}_{pm}	9^{01}_{pm}	10^{01}_{pm}	11^{01}_{pm}	12^{01}_{am}	1^{01}_{am}	2^{01}_{am}	3^{01}_{am}	4^{01}_{am}	5^{01}_{am}	6^{01}_{am}	7^{01}_{am}	8^{01}_{am}	9^{01}_{am}	10^{01}_{am}	11^{01}_{am}	1
Sun	Sun	Sun	Sun	Sun	Sun	Sun	Sun	Sun	Sun	Sun	Mon	Mon	Mon	Mon	Mon	Mon	Mon	Mon	Mon	Mon	Mon	Mon	

NIGERIA

Number of Time Zones: *1*
Standard Time: *Applicable for the entire year*
Advanced Time: *Not observed*
Time Zone: *13:00 (+1hr UTC)*

[a]	[b]	[c]	[d]	[e]	[f]	[g]	[h]	[i]	[j]	[k]	[l]	[m]	[n]	[o]	[p]	[q]	[r]	[s]	[t]	[u]	[v]	[w]	
13:01	14:01	15:01	16:01	17:01	18:01	19:01	20:01	21:01	22:01	23:01	00:01	01:01	02:01	03:01	04:01	05:01	06:01	07:01	08:01	09:01	10:01	11:01	12
1^{01}_{pm}	2^{01}_{pm}	3^{01}_{pm}	4^{01}_{pm}	5^{01}_{pm}	6^{01}_{pm}	7^{01}_{pm}	8^{01}_{pm}	9^{01}_{pm}	10^{01}_{pm}	11^{01}_{pm}	12^{01}_{am}	1^{01}_{am}	2^{01}_{am}	3^{01}_{am}	4^{01}_{am}	5^{01}_{am}	6^{01}_{am}	7^{01}_{am}	8^{01}_{am}	9^{01}_{am}	10^{01}_{am}	11^{01}_{am}	1
Sun	Sun	Sun	Sun	Sun	Sun	Sun	Sun	Sun	Sun	Sun	Mon	Mon	Mon	Mon	Mon	Mon	Mon	Mon	Mon	Mon	Mon	Mon	

NIUE

Number of Time Zones: *1*
Standard Time: *Applicable for the entire year*
Advanced Time: *Not observed*
Time Zone: *01:00 (-11hrs UTC)*

[a]	[b]	[c]	[d]	[e]	[f]	[g]	[h]	[i]	[j]	[k]	[l]	[m]	[n]	[o]	[p]	[q]	[r]	[s]	[t]	[u]	[v]	[w]	
01:01	02:01	03:01	04:01	05:01	06:01	07:01	08:01	09:01	10:01	11:01	12:01	13:01	14:01	15:01	16:01	17:01	18:01	19:01	20:01	21:01	22:01	23:01	00
1^{01}_{am}	2^{01}_{am}	3^{01}_{am}	4^{01}_{am}	5^{01}_{am}	6^{01}_{am}	7^{01}_{am}	8^{01}_{am}	9^{01}_{am}	10^{01}_{am}	11^{01}_{am}	12^{01}_{pm}	1^{01}_{pm}	2^{01}_{pm}	3^{01}_{pm}	4^{01}_{pm}	5^{01}_{pm}	6^{01}_{pm}	7^{01}_{pm}	8^{01}_{pm}	9^{01}_{pm}	10^{01}_{pm}	11^{01}_{pm}	12
Sun	Sun	Sun	Sun	Sun	Sun	Sun	Sun	Sun	Sun	Sun	Sun	Sun	Sun	Sun	Sun	Sun	Sun	Sun	Sun	Sun	Sun	Sun	

Note: Advanced Time = Daylight Saving Time = Summer Time

NORFOLK ISLAND
Number of Time Zones: *1*
Standard Time: *Applicable for the entire year*
Advanced Time: *Not observed*
Time Zone: *23:30 (+11hr 30mins UTC)*

[a]	[b]	[c]	[d]	[e]	[f]	[g]	[h]	[i]	[j]	[k]	[l]	[m]	[n]	[o]	[p]	[q]	[r]	[s]	[t]	[u]	[v]	[w]	[x]
23:31	00:31	01:31	02:31	03:31	04:31	05:31	06:31	07:31	08:31	09:31	10:31	11:31	12:31	13:31	14:31	15:31	16:31	17:31	18:31	19:31	20:31	21:31	22:31
11^{31}_{pm}	12^{31}_{am}	1^{31}_{am}	2^{31}_{am}	3^{31}_{am}	4^{31}_{am}	5^{31}_{am}	6^{31}_{am}	7^{31}_{am}	8^{31}_{am}	9^{31}_{am}	10^{31}_{am}	11^{31}_{am}	12^{31}_{pm}	1^{31}_{pm}	2^{31}_{pm}	3^{31}_{pm}	4^{31}_{pm}	5^{31}_{pm}	6^{31}_{pm}	7^{31}_{pm}	8^{31}_{pm}	9^{31}_{pm}	10^{31}_{pm}
Sun	Mon	Mon	Mon	Mon	Mon	Mon	Mon	Mon	Mon	Mon	Mon	Mon	Mon	Mon	Mon	Mon	Mon	Mon	Mon	Mon	Mon	Mon	Mon

NORTHERN MARIANA ISLANDS
Number of Time Zones: *1*
Standard Time: *Applicable for the entire year*
Advanced Time: *Not observed*
Time Zone: *22:00 (+10hrs UTC)*

[a]	[b]	[c]	[d]	[e]	[f]	[g]	[h]	[i]	[j]	[k]	[l]	[m]	[n]	[o]	[p]	[q]	[r]	[s]	[t]	[u]	[v]	[w]	[x]
22:01	23:01	00:01	01:01	02:01	03:01	04:01	05:01	06:01	07:01	08:01	09:01	10:01	11:01	12:01	13:01	14:01	15:01	16:01	17:01	18:01	19:01	20:01	21:01
10^{01}_{pm}	11^{01}_{pm}	12^{01}_{am}	1^{01}_{am}	2^{01}_{am}	3^{01}_{am}	4^{01}_{am}	5^{01}_{am}	6^{01}_{am}	7^{01}_{am}	8^{01}_{am}	9^{01}_{am}	10^{01}_{am}	11^{01}_{am}	12^{01}_{pm}	1^{01}_{pm}	2^{01}_{pm}	3^{01}_{pm}	4^{01}_{pm}	5^{01}_{pm}	6^{01}_{pm}	7^{01}_{pm}	8^{01}_{pm}	9^{01}_{pm}
Sun	Sun	Mon	Mon	Mon	Mon	Mon	Mon	Mon	Mon	Mon	Mon	Mon	Mon	Mon	Mon	Mon	Mon	Mon	Mon	Mon	Mon	Mon	Mon

NORWAY
Number of Time Zones: *1*

Standard Time
Period: *Last Sunday in September to Last Sunday in March*
Time Zone: *13:00 (+1hr UTC)*

[a]	[b]	[c]	[d]	[e]	[f]	[g]	[h]	[i]	[j]	[k]	[l]	[m]	[n]	[o]	[p]	[q]	[r]	[s]	[t]	[u]	[v]	[w]	[x]
13:01	14:01	15:01	16:01	17:01	18:01	19:01	20:01	21:01	22:01	23:01	00:01	01:01	02:01	03:01	04:01	05:01	06:01	07:01	08:01	09:01	10:01	11:01	12:01
1^{01}_{pm}	2^{01}_{pm}	3^{01}_{pm}	4^{01}_{pm}	5^{01}_{pm}	6^{01}_{pm}	7^{01}_{pm}	8^{01}_{pm}	9^{01}_{pm}	10^{01}_{pm}	11^{01}_{pm}	12^{01}_{am}	1^{01}_{am}	2^{01}_{am}	3^{01}_{am}	4^{01}_{am}	5^{01}_{am}	6^{01}_{am}	7^{01}_{am}	8^{01}_{am}	9^{01}_{am}	10^{01}_{am}	11^{01}_{am}	12^{01}_{pm}
Sun	Sun	Sun	Sun	Sun	Sun	Sun	Sun	Sun	Sun	Sun	Mon	Mon	Mon	Mon	Mon	Mon	Mon	Mon	Mon	Mon	Mon	Mon	Mon

Advanced Time
Period: *Last Sunday in March to Last Sunday in September*
Time Zone: *14:00 (+2hrs UTC)*

[a]	[b]	[c]	[d]	[e]	[f]	[g]	[h]	[i]	[j]	[k]	[l]	[m]	[n]	[o]	[p]	[q]	[r]	[s]	[t]	[u]	[v]	[w]	[x]
14:01	15:01	16:01	17:01	18:01	19:01	20:01	21:01	22:01	23:01	00:01	01:01	02:01	03:01	04:01	05:01	06:01	07:01	08:01	09:01	10:01	11:01	12:01	13:01
2^{01}_{pm}	3^{01}_{pm}	4^{01}_{pm}	5^{01}_{pm}	6^{01}_{pm}	7^{01}_{pm}	8^{01}_{pm}	9^{01}_{pm}	10^{01}_{pm}	11^{01}_{pm}	12^{01}_{am}	1^{01}_{am}	2^{01}_{am}	3^{01}_{am}	4^{01}_{am}	5^{01}_{am}	6^{01}_{am}	7^{01}_{am}	8^{01}_{am}	9^{01}_{am}	10^{01}_{am}	11^{01}_{am}	12^{01}_{pm}	1^{01}_{pm}
Sun	Sun	Sun	Sun	Sun	Sun	Sun	Sun	Sun	Sun	Mon	Mon	Mon	Mon	Mon	Mon	Mon	Mon	Mon	Mon	Mon	Mon	Mon	Mon

Note: Advanced Time = Daylight Saving Time = Summer Time

OKINAWA

Number of Time Zones: *1*
Standard Time: *Applicable for the entire year*
Advanced Time: *Not observed*
Time Zone: *21:00 (+9hrs UTC)*

[a]	[b]	[c]	[d]	[e]	[f]	[g]	[h]	[i]	[j]	[k]	[l]	[m]	[n]	[o]	[p]	[q]	[r]	[s]	[t]	[u]	[v]	[w]	[x]
21:01	22:01	23:01	00:01	01:01	02:01	03:01	04:01	05:01	06:01	07:01	08:01	09:01	10:01	11:01	12:01	13:01	14:01	15:01	16:01	17:01	18:01	19:01	20:0
9^{01}_{pm}	10^{01}_{pm}	11^{01}_{pm}	12^{01}_{am}	1^{01}_{am}	2^{01}_{am}	3^{01}_{am}	4^{01}_{am}	5^{01}_{am}	6^{01}_{am}	7^{01}_{am}	8^{01}_{am}	9^{01}_{am}	10^{01}_{am}	11^{01}_{am}	12^{01}_{pm}	1^{01}_{pm}	2^{01}_{pm}	3^{01}_{pm}	4^{01}_{pm}	5^{01}_{pm}	6^{01}_{pm}	7^{01}_{pm}	8^{0}_{p}
Sun	Sun	Sun	Mon	Mon	Mon	Mon	Mon	Mon	Mon	Mon	Mon	Mon	Mon	Mon	Mon	Mon	Mon	Mon	Mon	Mon	Mon	Mon	Mo

OMAN

Number of Time Zones: *1*
Standard Time: *Applicable for the entire year*
Advanced Time: *Not observed*
Time Zone: *16:00 (+4hrs UTC)*

[a]	[b]	[c]	[d]	[e]	[f]	[g]	[h]	[i]	[j]	[k]	[l]	[m]	[n]	[o]	[p]	[q]	[r]	[s]	[t]	[u]	[v]	[w]	[x]
16:01	17:01	18:01	19:01	20:01	21:01	22:01	23:01	00:01	01:01	02:01	03:01	04:01	05:01	06:01	07:01	08:01	09:01	10:01	11:01	12:01	13:01	14:01	15:0
4^{01}_{pm}	5^{01}_{pm}	6^{01}_{pm}	7^{01}_{pm}	8^{01}_{pm}	9^{01}_{pm}	10^{01}_{pm}	11^{01}_{pm}	12^{01}_{am}	1^{01}_{am}	2^{01}_{am}	3^{01}_{am}	4^{01}_{am}	5^{01}_{am}	6^{01}_{am}	7^{01}_{am}	8^{01}_{am}	9^{01}_{am}	10^{01}_{am}	11^{01}_{am}	12^{01}_{pm}	1^{01}_{pm}	2^{01}_{pm}	3^{01}_{p}
Sun	Sun	Sun	Sun	Sun	Sun	Sun	Sun	Mon	Mon	Mon	Mon	Mon	Mon	Mon	Mon	Mon	Mon	Mon	Mon	Mon	Mon	Mon	Mo

PAKISTAN

Number of Time Zones: *1*
Standard Time: *Applicable for the entire year*
Advanced Time: *Not observed*
Time Zone: *17:00 (+5hrs UTC)*

[a]	[b]	[c]	[d]	[e]	[f]	[g]	[h]	[i]	[j]	[k]	[l]	[m]	[n]	[o]	[p]	[q]	[r]	[s]	[t]	[u]	[v]	[w]	[x]
17:01	18:01	19:01	20:01	21:01	22:01	23:01	00:01	01:01	02:01	03:01	04:01	05:01	06:01	07:01	08:01	09:01	10:01	11:01	12:01	13:01	14:01	15:01	16:0
5^{01}_{pm}	6^{01}_{pm}	7^{01}_{pm}	8^{01}_{pm}	9^{01}_{pm}	10^{01}_{pm}	11^{01}_{pm}	12^{01}_{am}	1^{01}_{am}	2^{01}_{am}	3^{01}_{am}	4^{01}_{am}	5^{01}_{am}	6^{01}_{am}	7^{01}_{am}	8^{01}_{am}	9^{01}_{am}	10^{01}_{am}	11^{01}_{am}	12^{01}_{pm}	1^{01}_{pm}	2^{01}_{pm}	3^{01}_{pm}	4^{01}_{p}
Sun	Sun	Sun	Sun	Sun	Sun	Sun	Mon	Mon	Mon	Mon	Mon	Mon	Mon	Mon	Mon	Mon	Mon	Mon	Mon	Mon	Mon	Mon	Mon

PALAU

Number of Time Zones: *1*
Standard Time: *Applicable for the entire year*
Advanced Time: *Not observed*
Time Zone: *21:00 (+9hrs UTC)*

[a]	[b]	[c]	[d]	[e]	[f]	[g]	[h]	[i]	[j]	[k]	[l]	[m]	[n]	[o]	[p]	[q]	[r]	[s]	[t]	[u]	[v]	[w]	[x]
21:01	22:01	23:01	00:01	01:01	02:01	03:01	04:01	05:01	06:01	07:01	08:01	09:01	10:01	11:01	12:01	13:01	14:01	15:01	16:01	17:01	18:01	19:01	20:01
9^{01}_{pm}	10^{01}_{pm}	11^{01}_{pm}	12^{01}_{am}	1^{01}_{am}	2^{01}_{am}	3^{01}_{am}	4^{01}_{am}	5^{01}_{am}	6^{01}_{am}	7^{01}_{am}	8^{01}_{am}	9^{01}_{am}	10^{01}_{am}	11^{01}_{am}	12^{01}_{pm}	1^{01}_{pm}	2^{01}_{pm}	3^{01}_{pm}	4^{01}_{pm}	5^{01}_{pm}	6^{01}_{pm}	7^{01}_{pm}	8^{01}_{pm}
Sun	Sun	Sun	Mon	Mon	Mon	Mon	Mon	Mon	Mon	Mon	Mon	Mon	Mon	Mon	Mon	Mon	Mon	Mon	Mon	Mon	Mon	Mon	Mon

Note: Advanced Time = Daylight Saving Time = Summer Time

PANAMA

Number of Time Zones: *1*
Standard Time: *Applicable for the entire year*
Advanced Time: *Not observed*
Time Zone: *07:00 (-5hrs UTC)*

[a]	[b]	[c]	[d]	[e]	[f]	[g]	[h]	[i]	[j]	[k]	[l]	[m]	[n]	[o]	[p]	[q]	[r]	[s]	[t]	[u]	[v]	[w]	[x]
07:01	08:01	09:01	10:01	11:01	12:01	13:01	14:01	15:01	16:01	17:01	18:01	19:01	20:01	21:01	22:01	23:01	00:01	01:01	02:01	03:01	04:01	05:01	06:01
7^{01}_{am}	8^{01}_{am}	9^{01}_{am}	10^{01}_{am}	11^{01}_{am}	12^{01}_{pm}	1^{01}_{pm}	2^{01}_{pm}	3^{01}_{pm}	4^{01}_{pm}	5^{01}_{pm}	6^{01}_{pm}	7^{01}_{pm}	8^{01}_{pm}	9^{01}_{pm}	10^{01}_{pm}	11^{01}_{pm}	12^{01}_{am}	1^{01}_{am}	2^{01}_{am}	3^{01}_{am}	4^{01}_{am}	5^{01}_{am}	6^{01}_{am}
Sun	Sun	Sun	Sun	Sun	Sun	Sun	Sun	Sun	Sun	Sun	Sun	Sun	Sun	Sun	Sun	Sun	Mon	Mon	Mon	Mon	Mon	Mon	Mon

PAPUA NEW GUINEA

Number of Time Zones: *1*
Standard Time: *Applicable for the entire year*
Advanced Time: *Not observed*
Time Zone: *22:00 (+10hrs UTC)*

[a]	[b]	[c]	[d]	[e]	[f]	[g]	[h]	[i]	[j]	[k]	[l]	[m]	[n]	[o]	[p]	[q]	[r]	[s]	[t]	[u]	[v]	[w]	[x]
22:01	23:01	00:01	01:01	02:01	03:01	04:01	05:01	06:01	07:01	08:01	09:01	10:01	11:01	12:01	13:01	14:01	15:01	16:01	17:01	18:01	19:01	20:01	21:01
10^{01}_{pm}	11^{01}_{pm}	12^{01}_{am}	1^{01}_{am}	2^{01}_{am}	3^{01}_{am}	4^{01}_{am}	5^{01}_{am}	6^{01}_{am}	7^{01}_{am}	8^{01}_{am}	9^{01}_{am}	10^{01}_{am}	11^{01}_{am}	12^{01}_{pm}	1^{01}_{pm}	2^{01}_{pm}	3^{01}_{pm}	4^{01}_{pm}	5^{01}_{pm}	6^{01}_{pm}	7^{01}_{pm}	8^{01}_{pm}	9^{01}_{pm}
Sun	Sun	Mon	Mon	Mon	Mon	Mon	Mon	Mon	Mon	Mon	Mon	Mon	Mon	Mon	Mon	Mon	Mon	Mon	Mon	Mon	Mon	Mon	Mon

PARAGUAY

Number of Time Zones: *1*

Standard Time

Period: *April 1 to September 30*
Time Zone: *08:00 (-4hrs UTC)*

[a]	[b]	[c]	[d]	[e]	[f]	[g]	[h]	[i]	[j]	[k]	[l]	[m]	[n]	[o]	[p]	[q]	[r]	[s]	[t]	[u]	[v]	[w]	[x]
08:01	09:01	10:01	11:01	12:01	13:01	14:01	15:01	16:01	17:01	18:01	19:01	20:01	21:01	22:01	23:01	00:01	01:01	02:01	03:01	04:01	05:01	06:01	07:01
8^{01}_{am}	9^{01}_{am}	10^{01}_{am}	11^{01}_{am}	12^{01}_{pm}	1^{01}_{pm}	2^{01}_{pm}	3^{01}_{pm}	4^{01}_{pm}	5^{01}_{pm}	6^{01}_{pm}	7^{01}_{pm}	8^{01}_{pm}	9^{01}_{pm}	10^{01}_{pm}	11^{01}_{pm}	12^{01}_{am}	1^{01}_{am}	2^{01}_{am}	3^{01}_{am}	4^{01}_{am}	5^{01}_{am}	6^{01}_{am}	7^{01}_{am}
Sun	Sun	Sun	Sun	Sun	Sun	Sun	Sun	Sun	Sun	Sun	Sun	Sun	Sun	Sun	Sun	Mon	Mon	Mon	Mon	Mon	Mon	Mon	Mon

Advanced Time

Period: *September 30 to April 1*
Time Zone: *09:00 (-3hrs UTC)*

[a]	[b]	[c]	[d]	[e]	[f]	[g]	[h]	[i]	[j]	[k]	[l]	[m]	[n]	[o]	[p]	[q]	[r]	[s]	[t]	[u]	[v]	[w]	[x]
09:01	10:01	11:01	12:01	13:01	14:01	15:01	16:01	17:01	18:01	19:01	20:01	21:01	22:01	23:01	00:01	01:01	02:01	03:01	04:01	05:01	06:01	07:01	08:01
9^{01}_{am}	10^{01}_{am}	11^{01}_{am}	12^{01}_{pm}	1^{01}_{pm}	2^{01}_{pm}	3^{01}_{pm}	4^{01}_{pm}	5^{01}_{pm}	6^{01}_{pm}	7^{01}_{pm}	8^{01}_{pm}	9^{01}_{pm}	10^{01}_{pm}	11^{01}_{pm}	12^{01}_{am}	1^{01}_{am}	2^{01}_{am}	3^{01}_{am}	4^{01}_{am}	5^{01}_{am}	6^{01}_{am}	7^{01}_{am}	8^{01}_{am}
Sun	Sun	Sun	Sun	Sun	Sun	Sun	Sun	Sun	Sun	Sun	Sun	Sun	Sun	Sun	Mon	Mon	Mon	Mon	Mon	Mon	Mon	Mon	Mon

Note: Advanced Time = Daylight Saving Time = Summer Time

PERU

Number of Time Zones: *1*
Standard Time: *Applicable for the entire year*
Advanced Time: *Not observed*
Time Zone: *07:00 (-5hrs UTC)*

[a]	[b]	[c]	[d]	[e]	[f]	[g]	[h]	[i]	[j]	[k]	[l]	[m]	[n]	[o]	[p]	[q]	[r]	[s]	[t]	[u]	[v]	[w]	
07:01	08:01	09:01	10:01	11:01	12:01	13:01	14:01	15:01	16:01	17:01	18:01	19:01	20:01	21:01	22:01	23:01	00:01	01:01	02:01	03:01	04:01	05:01	06:
7^{01}_{am}	8^{01}_{am}	9^{01}_{am}	10^{01}_{am}	11^{01}_{am}	12^{01}_{pm}	1^{01}_{pm}	2^{01}_{pm}	3^{01}_{pm}	4^{01}_{pm}	5^{01}_{pm}	6^{01}_{pm}	7^{01}_{pm}	8^{01}_{pm}	9^{01}_{pm}	10^{01}_{pm}	11^{01}_{pm}	12^{01}_{am}	1^{01}_{am}	2^{01}_{am}	3^{01}_{am}	4^{01}_{am}	5^{01}_{am}	6
Sun	Sun	Sun	Sun	Sun	Sun	Sun	Sun	Sun	Sun	Sun	Sun	Sun	Sun	Sun	Sun	Sun	Mon	Mon	Mon	Mon	Mon	Mon	M

PHILIPPINES

Number of Time Zones: *1*
Standard Time: *Applicable for the entire year*
Advanced Time: *Not observed*
Time Zone: *20:00 (+8hrs UTC)*

[a]	[b]	[c]	[d]	[e]	[f]	[g]	[h]	[i]	[j]	[k]	[l]	[m]	[n]	[o]	[p]	[q]	[r]	[s]	[t]	[u]	[v]	[w]	[
20:01	21:01	22:01	23:01	00:01	01:01	02:01	03:01	04:01	05:01	06:01	07:01	08:01	09:01	10:01	11:01	12:01	13:01	14:01	15:01	16:01	17:01	18:01	19:
8^{01}_{pm}	9^{01}_{pm}	10^{01}_{pm}	11^{01}_{pm}	12^{01}_{am}	1^{01}_{am}	2^{01}_{am}	3^{01}_{am}	4^{01}_{am}	5^{01}_{am}	6^{01}_{am}	7^{01}_{am}	8^{01}_{am}	9^{01}_{am}	10^{01}_{am}	11^{01}_{am}	12^{01}_{pm}	1^{01}_{pm}	2^{01}_{pm}	3^{01}_{pm}	4^{01}_{pm}	5^{01}_{pm}	6^{01}_{pm}	7
Sun	Sun	Sun	Sun	Mon	Mon	Mon	Mon	Mon	Mon	Mon	Mon	Mon	Mon	Mon	Mon	Mon	Mon	Mon	Mon	Mon	Mon	Mon	M

PITCAIRN ISLANDS

Number of Time Zones: *1*
Standard Time: *Applicable for the entire year*
Advanced Time: *Not observed*
Time Zone: *03:30 (-8hrs 30mins UTC)*

[a]	[b]	[c]	[d]	[e]	[f]	[g]	[h]	[i]	[j]	[k]	[l]	[m]	[n]	[o]	[p]	[q]	[r]	[s]	[t]	[u]	[v]	[w]	[
03:31	04:31	05:31	06:31	07:31	08:31	09:31	10:31	11:31	12:31	13:31	14:31	15:31	16:31	17:31	18:31	19:31	20:31	21:31	22:31	23:31	00:31	01:31	02:
3^{31}_{am}	4^{31}_{am}	5^{31}_{am}	6^{31}_{am}	7^{31}_{am}	8^{31}_{am}	9^{31}_{am}	10^{31}_{am}	11^{31}_{am}	12^{31}_{pm}	1^{31}_{pm}	2^{31}_{pm}	3^{31}_{pm}	4^{31}_{pm}	5^{31}_{pm}	6^{31}_{pm}	7^{31}_{pm}	8^{31}_{pm}	9^{31}_{pm}	10^{31}_{pm}	11^{31}_{pm}	12^{31}_{am}	1^{31}_{am}	2
Sun	Sun	Sun	Sun	Sun	Sun	Sun	Sun	Sun	Sun	Sun	Sun	Sun	Sun	Sun	Sun	Sun	Sun	Sun	Sun	Sun	Mon	Mon	M

Note: Advanced Time = Daylight Saving Time = Summer Time

POLAND

Number of Time Zones: *1*

Standard Time

Period: *Last Sunday in September to Last Sunday in March*
Time Zone: *13:00 (+1hr UTC)*

[a]	[b]	[c]	[d]	[e]	[f]	[g]	[h]	[i]	[j]	[k]	[l]	[m]	[n]	[o]	[p]	[q]	[r]	[s]	[t]	[u]	[v]	[w]	[x]
13:01	14:01	15:01	16:01	17:01	18:01	19:01	20:01	21:01	22:01	23:01	00:01	01:01	02:01	03:01	04:01	05:01	06:01	07:01	08:01	09:01	10:01	11:01	12:01
1^{01}_{pm}	2^{01}_{pm}	3^{01}_{pm}	4^{01}_{pm}	5^{01}_{pm}	6^{01}_{pm}	7^{01}_{pm}	8^{01}_{pm}	9^{01}_{pm}	10^{01}_{pm}	11^{01}_{pm}	12^{01}_{am}	1^{01}_{am}	2^{01}_{am}	3^{01}_{am}	4^{01}_{am}	5^{01}_{am}	6^{01}_{am}	7^{01}_{am}	8^{01}_{am}	9^{01}_{am}	10^{01}_{am}	11^{01}_{am}	12^{01}_{pm}
Sun	Sun	Sun	Sun	Sun	Sun	Sun	Sun	Sun	Sun	Sun	Mon	Mon	Mon	Mon	Mon	Mon	Mon	Mon	Mon	Mon	Mon	Mon	Mon

Advanced Time

Period: *Last Sunday in March to Last Sunday in September*
Time Zone: *14:00 (+2hrs UTC)*

[a]	[b]	[c]	[d]	[e]	[f]	[g]	[h]	[i]	[j]	[k]	[l]	[m]	[n]	[o]	[p]	[q]	[r]	[s]	[t]	[u]	[v]	[w]	[x]
14:01	15:01	16:01	17:01	18:01	19:01	20:01	21:01	22:01	23:01	00:01	01:01	02:01	03:01	04:01	05:01	06:01	07:01	08:01	09:01	10:01	11:01	12:01	13:01
2^{01}_{pm}	3^{01}_{pm}	4^{01}_{pm}	5^{01}_{pm}	6^{01}_{pm}	7^{01}_{pm}	8^{01}_{pm}	9^{01}_{pm}	10^{01}_{pm}	11^{01}_{pm}	12^{01}_{am}	1^{01}_{am}	2^{01}_{am}	3^{01}_{am}	4^{01}_{am}	5^{01}_{am}	6^{01}_{am}	7^{01}_{am}	8^{01}_{am}	9^{01}_{am}	10^{01}_{am}	11^{01}_{am}	12^{01}_{pm}	1^{01}_{pm}
Sun	Sun	Sun	Sun	Sun	Sun	Sun	Sun	Sun	Sun	Mon	Mon	Mon	Mon	Mon	Mon	Mon	Mon	Mon	Mon	Mon	Mon	Mon	Mon

PORTUGAL

Number of Time Zones: *1*

Standard Time

Period: *Last Sunday in September to Last Sunday in March*
Time Zone: *12:00 (UTC)*

[a]	[b]	[c]	[d]	[e]	[f]	[g]	[h]	[i]	[j]	[k]	[l]	[m]	[n]	[o]	[p]	[q]	[r]	[s]	[t]	[u]	[v]	[w]	[x]
12:01	13:01	14:01	15:01	16:01	17:01	18:01	19:01	20:01	21:01	22:01	23:01	00:01	01:01	02:01	03:01	04:01	05:01	06:01	07:01	08:01	09:01	10:01	11:01
12^{01}_{pm}	1^{01}_{pm}	2^{01}_{pm}	3^{01}_{pm}	4^{01}_{pm}	5^{01}_{pm}	6^{01}_{pm}	7^{01}_{pm}	8^{01}_{pm}	9^{01}_{pm}	10^{01}_{pm}	11^{01}_{pm}	12^{01}_{am}	1^{01}_{am}	2^{01}_{am}	3^{01}_{am}	4^{01}_{am}	5^{01}_{am}	6^{01}_{am}	7^{01}_{am}	8^{01}_{am}	9^{01}_{am}	10^{01}_{am}	11^{01}_{am}
Sun	Sun	Sun	Sun	Sun	Sun	Sun	Sun	Sun	Sun	Sun	Sun	Mon	Mon	Mon	Mon	Mon	Mon	Mon	Mon	Mon	Mon	Mon	Mon

Advanced Time

Period: *Last Sunday in March to Last Sunday in September*
Time Zone: *13:00 (+1hr UTC)*

[a]	[b]	[c]	[d]	[e]	[f]	[g]	[h]	[i]	[j]	[k]	[l]	[m]	[n]	[o]	[p]	[q]	[r]	[s]	[t]	[u]	[v]	[w]	[x]
13:01	14:01	15:01	16:01	17:01	18:01	19:01	20:01	21:01	22:01	23:01	00:01	01:01	02:01	03:01	04:01	05:01	06:01	07:01	08:01	09:01	10:01	11:01	12:01
1^{01}_{pm}	2^{01}_{pm}	3^{01}_{pm}	4^{01}_{pm}	5^{01}_{pm}	6^{01}_{pm}	7^{01}_{pm}	8^{01}_{pm}	9^{01}_{pm}	10^{01}_{pm}	11^{01}_{pm}	12^{01}_{am}	1^{01}_{am}	2^{01}_{am}	3^{01}_{am}	4^{01}_{am}	5^{01}_{am}	6^{01}_{am}	7^{01}_{am}	8^{01}_{am}	9^{01}_{am}	10^{01}_{am}	11^{01}_{am}	12^{01}_{pm}
Sun	Sun	Sun	Sun	Sun	Sun	Sun	Sun	Sun	Sun	Sun	Mon	Mon	Mon	Mon	Mon	Mon	Mon	Mon	Mon	Mon	Mon	Mon	Mon

Note: Advanced Time = Daylight Saving Time = Summer Time

PUERTO RICO
Number of Time Zones: *1*
Standard Time: *Applicable for the entire year*
Advanced Time: *Not observed*
Time Zone: *08:00 (-4hrs UTC)*

[a]	[b]	[c]	[d]	[e]	[f]	[g]	[h]	[i]	[j]	[k]	[l]	[m]	[n]	[o]	[p]	[q]	[r]	[s]	[t]	[u]	[v]	[w]	[
08:01	09:01	10:01	11:01	12:01	13:01	14:01	15:01	16:01	17:01	18:01	19:01	20:01	21:01	22:01	23:01	00:01	01:01	02:01	03:01	04:01	05:01	06:01	07:
8^{01}_{am}	9^{01}_{am}	10^{01}_{am}	11^{01}_{am}	12^{01}_{pm}	1^{01}_{pm}	2^{01}_{pm}	3^{01}_{pm}	4^{01}_{pm}	5^{01}_{pm}	6^{01}_{pm}	7^{01}_{pm}	8^{01}_{pm}	9^{01}_{pm}	10^{01}_{pm}	11^{01}_{pm}	12^{01}_{am}	1^{01}_{am}	2^{01}_{am}	3^{01}_{am}	4^{01}_{am}	5^{01}_{am}	6^{01}_{am}	
Sun	Sun	Sun	Sun	Sun	Sun	Sun	Sun	Sun	Sun	Sun	Sun	Sun	Sun	Sun	Sun	Mon	Mon	Mon	Mon	Mon	Mon	Mon	M

QATAR
Number of Time Zones: *1*
Standard Time: *Applicable for the entire year*
Advanced Time: *Not observed*
Time Zone: *15:00 (+3hrs UTC)*

[a]	[b]	[c]	[d]	[e]	[f]	[g]	[h]	[i]	[j]	[k]	[l]	[m]	[n]	[o]	[p]	[q]	[r]	[s]	[t]	[u]	[v]	[w]	[
15:01	16:01	17:01	18:01	19:01	20:01	21:01	22:01	23:01	00:01	01:01	02:01	03:01	04:01	05:01	06:01	07:01	08:01	09:01	10:01	11:01	12:01	13:01	14:
3^{01}_{pm}	4^{01}_{pm}	5^{01}_{pm}	6^{01}_{pm}	7^{01}_{pm}	8^{01}_{pm}	9^{01}_{pm}	10^{01}_{pm}	11^{01}_{pm}	12^{01}_{am}	1^{01}_{am}	2^{01}_{am}	3^{01}_{am}	4^{01}_{am}	5^{01}_{am}	6^{01}_{am}	7^{01}_{am}	8^{01}_{am}	9^{01}_{am}	10^{01}_{am}	11^{01}_{am}	12^{01}_{pm}	1^{01}_{pm}	2
Sun	Sun	Sun	Sun	Sun	Sun	Sun	Sun	Sun	Mon	Mon	Mon	Mon	Mon	Mon	Mon	Mon	Mon	Mon	Mon	Mon	Mon	Mon	M

REUNION
Number of Time Zones: *1*
Standard Time: *Applicable for the entire year*
Advanced Time: *Not observed*
Time Zone: *16:00 (+4hrs UTC)*

[a]	[b]	[c]	[d]	[e]	[f]	[g]	[h]	[i]	[j]	[k]	[l]	[m]	[n]	[o]	[p]	[q]	[r]	[s]	[t]	[u]	[v]	[w]	[
16:01	17:01	18:01	19:01	20:01	21:01	22:01	23:01	00:01	01:01	02:01	03:01	04:01	05:01	06:01	07:01	08:01	09:01	10:01	11:01	12:01	13:01	14:01	15:
4^{01}_{pm}	5^{01}_{pm}	6^{01}_{pm}	7^{01}_{pm}	8^{01}_{pm}	9^{01}_{pm}	10^{01}_{pm}	11^{01}_{pm}	12^{01}_{am}	1^{01}_{am}	2^{01}_{am}	3^{01}_{am}	4^{01}_{am}	5^{01}_{am}	6^{01}_{am}	7^{01}_{am}	8^{01}_{am}	9^{01}_{am}	10^{01}_{am}	11^{01}_{am}	12^{01}_{pm}	1^{01}_{pm}	2^{01}_{pm}	3
Sun	Sun	Sun	Sun	Sun	Sun	Sun	Sun	Mon	Mon	Mon	Mon	Mon	Mon	Mon	Mon	Mon	Mon	Mon	Mon	Mon	Mon	Mon	M

Note: Advanced Time = Daylight Saving Time = Summer Time

ROMANIA
Number of Time Zones: *1*

Standard Time
Period: *Last Sunday in September to Last Sunday in March*
Time Zone: *14:00 (+2hrs UTC)*

[a]	[b]	[c]	[d]	[e]	[f]	[g]	[h]	[i]	[j]	[k]	[l]	[m]	[n]	[o]	[p]	[q]	[r]	[s]	[t]	[u]	[v]	[w]	[x]
4:01	15:01	16:01	17:01	18:01	19:01	20:01	21:01	22:01	23:01	00:01	01:01	02:01	03:01	04:01	05:01	06:01	07:01	08:01	09:01	10:01	11:01	12:01	13:01
2^{01}pm	3^{01}pm	4^{01}pm	5^{01}pm	6^{01}pm	7^{01}pm	8^{01}pm	9^{01}pm	10^{01}pm	11^{01}pm	12^{01}am	1^{01}am	2^{01}am	3^{01}am	4^{01}am	5^{01}am	6^{01}am	7^{01}am	8^{01}am	9^{01}am	10^{01}am	11^{01}am	12^{01}pm	1^{01}pm
Sun	Sun	Sun	Sun	Sun	Sun	Sun	Sun	Sun	Sun	Mon	Mon	Mon	Mon	Mon	Mon	Mon	Mon	Mon	Mon	Mon	Mon	Mon	Mon

Advanced Time
Period: *Last Sunday in March to Last Sunday in September*
Time Zone: *15:00 (+3hrs UTC)*

[a]	[b]	[c]	[d]	[e]	[f]	[g]	[h]	[i]	[j]	[k]	[l]	[m]	[n]	[o]	[p]	[q]	[r]	[s]	[t]	[u]	[v]	[w]	[x]
5:01	16:01	17:01	18:01	19:01	20:01	21:01	22:01	23:01	00:01	01:01	02:01	03:01	04:01	05:01	06:01	07:01	08:01	09:01	10:01	11:01	12:01	13:01	14:01
3^{01}pm	4^{01}pm	5^{01}pm	6^{01}pm	7^{01}pm	8^{01}pm	9^{01}pm	10^{01}pm	11^{01}pm	12^{01}am	1^{01}am	2^{01}am	3^{01}am	4^{01}am	5^{01}am	6^{01}am	7^{01}am	8^{01}am	9^{01}am	10^{01}am	11^{01}am	12^{01}pm	1^{01}pm	2^{01}pm
Sun	Sun	Sun	Sun	Sun	Sun	Sun	Sun	Sun	Mon	Mon	Mon	Mon	Mon	Mon	Mon	Mon	Mon	Mon	Mon	Mon	Mon	Mon	Mon

RWANDA
Number of Time Zones: *1*
Standard Time: *Applicable for the entire year*
Advanced Time: *Not observed*
Time Zone: *14:00 (+2hrs UTC)*

[a]	[b]	[c]	[d]	[e]	[f]	[g]	[h]	[i]	[j]	[k]	[l]	[m]	[n]	[o]	[p]	[q]	[r]	[s]	[t]	[u]	[v]	[w]	[x]
4:01	15:01	16:01	17:01	18:01	19:01	20:01	21:01	22:01	23:01	00:01	01:01	02:01	03:01	04:01	05:01	06:01	07:01	08:01	09:01	10:01	11:01	12:01	13:01
2^{01}pm	3^{01}pm	4^{01}pm	5^{01}pm	6^{01}pm	7^{01}pm	8^{01}pm	9^{01}pm	10^{01}pm	11^{01}pm	12^{01}am	1^{01}am	2^{01}am	3^{01}am	4^{01}am	5^{01}am	6^{01}am	7^{01}am	8^{01}am	9^{01}am	10^{01}am	11^{01}am	12^{01}pm	1^{01}pm
Sun	Sun	Sun	Sun	Sun	Sun	Sun	Sun	Sun	Sun	Mon	Mon	Mon	Mon	Mon	Mon	Mon	Mon	Mon	Mon	Mon	Mon	Mon	Mon

SABA
Number of Time Zones: *1*
Standard Time: *Applicable for the entire year*
Advanced Time: *Not observed*
Time Zone: *08:00 (-4hrs UTC)*

[a]	[b]	[c]	[d]	[e]	[f]	[g]	[h]	[i]	[j]	[k]	[l]	[m]	[n]	[o]	[p]	[q]	[r]	[s]	[t]	[u]	[v]	[w]	[x]
08:01	09:01	10:01	11:01	12:01	13:01	14:01	15:01	16:01	17:01	18:01	19:01	20:01	21:01	22:01	23:01	00:01	01:01	02:01	03:01	04:01	05:01	06:01	07:01
8^{01}am	9^{01}am	10^{01}am	11^{01}am	12^{01}pm	1^{01}pm	2^{01}pm	3^{01}pm	4^{01}pm	5^{01}pm	6^{01}pm	7^{01}pm	8^{01}pm	9^{01}pm	10^{01}pm	11^{01}pm	12^{01}am	1^{01}am	2^{01}am	3^{01}am	4^{01}am	5^{01}am	6^{01}am	7^{01}am
Sun	Sun	Sun	Sun	Sun	Sun	Sun	Sun	Sun	Sun	Sun	Sun	Sun	Sun	Sun	Sun	Sun	Mon	Mon	Mon	Mon	Mon	Mon	Mon

Note: Advanced Time = Daylight Saving Time = Summer Time

ST. BARTHELEMY

Number of Time Zones: *1*
Standard Time: *Applicable for the entire year*
Advanced Time: *Not observed*
Time Zone: *08:00 (-4hrs UTC)*

[a]	[b]	[c]	[d]	[e]	[f]	[g]	[h]	[i]	[j]	[k]	[l]	[m]	[n]	[o]	[p]	[q]	[r]	[s]	[t]	[u]	[v]	[w]	[x]
08:01	09:01	10:01	11:01	12:01	13:01	14:01	15:01	16:01	17:01	18:01	19:01	20:01	21:01	22:01	23:01	00:01	01:01	02:01	03:01	04:01	05:01	06:01	07:0
8^{01}_{am}	9^{01}_{am}	10^{01}_{am}	11^{01}_{am}	12^{01}_{pm}	1^{01}_{pm}	2^{01}_{pm}	3^{01}_{pm}	4^{01}_{pm}	5^{01}_{pm}	6^{01}_{pm}	7^{01}_{pm}	8^{01}_{pm}	9^{01}_{pm}	10^{01}_{pm}	11^{01}_{pm}	12^{01}_{am}	1^{01}_{am}	2^{01}_{am}	3^{01}_{am}	4^{01}_{am}	5^{01}_{am}	6^{01}_{am}	7^{0}_{a}
Sun	Sun	Sun	Sun	Sun	Sun	Sun	Sun	Sun	Sun	Sun	Sun	Sun	Sun	Sun	Sun	Mon	Mon	Mon	Mon	Mon	Mon	Mon	Mo

ST. EUSTATIUS

Number of Time Zones: *1*
Standard Time: *Applicable for the entire year*
Advanced Time: *Not observed*
Time Zone: *08:00 (-4hrs UTC)*

[a]	[b]	[c]	[d]	[e]	[f]	[g]	[h]	[i]	[j]	[k]	[l]	[m]	[n]	[o]	[p]	[q]	[r]	[s]	[t]	[u]	[v]	[w]	[x]
08:01	09:01	10:01	11:01	12:01	13:01	14:01	15:01	16:01	17:01	18:01	19:01	20:01	21:01	22:01	23:01	00:01	01:01	02:01	03:01	04:01	05:01	06:01	07:0
8^{01}_{am}	9^{01}_{am}	10^{01}_{am}	11^{01}_{am}	12^{01}_{pm}	1^{01}_{pm}	2^{01}_{pm}	3^{01}_{pm}	4^{01}_{pm}	5^{01}_{pm}	6^{01}_{pm}	7^{01}_{pm}	8^{01}_{pm}	9^{01}_{pm}	10^{01}_{pm}	11^{01}_{pm}	12^{01}_{am}	1^{01}_{am}	2^{01}_{am}	3^{01}_{am}	4^{01}_{am}	5^{01}_{am}	6^{01}_{am}	7^{0}_{a}
Sun	Sun	Sun	Sun	Sun	Sun	Sun	Sun	Sun	Sun	Sun	Sun	Sun	Sun	Sun	Sun	Mon	Mon	Mon	Mon	Mon	Mon	Mon	Mor

ST. HELENA

Number of Time Zones: *1*
Standard Time: *Applicable for the entire year*
Advanced Time: *Not observed*
Time Zone: *12:00 (UTC)*

[a]	[b]	[c]	[d]	[e]	[f]	[g]	[h]	[i]	[j]	[k]	[l]	[m]	[n]	[o]	[p]	[q]	[r]	[s]	[t]	[u]	[v]	[w]	[x]
12:01	13:01	14:01	15:01	16:01	17:01	18:01	19:01	20:01	21:01	22:01	23:01	00:01	01:01	02:01	03:01	04:01	05:01	06:01	07:01	08:01	09:01	10:01	11:01
12^{01}_{pm}	1^{01}_{pm}	2^{01}_{pm}	3^{01}_{pm}	4^{01}_{pm}	5^{01}_{pm}	6^{01}_{pm}	7^{01}_{pm}	8^{01}_{pm}	9^{01}_{pm}	10^{01}_{pm}	11^{01}_{pm}	12^{01}_{am}	1^{01}_{am}	2^{01}_{am}	3^{01}_{am}	4^{01}_{am}	5^{01}_{am}	6^{01}_{am}	7^{01}_{am}	8^{01}_{am}	9^{01}_{am}	10^{01}_{am}	11^{01}_{am}
Sun	Sun	Sun	Sun	Sun	Sun	Sun	Sun	Sun	Sun	Sun	Sun	Mon	Mon	Mon	Mon	Mon	Mon	Mon	Mon	Mon	Mon	Mon	Mon

ST. KITTS AND NEVIS

Number of Time Zones: *1*
Standard Time: *Applicable for the entire year*
Advanced Time: *Not observed*
Time Zone: *08:00 (-4hrs UTC)*

[a]	[b]	[c]	[d]	[e]	[f]	[g]	[h]	[i]	[j]	[k]	[l]	[m]	[n]	[o]	[p]	[q]	[r]	[s]	[t]	[u]	[v]	[w]	[x]
08:01	09:01	10:01	11:01	12:01	13:01	14:01	15:01	16:01	17:01	18:01	19:01	20:01	21:01	22:01	23:01	00:01	01:01	02:01	03:01	04:01	05:01	06:01	07:01
8^{01}_{am}	9^{01}_{am}	10^{01}_{am}	11^{01}_{am}	12^{01}_{pm}	1^{01}_{pm}	2^{01}_{pm}	3^{01}_{pm}	4^{01}_{pm}	5^{01}_{pm}	6^{01}_{pm}	7^{01}_{pm}	8^{01}_{pm}	9^{01}_{pm}	10^{01}_{pm}	11^{01}_{pm}	12^{01}_{am}	1^{01}_{am}	2^{01}_{am}	3^{01}_{am}	4^{01}_{am}	5^{01}_{am}	6^{01}_{am}	7^{01}_{am}
Sun	Sun	Sun	Sun	Sun	Sun	Sun	Sun	Sun	Sun	Sun	Sun	Sun	Sun	Sun	Sun	Mon	Mon	Mon	Mon	Mon	Mon	Mon	Mon

Note: Advanced Time = Daylight Saving Time = Summer Time

ST. LUCIA
Number of Time Zones: *1*
Standard Time: *Applicable for the entire year*
Advanced Time: *Not observed*
Time Zone: *08:00 (-4hrs UTC)*

[a]	[b]	[c]	[d]	[e]	[f]	[g]	[h]	[i]	[J]	[k]	[l]	[m]	[n]	[o]	[p]	[q]	[r]	[s]	[t]	[u]	[v]	[w]	[x]
08:01	09:01	10:01	11:01	12:01	13:01	14:01	15:01	16:01	17:01	18:01	19:01	20:01	21:01	22:01	23:01	00:01	01:01	02:01	03:01	04:01	05:01	06:01	07:01
8_{am}^{01}	9_{am}^{01}	10_{am}^{01}	11_{am}^{01}	12_{pm}^{01}	1_{pm}^{01}	2_{pm}^{01}	3_{pm}^{01}	4_{pm}^{01}	5_{pm}^{01}	6_{pm}^{01}	7_{pm}^{01}	8_{pm}^{01}	9_{pm}^{01}	10_{pm}^{01}	11_{pm}^{01}	12_{am}^{01}	1_{am}^{01}	2_{am}^{01}	3_{am}^{01}	4_{am}^{01}	5_{am}^{01}	6_{am}^{01}	7_{am}^{01}
Sun	Sun	Sun	Sun	Sun	Sun	Sun	Sun	Sun	Sun	Sun	Sun	Sun	Sun	Sun	Sun	Mon	Mon	Mon	Mon	Mon	Mon	Mon	Mon

ST. MARTIN (ST. MAARTEN)
Number of Time Zones: *1*
Standard Time: *Applicable for the entire year*
Advanced Time: *Not observed*
Time Zone: *08:00 (-4hrs UTC)*

[a]	[b]	[c]	[d]	[e]	[f]	[g]	[h]	[i]	[J]	[k]	[l]	[m]	[n]	[o]	[p]	[q]	[r]	[s]	[t]	[u]	[v]	[w]	[x]
08:01	09:01	10:01	11:01	12:01	13:01	14:01	15:01	16:01	17:01	18:01	19:01	20:01	21:01	22:01	23:01	00:01	01:01	02:01	03:01	04:01	05:01	06:01	07:01
8_{am}^{01}	9_{am}^{01}	10_{am}^{01}	11_{am}^{01}	12_{pm}^{01}	1_{pm}^{01}	2_{pm}^{01}	3_{pm}^{01}	4_{pm}^{01}	5_{pm}^{01}	6_{pm}^{01}	7_{pm}^{01}	8_{pm}^{01}	9_{pm}^{01}	10_{pm}^{01}	11_{pm}^{01}	12_{am}^{01}	1_{am}^{01}	2_{am}^{01}	3_{am}^{01}	4_{am}^{01}	5_{am}^{01}	6_{am}^{01}	7_{am}^{01}
Sun	Sun	Sun	Sun	Sun	Sun	Sun	Sun	Sun	Sun	Sun	Sun	Sun	Sun	Sun	Sun	Mon	Mon	Mon	Mon	Mon	Mon	Mon	Mon

ST. PIERRE AND MIQUELON
Number of Time Zones: *1*

Standard Time
Period: *Last Sunday in October to First Sunday in April*
Time Zone: *09:00 (-3hrs UTC)*

[a]	[b]	[c]	[d]	[e]	[f]	[g]	[h]	[i]	[J]	[k]	[l]	[m]	[n]	[o]	[p]	[q]	[r]	[s]	[t]	[u]	[v]	[w]	[x]
09:01	10:01	11:01	12:01	13:01	14:01	15:01	16:01	17:01	18:01	19:01	20:01	21:01	22:01	23:01	00:01	01:01	02:01	03:01	04:01	05:01	06:01	07:01	08:01
9_{am}^{01}	10_{am}^{01}	11_{am}^{01}	12_{pm}^{01}	1_{pm}^{01}	2_{pm}^{01}	3_{pm}^{01}	4_{pm}^{01}	5_{pm}^{01}	6_{pm}^{01}	7_{pm}^{01}	8_{pm}^{01}	9_{pm}^{01}	10_{pm}^{01}	11_{pm}^{01}	12_{am}^{01}	1_{am}^{01}	2_{am}^{01}	3_{am}^{01}	4_{am}^{01}	5_{am}^{01}	6_{am}^{01}	7_{am}^{01}	8_{am}^{01}
Sun	Sun	Sun	Sun	Sun	Sun	Sun	Sun	Sun	Sun	Sun	Sun	Sun	Sun	Sun	Mon	Mon	Mon	Mon	Mon	Mon	Mon	Mon	Mon

Advanced Time
Period: *First Sunday in April to Last Sunday in October*
Time Zone: *10:00 (-2hrs UTC)*

[a]	[b]	[c]	[d]	[e]	[f]	[g]	[h]	[i]	[J]	[k]	[l]	[m]	[n]	[o]	[p]	[q]	[r]	[s]	[t]	[u]	[v]	[w]	[x]
10:01	11:01	12:01	13:01	14:01	15:01	16:01	17:01	18:01	19:01	20:01	21:01	22:01	23:01	00:01	01:01	02:01	03:01	04:01	05:01	06:01	07:01	08:01	09:01
10_{am}^{01}	11_{am}^{01}	12_{pm}^{01}	1_{pm}^{01}	2_{pm}^{01}	3_{pm}^{01}	4_{pm}^{01}	5_{pm}^{01}	6_{pm}^{01}	7_{pm}^{01}	8_{pm}^{01}	9_{pm}^{01}	10_{pm}^{01}	11_{pm}^{01}	12_{am}^{01}	1_{am}^{01}	2_{am}^{01}	3_{am}^{01}	4_{am}^{01}	5_{am}^{01}	6_{am}^{01}	7_{am}^{01}	8_{am}^{01}	9_{am}^{01}
Sun	Sun	Sun	Sun	Sun	Sun	Sun	Sun	Sun	Sun	Sun	Sun	Sun	Sun	Sun	Mon	Mon	Mon	Mon	Mon	Mon	Mon	Mon	Mon

Note: Advanced Time = Daylight Saving Time = Summer Time

ST. VINCENT AND THE GRENADINES

Number of Time Zones: *1*
Standard Time: *Applicable for the entire year*
Advanced Time: *Not observed*
Time Zone: *08:00 (-4hrs UTC)*

[a]	[b]	[c]	[d]	[e]	[f]	[g]	[h]	[i]	[j]	[k]	[l]	[m]	[n]	[o]	[p]	[q]	[r]	[s]	[t]	[u]	[v]	[w]	[x]
08:01	09:01	10:01	11:01	12:01	13:01	14:01	15:01	16:01	17:01	18:01	19:01	20:01	21:01	22:01	23:01	00:01	01:01	02:01	03:01	04:01	05:01	06:01	07:0
8^{01}_{am}	9^{01}_{am}	10^{01}_{am}	11^{01}_{am}	12^{01}_{pm}	1^{01}_{pm}	2^{01}_{pm}	3^{01}_{pm}	4^{01}_{pm}	5^{01}_{pm}	6^{01}_{pm}	7^{01}_{pm}	8^{01}_{pm}	9^{01}_{pm}	10^{01}_{pm}	11^{01}_{pm}	12^{01}_{am}	1^{01}_{am}	2^{01}_{am}	3^{01}_{am}	4^{01}_{am}	5^{01}_{am}	6^{01}_{am}	7
Sun	Sun	Sun	Sun	Sun	Sun	Sun	Sun	Sun	Sun	Sun	Sun	Sun	Sun	Sun	Sun	Mon	Mon	Mon	Mon	Mon	Mon	Mon	Mo

SAN MARINO

Number of Time Zones: *1*

Standard Time

Period: *Last Sunday in September to Last Sunday in March*
Time Zone: *13:00 (+1hr UTC)*

[a]	[b]	[c]	[d]	[e]	[f]	[g]	[h]	[i]	[j]	[k]	[l]	[m]	[n]	[o]	[p]	[q]	[r]	[s]	[t]	[u]	[v]	[w]	[x]
13:01	14:01	15:01	16:01	17:01	18:01	19:01	20:01	21:01	22:01	23:01	00:01	01:01	02:01	03:01	04:01	05:01	06:01	07:01	08:01	09:01	10:01	11:01	12:0
1^{01}_{pm}	2^{01}_{pm}	3^{01}_{pm}	4^{01}_{pm}	5^{01}_{pm}	6^{01}_{pm}	7^{01}_{pm}	8^{01}_{pm}	9^{01}_{pm}	10^{01}_{pm}	11^{01}_{pm}	12^{01}_{am}	1^{01}_{am}	2^{01}_{am}	3^{01}_{am}	4^{01}_{am}	5^{01}_{am}	6^{01}_{am}	7^{01}_{am}	8^{01}_{am}	9^{01}_{am}	10^{01}_{am}	11^{01}_{am}	$12^{}_{p}$
Sun	Sun	Sun	Sun	Sun	Sun	Sun	Sun	Sun	Sun	Sun	Mon	Mon	Mon	Mon	Mon	Mon	Mon	Mon	Mon	Mon	Mon	Mon	Mo

Advanced Time

Period: *Last Sunday in March to Last Sunday in September*
Time Zone: *14:00 (+2hrs UTC)*

[a]	[b]	[c]	[d]	[e]	[f]	[g]	[h]	[i]	[j]	[k]	[l]	[m]	[n]	[o]	[p]	[q]	[r]	[s]	[t]	[u]	[v]	[w]	[x]
14:01	15:01	16:01	17:01	18:01	19:01	20:01	21:01	22:01	23:01	00:01	01:01	02:01	03:01	04:01	05:01	06:01	07:01	08:01	09:01	10:01	11:01	12:01	13:0
2^{01}_{pm}	3^{01}_{pm}	4^{01}_{pm}	5^{01}_{pm}	6^{01}_{pm}	7^{01}_{pm}	8^{01}_{pm}	9^{01}_{pm}	10^{01}_{pm}	11^{01}_{pm}	12^{01}_{am}	1^{01}_{am}	2^{01}_{am}	3^{01}_{am}	4^{01}_{am}	5^{01}_{am}	6^{01}_{am}	7^{01}_{am}	8^{01}_{am}	9^{01}_{am}	10^{01}_{am}	11^{01}_{am}	12^{01}_{pm}	$1^{}_{p}$
Sun	Sun	Sun	Sun	Sun	Sun	Sun	Sun	Sun	Sun	Mon	Mon	Mon	Mon	Mon	Mon	Mon	Mon	Mon	Mon	Mon	Mon	Mon	Mo

SAO TOME AND PRINCIPE

Number of Time Zones: *1*
Standard Time: *Applicable for the entire year*
Advanced Time: *Not observed*
Time Zone: *12:00 (UTC)*

[a]	[b]	[c]	[d]	[e]	[f]	[g]	[h]	[i]	[j]	[k]	[l]	[m]	[n]	[o]	[p]	[q]	[r]	[s]	[t]	[u]	[v]	[w]	[x]
12:01	13:01	14:01	15:01	16:01	17:01	18:01	19:01	20:01	21:01	22:01	23:01	00:01	01:01	02:01	03:01	04:01	05:01	06:01	07:01	08:01	09:01	10:01	11:0
12^{01}_{pm}	1^{01}_{pm}	2^{01}_{pm}	3^{01}_{pm}	4^{01}_{pm}	5^{01}_{pm}	6^{01}_{pm}	7^{01}_{pm}	8^{01}_{pm}	9^{01}_{pm}	10^{01}_{pm}	11^{01}_{pm}	12^{01}_{am}	1^{01}_{am}	2^{01}_{am}	3^{01}_{am}	4^{01}_{am}	5^{01}_{am}	6^{01}_{am}	7^{01}_{am}	8^{01}_{am}	9^{01}_{am}	10^{01}_{am}	$11^{}_{ar}$
Sun	Sun	Sun	Sun	Sun	Sun	Sun	Sun	Sun	Sun	Sun	Sun	Mon	Mon	Mon	Mon	Mon	Mon	Mon	Mon	Mon	Mon	Mon	Mo

Note: Advanced Time = Daylight Saving Time = Summer Time

SAUDI ARABIA

Number of Time Zones: *1*
Standard Time: *Applicable for the entire year*
Advanced Time: *Not observed*
Time Zone: *15:00 (+3hrs UTC)*

[a]	[b]	[c]	[d]	[e]	[f]	[g]	[h]	[i]	[j]	[k]	[l]	[m]	[n]	[o]	[p]	[q]	[r]	[s]	[t]	[u]	[v]	[w]	[x]
15:01	16:01	17:01	18:01	19:01	20:01	21:01	22:01	23:01	00:01	01:01	02:01	03:01	04:01	05:01	06:01	07:01	08:01	09:01	10:01	11:01	12:01	13:01	14:01
3^{01}_{pm}	4^{01}_{pm}	5^{01}_{pm}	6^{01}_{pm}	7^{01}_{pm}	8^{01}_{pm}	9^{01}_{pm}	10^{01}_{pm}	11^{01}_{pm}	12^{01}_{am}	1^{01}_{am}	2^{01}_{am}	3^{01}_{am}	4^{01}_{am}	5^{01}_{am}	6^{01}_{am}	7^{01}_{am}	8^{01}_{am}	9^{01}_{am}	10^{01}_{am}	11^{01}_{am}	12^{01}_{pm}	1^{01}_{pm}	2^{01}_{pm}
Sun	Sun	Sun	Sun	Sun	Sun	Sun	Sun	Sun	Mon	Mon	Mon	Mon	Mon	Mon	Mon	Mon	Mon	Mon	Mon	Mon	Mon	Mon	Mon

SENEGAL

Number of Time Zones: *1*
Standard Time: *Applicable for the entire year*
Advanced Time: *Not observed*
Time Zone: *12:00 (UTC)*

[a]	[b]	[c]	[d]	[e]	[f]	[g]	[h]	[i]	[j]	[k]	[l]	[m]	[n]	[o]	[p]	[q]	[r]	[s]	[t]	[u]	[v]	[w]	[x]
12:01	13:01	14:01	15:01	16:01	17:01	18:01	19:01	20:01	21:01	22:01	23:01	00:01	01:01	02:01	03:01	04:01	05:01	06:01	07:01	08:01	09:01	10:01	11:01
12^{01}_{pm}	1^{01}_{pm}	2^{01}_{pm}	3^{01}_{pm}	4^{01}_{pm}	5^{01}_{pm}	6^{01}_{pm}	7^{01}_{pm}	8^{01}_{pm}	9^{01}_{pm}	10^{01}_{pm}	11^{01}_{pm}	12^{01}_{am}	1^{01}_{am}	2^{01}_{am}	3^{01}_{am}	4^{01}_{am}	5^{01}_{am}	6^{01}_{am}	7^{01}_{am}	8^{01}_{am}	9^{01}_{am}	10^{01}_{am}	11^{01}_{am}
Sun	Sun	Sun	Sun	Sun	Sun	Sun	Sun	Sun	Sun	Sun	Sun	Mon	Mon	Mon	Mon	Mon	Mon	Mon	Mon	Mon	Mon	Mon	Mon

SEYCHELLES

Number of Time Zones: *1*
Standard Time: *Applicable for the entire year*
Advanced Time: *Not observed*
Time Zone: *16:00 (+4hrs UTC)*

[a]	[b]	[c]	[d]	[e]	[f]	[g]	[h]	[i]	[j]	[k]	[l]	[m]	[n]	[o]	[p]	[q]	[r]	[s]	[t]	[u]	[v]	[w]	[x]
16:01	17:01	18:01	19:01	20:01	21:01	22:01	23:01	00:01	01:01	02:01	03:01	04:01	05:01	06:01	07:01	08:01	09:01	10:01	11:01	12:01	13:01	14:01	15:01
4^{01}_{pm}	5^{01}_{pm}	6^{01}_{pm}	7^{01}_{pm}	8^{01}_{pm}	9^{01}_{pm}	10^{01}_{pm}	11^{01}_{pm}	12^{01}_{am}	1^{01}_{am}	2^{01}_{am}	3^{01}_{am}	4^{01}_{am}	5^{01}_{am}	6^{01}_{am}	7^{01}_{am}	8^{01}_{am}	9^{01}_{am}	10^{01}_{am}	11^{01}_{am}	12^{01}_{pm}	1^{01}_{pm}	2^{01}_{pm}	3^{01}_{pm}
Sun	Sun	Sun	Sun	Sun	Sun	Sun	Sun	Mon	Mon	Mon	Mon	Mon	Mon	Mon	Mon	Mon	Mon	Mon	Mon	Mon	Mon	Mon	Mon

SIERRA LEONE

Number of Time Zones: *1*
Standard Time: *Applicable for the entire year*
Advanced Time: *Not observed*
Time Zone: *12:00 (UTC)*

[a]	[b]	[c]	[d]	[e]	[f]	[g]	[h]	[i]	[j]	[k]	[l]	[m]	[n]	[o]	[p]	[q]	[r]	[s]	[t]	[u]	[v]	[w]	[x]
12:01	13:01	14:01	15:01	16:01	17:01	18:01	19:01	20:01	21:01	22:01	23:01	00:01	01:01	02:01	03:01	04:01	05:01	06:01	07:01	08:01	09:01	10:01	11:01
12^{01}_{pm}	1^{01}_{pm}	2^{01}_{pm}	3^{01}_{pm}	4^{01}_{pm}	5^{01}_{pm}	6^{01}_{pm}	7^{01}_{pm}	8^{01}_{pm}	9^{01}_{pm}	10^{01}_{pm}	11^{01}_{pm}	12^{01}_{am}	1^{01}_{am}	2^{01}_{am}	3^{01}_{am}	4^{01}_{am}	5^{01}_{am}	6^{01}_{am}	7^{01}_{am}	8^{01}_{am}	9^{01}_{am}	10^{01}_{am}	11^{01}_{am}
Sun	Sun	Sun	Sun	Sun	Sun	Sun	Sun	Sun	Sun	Sun	Sun	Mon	Mon	Mon	Mon	Mon	Mon	Mon	Mon	Mon	Mon	Mon	Mon

Note: Advanced Time = Daylight Saving Time = Summer Time

SINGAPORE

Number of Time Zones: *1*
Standard Time: *Applicable for the entire year*
Advanced Time: *Not observed*
Time Zone: *20:00 (+8hrs UTC)*

[a]	[b]	[c]	[d]	[e]	[f]	[g]	[h]	[i]	[j]	[k]	[l]	[m]	[n]	[o]	[p]	[q]	[r]	[s]	[t]	[u]	[v]	[w]	[x]
20:01	21:01	22:01	23:01	00:01	01:01	02:01	03:01	04:01	05:01	06:01	07:01	08:01	09:01	10:01	11:01	12:01	13:01	14:01	15:01	16:01	17:01	18:01	19:01
8^{01}_{pm}	9^{01}_{pm}	10^{01}_{pm}	11^{01}_{pm}	12^{01}_{am}	1^{01}_{am}	2^{01}_{am}	3^{01}_{am}	4^{01}_{am}	5^{01}_{am}	6^{01}_{am}	7^{01}_{am}	8^{01}_{am}	9^{01}_{am}	10^{01}_{am}	11^{01}_{am}	12^{01}_{pm}	1^{01}_{pm}	2^{01}_{pm}	3^{01}_{pm}	4^{01}_{pm}	5^{01}_{pm}	6^{01}_{pm}	7^{01}_{pm}
Sun	Sun	Sun	Sun	Mon	Mon	Mon	Mon	Mon	Mon	Mon	Mon	Mon	Mon	Mon	Mon	Mon	Mon	Mon	Mon	Mon	Mon	Mon	Mon

SOLOMON ISLANDS

Number of Time Zones: *1*
Standard Time: *Applicable for the entire year*
Advanced Time: *Not observed*
Time Zone: *23:00 (+11hrs UTC)*

[a]	[b]	[c]	[d]	[e]	[f]	[g]	[h]	[i]	[j]	[k]	[l]	[m]	[n]	[o]	[p]	[q]	[r]	[s]	[t]	[u]	[v]	[w]	[x]
23:01	00:01	01:01	02:01	03:01	04:01	05:01	06:01	07:01	08:01	09:01	10:01	11:01	12:01	13:01	14:01	15:01	16:01	17:01	18:01	19:01	20:01	21:01	22:01
11^{01}_{pm}	12^{01}_{am}	1^{01}_{am}	2^{01}_{am}	3^{01}_{am}	4^{01}_{am}	5^{01}_{am}	6^{01}_{am}	7^{01}_{am}	8^{01}_{am}	9^{01}_{am}	10^{01}_{am}	11^{01}_{am}	12^{01}_{pm}	1^{01}_{pm}	2^{01}_{pm}	3^{01}_{pm}	4^{01}_{pm}	5^{01}_{pm}	6^{01}_{pm}	7^{01}_{pm}	8^{01}_{pm}	9^{01}_{pm}	10^{01}_{pm}
Sun	Mon	Mon	Mon	Mon	Mon	Mon	Mon	Mon	Mon	Mon	Mon	Mon	Mon	Mon	Mon	Mon	Mon	Mon	Mon	Mon	Mon	Mon	Mon

SOMALIA

Number of Time Zones: *1*
Standard Time: *Applicable for the entire year*
Advanced Time: *Not observed*
Time Zone: *15:00 (+3hrs UTC)*

[a]	[b]	[c]	[d]	[e]	[f]	[g]	[h]	[i]	[j]	[k]	[l]	[m]	[n]	[o]	[p]	[q]	[r]	[s]	[t]	[u]	[v]	[w]	[x]
15:01	16:01	17:01	18:01	19:01	20:01	21:01	22:01	23:01	00:01	01:01	02:01	03:01	04:01	05:01	06:01	07:01	08:01	09:01	10:01	11:01	12:01	13:01	14:01
3^{01}_{pm}	4^{01}_{pm}	5^{01}_{pm}	6^{01}_{pm}	7^{01}_{pm}	8^{01}_{pm}	9^{01}_{pm}	10^{01}_{pm}	11^{01}_{pm}	12^{01}_{am}	1^{01}_{am}	2^{01}_{am}	3^{01}_{am}	4^{01}_{am}	5^{01}_{am}	6^{01}_{am}	7^{01}_{am}	8^{01}_{am}	9^{01}_{am}	10^{01}_{am}	11^{01}_{am}	12^{01}_{pm}	1^{01}_{pm}	2^{01}_{pm}
Sun	Sun	Sun	Sun	Sun	Sun	Sun	Sun	Sun	Mon	Mon	Mon	Mon	Mon	Mon	Mon	Mon	Mon	Mon	Mon	Mon	Mon	Mon	Mon

Note: Advanced Time = Daylight Saving Time = Summer Time

SOUTH AFRICA

Number of Time Zones: *1*
Standard Time: *Applicable for the entire year*
Advanced Time: *Not observed*
Time Zone: *14:00 (+2hrs UTC)*

[a]	[b]	[c]	[d]	[e]	[f]	[g]	[h]	[i]	[j]	[k]	[l]	[m]	[n]	[o]	[p]	[q]	[r]	[s]	[t]	[u]	[v]	[w]	[x]
14:01	15:01	16:01	17:01	18:01	19:01	20:01	21:01	22:01	23:01	00:01	01:01	02:01	03:01	04:01	05:01	06:01	07:01	08:01	09:01	10:01	11:01	12:01	13:01
2:01pm	3:01pm	4:01pm	5:01pm	6:01pm	7:01pm	8:01pm	9:01pm	10:01pm	11:01pm	12:01am	1:01am	2:01am	3:01am	4:01am	5:01am	6:01am	7:01am	8:01am	9:01am	10:01am	11:01am	12:01pm	1:01pm
Sun	Sun	Sun	Sun	Sun	Sun	Sun	Sun	Sun	Sun	Mon	Mon	Mon	Mon	Mon	Mon	Mon	Mon	Mon	Mon	Mon	Mon	Mon	Mon

SOUTH GEORGIA ISLAND

Number of Time Zones: *1*

Standard Time

Period: *Third Sunday in April to Second Sunday in September*
Time Zone: *10:00 (-2hrs UTC)*

[a]	[b]	[c]	[d]	[e]	[f]	[g]	[h]	[i]	[j]	[k]	[l]	[m]	[n]	[o]	[p]	[q]	[r]	[s]	[t]	[u]	[v]	[w]	[x]
10:01	11:01	12:01	13:01	14:01	15:01	16:01	17:01	18:01	19:01	20:01	21:01	22:01	23:01	00:01	01:01	02:01	03:01	04:01	05:01	06:01	07:01	08:01	09:01
10:01am	11:01am	12:01pm	1:01pm	2:01pm	3:01pm	4:01pm	5:01pm	6:01pm	7:01pm	8:01pm	9:01pm	10:01pm	11:01pm	12:01am	1:01am	2:01am	3:01am	4:01am	5:01am	6:01am	7:01am	8:01am	9:01am
Sun	Sun	Sun	Sun	Sun	Sun	Sun	Sun	Sun	Sun	Sun	Sun	Sun	Sun	Mon	Mon	Mon	Mon	Mon	Mon	Mon	Mon	Mon	Mon

Advanced Time

Period: *Second Sunday in September to Third Sunday in April*
Time Zone: *11:00 (-1hr UTC)*

[a]	[b]	[c]	[d]	[e]	[f]	[g]	[h]	[i]	[j]	[k]	[l]	[m]	[n]	[o]	[p]	[q]	[r]	[s]	[t]	[u]	[v]	[w]	[x]
11:01	12:01	13:01	14:01	15:01	16:01	17:01	18:01	19:01	20:01	21:01	22:01	23:01	00:01	01:01	02:01	03:01	04:01	05:01	06:01	07:01	08:01	09:01	10:01
11:01am	12:01pm	1:01pm	2:01pm	3:01pm	4:01pm	5:01pm	6:01pm	7:01pm	8:01pm	9:01pm	10:01pm	11:01pm	12:01am	1:01am	2:01am	3:01am	4:01am	5:01am	6:01am	7:01am	8:01am	9:01am	10:01am
Sun	Sun	Sun	Sun	Sun	Sun	Sun	Sun	Sun	Sun	Sun	Sun	Sun	Mon	Mon	Mon	Mon	Mon	Mon	Mon	Mon	Mon	Mon	Mon

Note: Advanced Time = Daylight Saving Time = Summer Time

SOVIET UNION

Number of Time Zones: *11*
Notes: *Advanced Time observed;*
See Reference Map II for graphic depiction of time zones;
Numbers of following time zones keyed to Reference Map II

TIME ZONE II

Note: *Includes Arkhangelsk, Kiev, Leningrad, Moscow, and Odessa*

Standard Time

Period: *Last Sunday in September to Last Sunday in March*
Time Zone: *15:00 (+3hrs UTC)*

[a]	[b]	[c]	[d]	[e]	[f]	[g]	[h]	[i]	[j]	[k]	[l]	[m]	[n]	[o]	[p]	[q]	[r]	[s]	[t]	[u]	[v]	[w]	[x]
15:01	16:01	17:01	18:01	19:01	20:01	21:01	22:01	23:01	00:01	01:01	02:01	03:01	04:01	05:01	06:01	07:01	08:01	09:01	10:01	11:01	12:01	13:01	14:01
3:01pm	4:01pm	5:01pm	6:01pm	7:01pm	8:01pm	9:01pm	10:01pm	11:01pm	12:01am	1:01am	2:01am	3:01am	4:01am	5:01am	6:01am	7:01am	8:01am	9:01am	10:01am	11:01am	12:01pm	1:01pm	2:01pm
Sun	Sun	Sun	Sun	Sun	Sun	Sun	Sun	Sun	Mon	Mon	Mon	Mon	Mon	Mon	Mon	Mon	Mon	Mon	Mon	Mon	Mon	Mon	Mon

Advanced Time

Period: *Last Sunday in March to Last Sunday in September*
Time Zone: *16:00 (+4hrs UTC)*

[a]	[b]	[c]	[d]	[e]	[f]	[g]	[h]	[i]	[j]	[k]	[l]	[m]	[n]	[o]	[p]	[q]	[r]	[s]	[t]	[u]	[v]	[w]	[x]
16:01	17:01	18:01	19:01	20:01	21:01	22:01	23:01	00:01	01:01	02:01	03:01	04:01	05:01	06:01	07:01	08:01	09:01	10:01	11:01	12:01	13:01	14:01	15:01
4:01pm	5:01pm	6:01pm	7:01pm	8:01pm	9:01pm	10:01pm	11:01pm	12:01am	1:01am	2:01am	3:01am	4:01am	5:01am	6:01am	7:01am	8:01am	9:01am	10:01am	11:01am	12:01pm	1:01pm	2:01pm	3:01pm
Sun	Sun	Sun	Sun	Sun	Sun	Sun	Sun	Mon	Mon	Mon	Mon	Mon	Mon	Mon	Mon	Mon	Mon	Mon	Mon	Mon	Mon	Mon	Mon

TIME ZONE III

Note: *Includes Baku, Tbilisi, and Volgograd*

Standard Time

Period: *Last Sunday in September to Last Sunday in March*
Time Zone: *16:00 (+4hrs UTC)*

[a]	[b]	[c]	[d]	[e]	[f]	[g]	[h]	[i]	[j]	[k]	[l]	[m]	[n]	[o]	[p]	[q]	[r]	[s]	[t]	[u]	[v]	[w]	[x]
16:01	17:01	18:01	19:01	20:01	21:01	22:01	23:01	00:01	01:01	02:01	03:01	04:01	05:01	06:01	07:01	08:01	09:01	10:01	11:01	12:01	13:01	14:01	15:01
4:01pm	5:01pm	6:01pm	7:01pm	8:01pm	9:01pm	10:01pm	11:01pm	12:01am	1:01am	2:01am	3:01am	4:01am	5:01am	6:01am	7:01am	8:01am	9:01am	10:01am	11:01am	12:01pm	1:01pm	2:01pm	3:01pm
Sun	Sun	Sun	Sun	Sun	Sun	Sun	Sun	Mon	Mon	Mon	Mon	Mon	Mon	Mon	Mon	Mon	Mon	Mon	Mon	Mon	Mon	Mon	Mon

Advanced Time

Period: *Last Sunday in March to Last Sunday in September*
Time Zone: *17:00 (+5hrs UTC)*

[a]	[b]	[c]	[d]	[e]	[f]	[g]	[h]	[i]	[j]	[k]	[l]	[m]	[n]	[o]	[p]	[q]	[r]	[s]	[t]	[u]	[v]	[w]	[x]
17:01	18:01	19:01	20:01	21:01	22:01	23:01	00:01	01:01	02:01	03:01	04:01	05:01	06:01	07:01	08:01	09:01	10:01	11:01	12:01	13:01	14:01	15:01	16:01
5:01pm	6:01pm	7:01pm	8:01pm	9:01pm	10:01pm	11:01pm	12:01am	1:01am	2:01am	3:01am	4:01am	5:01am	6:01am	7:01am	8:01am	9:01am	10:01am	11:01am	12:01pm	1:01pm	2:01pm	3:01pm	4:01pm
Sun	Sun	Sun	Sun	Sun	Sun	Sun	Mon	Mon	Mon	Mon	Mon	Mon	Mon	Mon	Mon	Mon	Mon	Mon	Mon	Mon	Mon	Mon	Mon

Note: Advanced Time = Daylight Saving Time = Summer Time

SOVIET UNION *(Continued)*

TIME ZONE IV
Note: *Includes Ashkabad, Novvy Port, and Sverdlovsk*

Standard Time
Period: *Last Sunday in September to Last Sunday in March*
Time Zone: *17:00 (+5hrs UTC)*

[a]	[b]	[c]	[d]	[e]	[f]	[g]	[h]	[i]	[j]	[k]	[l]	[m]	[n]	[o]	[p]	[q]	[r]	[s]	[t]	[u]	[v]	[w]	[x]
17:01	18:01	19:01	20:01	21:01	22:01	23:01	00:01	01:01	02:01	03:01	04:01	05:01	06:01	07:01	08:01	09:01	10:01	11:01	12:01	13:01	14:01	15:01	16:01
5^{01}pm	6^{01}pm	7^{01}pm	8^{01}pm	9^{01}pm	10^{01}pm	11^{01}pm	12^{01}am	1^{01}am	2^{01}am	3^{01}am	4^{01}am	5^{01}am	6^{01}am	7^{01}am	8^{01}am	9^{01}am	10^{01}am	11^{01}am	12^{01}pm	1^{01}pm	2^{01}pm	3^{01}pm	4^{01}pm
Sun	Sun	Sun	Sun	Sun	Sun	Sun	Mon	Mon	Mon	Mon	Mon	Mon	Mon	Mon	Mon	Mon	Mon	Mon	Mon	Mon	Mon	Mon	Mon

Advanced Time
Period: *Last Sunday in March to Last Sunday in September*
Time Zone: *18:00 (+6hrs UTC)*

[a]	[b]	[c]	[d]	[e]	[f]	[g]	[h]	[i]	[j]	[k]	[l]	[m]	[n]	[o]	[p]	[q]	[r]	[s]	[t]	[u]	[v]	[w]	[x]
18:01	19:01	20:01	21:01	22:01	23:01	00:01	01:01	02:01	03:01	04:01	05:01	06:01	07:01	08:01	09:01	10:01	11:01	12:01	13:01	14:01	15:01	16:01	17:01
6^{01}pm	7^{01}pm	8^{01}pm	9^{01}pm	10^{01}pm	11^{01}pm	12^{01}am	1^{01}am	2^{01}am	3^{01}am	4^{01}am	5^{01}am	6^{01}am	7^{01}am	8^{01}am	9^{01}am	10^{01}am	11^{01}am	12^{01}pm	1^{01}pm	2^{01}pm	3^{01}pm	4^{01}pm	5^{01}pm
Sun	Sun	Sun	Sun	Sun	Sun	Mon	Mon	Mon	Mon	Mon	Mon	Mon	Mon	Mon	Mon	Mon	Mon	Mon	Mon	Mon	Mon	Mon	Mon

TIME ZONE V
Note: *Includes Alma-Ata, Omsk, and Tashkent*

Standard Time
Period: *Last Sunday in September to Last Sunday in March*
Time Zone: *18:00 (+6hrs UTC)*

[a]	[b]	[c]	[d]	[e]	[f]	[g]	[h]	[i]	[j]	[k]	[l]	[m]	[n]	[o]	[p]	[q]	[r]	[s]	[t]	[u]	[v]	[w]	[x]
18:01	19:01	20:01	21:01	22:01	23:01	00:01	01:01	02:01	03:01	04:01	05:01	06:01	07:01	08:01	09:01	10:01	11:01	12:01	13:01	14:01	15:01	16:01	17:01
6^{01}pm	7^{01}pm	8^{01}pm	9^{01}pm	10^{01}pm	11^{01}pm	12^{01}am	1^{01}am	2^{01}am	3^{01}am	4^{01}am	5^{01}am	6^{01}am	7^{01}am	8^{01}am	9^{01}am	10^{01}am	11^{01}am	12^{01}pm	1^{01}pm	2^{01}pm	3^{01}pm	4^{01}pm	5^{01}pm
Sun	Sun	Sun	Sun	Sun	Sun	Mon	Mon	Mon	Mon	Mon	Mon	Mon	Mon	Mon	Mon	Mon	Mon	Mon	Mon	Mon	Mon	Mon	Mon

Advanced Time
Period: *Last Sunday in March to Last Sunday in September*
Time Zone: *19:00 (+7hrs UTC)*

[a]	[b]	[c]	[d]	[e]	[f]	[g]	[h]	[i]	[j]	[k]	[l]	[m]	[n]	[o]	[p]	[q]	[r]	[s]	[t]	[u]	[v]	[w]	[x]
19:01	20:01	21:01	22:01	23:01	00:01	01:01	02:01	03:01	04:01	05:01	06:01	07:01	08:01	09:01	10:01	11:01	12:01	13:01	14:01	15:01	16:01	17:01	18:01
7^{01}pm	8^{01}pm	9^{01}pm	10^{01}pm	11^{01}pm	12^{01}am	1^{01}am	2^{01}am	3^{01}am	4^{01}am	5^{01}am	6^{01}am	7^{01}am	8^{01}am	9^{01}am	10^{01}am	11^{01}am	12^{01}pm	1^{01}pm	2^{01}pm	3^{01}pm	4^{01}pm	5^{01}pm	6^{01}pm
Sun	Sun	Sun	Sun	Sun	Mon	Mon	Mon	Mon	Mon	Mon	Mon	Mon	Mon	Mon	Mon	Mon	Mon	Mon	Mon	Mon	Mon	Mon	Mon

Note: Advanced Time = Daylight Saving Time = Summer Time

SOVIET UNION *(Continued)*

TIME ZONE VI
Note: *Includes Krasnoyarsk and Novosibirsk*

Standard Time
Period: *Last Sunday in September to Last Sunday in March*
Time Zone: *19:00 (+7hrs UTC)*

[a]	[b]	[c]	[d]	[e]	[f]	[g]	[h]	[i]	[j]	[k]	[l]	[m]	[n]	[o]	[p]	[q]	[r]	[s]	[t]	[u]	[v]	[w]	
19:01	20:01	21:01	22:01	23:01	00:01	01:01	02:01	03:01	04:01	05:01	06:01	07:01	08:01	09:01	10:01	11:01	12:01	13:01	14:01	15:01	16:01	17:01	18:
7:01pm	8:01pm	9:01pm	10:01pm	11:01pm	12:01am	1:01am	2:01am	3:01am	4:01am	5:01am	6:01am	7:01am	8:01am	9:01am	10:01am	11:01am	12:01pm	1:01pm	2:01pm	3:01pm	4:01pm	5:01pm	6
Sun	Sun	Sun	Sun	Sun	Mon	Mon	Mon	Mon	Mon	Mon	Mon	Mon	Mon	Mon	Mon	Mon	Mon	Mon	Mon	Mon	Mon	Mon	M

Advanced Time
Period: *Last Sunday in March to Last Sunday in September*
Time Zone: *20:00 (+8hrs UTC)*

[a]	[b]	[c]	[d]	[e]	[f]	[g]	[h]	[i]	[j]	[k]	[l]	[m]	[n]	[o]	[p]	[q]	[r]	[s]	[t]	[u]	[v]	[w]	
20:01	21:01	22:01	23:01	00:01	01:01	02:01	03:01	04:01	05:01	06:01	07:01	08:01	09:01	10:01	11:01	12:01	13:01	14:01	15:01	16:01	17:01	18:01	19:
8:01pm	9:01pm	10:01pm	11:01pm	12:01am	1:01am	2:01am	3:01am	4:01am	5:01am	6:01am	7:01am	8:01am	9:01am	10:01am	11:01am	12:01pm	1:01pm	2:01pm	3:01pm	4:01pm	5:01pm	6:01pm	7
Sun	Sun	Sun	Sun	Mon	Mon	Mon	Mon	Mon	Mon	Mon	Mon	Mon	Mon	Mon	Mon	Mon	Mon	Mon	Mon	Mon	Mon	Mon	M

TIME ZONE VII
Note: *Includes Irkutsk*

Standard Time
Period: *Last Sunday in September to Last Sunday in March*
Time Zone: *20:00 (+8hrs UTC)*

[a]	[b]	[c]	[d]	[e]	[f]	[g]	[h]	[i]	[j]	[k]	[l]	[m]	[n]	[o]	[p]	[q]	[r]	[s]	[t]	[u]	[v]	[w]	
20:01	21:01	22:01	23:01	00:01	01:01	02:01	03:01	04:01	05:01	06:01	07:01	08:01	09:01	10:01	11:01	12:01	13:01	14:01	15:01	16:01	17:01	18:01	19
8:01pm	9:01pm	10:01pm	11:01pm	12:01am	1:01am	2:01am	3:01am	4:01am	5:01am	6:01am	7:01am	8:01am	9:01am	10:01am	11:01am	12:01pm	1:01pm	2:01pm	3:01pm	4:01pm	5:01pm	6:01pm	
Sun	Sun	Sun	Sun	Mon	Mon	Mon	Mon	Mon	Mon	Mon	Mon	Mon	Mon	Mon	Mon	Mon	Mon	Mon	Mon	Mon	Mon	Mon	

Advanced Time
Period: *Last Sunday in March to Last Sunday in September*
Time Zone: *21:00 (+9hrs UTC)*

[a]	[b]	[c]	[d]	[e]	[f]	[g]	[h]	[i]	[j]	[k]	[l]	[m]	[n]	[o]	[p]	[q]	[r]	[s]	[t]	[u]	[v]	[w]	
21:01	22:01	23:01	00:01	01:01	02:01	03:01	04:01	05:01	06:01	07:01	08:01	09:01	10:01	11:01	12:01	13:01	14:01	15:01	16:01	17:01	18:01	19:01	20
9:01pm	10:01pm	11:01pm	12:01am	1:01am	2:01am	3:01am	4:01am	5:01am	6:01am	7:01am	8:01am	9:01am	10:01am	11:01am	12:01pm	1:01pm	2:01pm	3:01pm	4:01pm	5:01pm	6:01pm	7:01pm	
Sun	Sun	Sun	Mon	Mon	Mon	Mon	Mon	Mon	Mon	Mon	Mon	Mon	Mon	Mon	Mon	Mon	Mon	Mon	Mon	Mon	Mon	Mon	

Note: Advanced Time = Daylight Saving Time = Summer Time

SOVIET UNION *(Continued)*

TIME ZONE VIII
Note: *Includes Tiksi and Yakutsk*

Standard Time
Period: *Last Sunday in September to Last Sunday in March*
Time Zone: *21:00 (+9hrs UTC)*

[a]	[b]	[c]	[d]	[e]	[f]	[g]	[h]	[i]	[j]	[k]	[l]	[m]	[n]	[o]	[p]	[q]	[r]	[s]	[t]	[u]	[v]	[w]	[x]
21:01	22:01	23:01	00:01	01:01	02:01	03:01	04:01	05:01	06:01	07:01	08:01	09:01	10:01	11:01	12:01	13:01	14:01	15:01	16:01	17:01	18:01	19:01	20:01
9^{01}_{pm}	10^{01}_{pm}	11^{01}_{pm}	12^{01}_{am}	1^{01}_{am}	2^{01}_{am}	3^{01}_{am}	4^{01}_{am}	5^{01}_{am}	6^{01}_{am}	7^{01}_{am}	8^{01}_{am}	9^{01}_{am}	10^{01}_{am}	11^{01}_{am}	12^{01}_{pm}	1^{01}_{pm}	2^{01}_{pm}	3^{01}_{pm}	4^{01}_{pm}	5^{01}_{pm}	6^{01}_{pm}	7^{01}_{pm}	8^{01}_{pm}
Sun	Sun	Sun	Mon	Mon	Mon	Mon	Mon	Mon	Mon	Mon	Mon	Mon	Mon	Mon	Mon	Mon	Mon	Mon	Mon	Mon	Mon	Mon	Mon

Advanced Time
Period: *Last Sunday in March to Last Sunday in September*
Time Zone: *22:00 (+10hrs UTC)*

[a]	[b]	[c]	[d]	[e]	[f]	[g]	[h]	[i]	[j]	[k]	[l]	[m]	[n]	[o]	[p]	[q]	[r]	[s]	[t]	[u]	[v]	[w]	[x]
22:01	23:01	00:01	01:01	02:01	03:01	04:01	05:01	06:01	07:01	08:01	09:01	10:01	11:01	12:01	13:01	14:01	15:01	16:01	17:01	18:01	19:01	20:01	21:01
10^{01}_{pm}	11^{01}_{pm}	12^{01}_{am}	1^{01}_{am}	2^{01}_{am}	3^{01}_{am}	4^{01}_{am}	5^{01}_{am}	6^{01}_{am}	7^{01}_{am}	8^{01}_{am}	9^{01}_{am}	10^{01}_{am}	11^{01}_{am}	12^{01}_{pm}	1^{01}_{pm}	2^{01}_{pm}	3^{01}_{pm}	4^{01}_{pm}	5^{01}_{pm}	6^{01}_{pm}	7^{01}_{pm}	8^{01}_{pm}	9^{01}_{pm}
Sun	Sun	Mon	Mon	Mon	Mon	Mon	Mon	Mon	Mon	Mon	Mon	Mon	Mon	Mon	Mon	Mon	Mon	Mon	Mon	Mon	Mon	Mon	Mon

TIME ZONE IX
Note: *Includes Khabarovsk, Okhotsk, and Vladivostok*

Standard Time
Period: *Last Sunday in September to Last Sunday in March*
Time Zone: *22:00 (+10hrs UTC)*

[a]	[b]	[c]	[d]	[e]	[f]	[g]	[h]	[i]	[j]	[k]	[l]	[m]	[n]	[o]	[p]	[q]	[r]	[s]	[t]	[u]	[v]	[w]	[x]
22:01	23:01	00:01	01:01	02:01	03:01	04:01	05:01	06:01	07:01	08:01	09:01	10:01	11:01	12:01	13:01	14:01	15:01	16:01	17:01	18:01	19:01	20:01	21:01
10^{01}_{pm}	11^{01}_{pm}	12^{01}_{am}	1^{01}_{am}	2^{01}_{am}	3^{01}_{am}	4^{01}_{am}	5^{01}_{am}	6^{01}_{am}	7^{01}_{am}	8^{01}_{am}	9^{01}_{am}	10^{01}_{am}	11^{01}_{am}	12^{01}_{pm}	1^{01}_{pm}	2^{01}_{pm}	3^{01}_{pm}	4^{01}_{pm}	5^{01}_{pm}	6^{01}_{pm}	7^{01}_{pm}	8^{01}_{pm}	9^{01}_{pm}
Sun	Sun	Mon	Mon	Mon	Mon	Mon	Mon	Mon	Mon	Mon	Mon	Mon	Mon	Mon	Mon	Mon	Mon	Mon	Mon	Mon	Mon	Mon	Mon

Advanced Time
Period: *Last Sunday in March to Last Sunday in September*
Time Zone: *23:00 (+11hrs UTC)*

[a]	[b]	[c]	[d]	[e]	[f]	[g]	[h]	[i]	[j]	[k]	[l]	[m]	[n]	[o]	[p]	[q]	[r]	[s]	[t]	[u]	[v]	[w]	[x]
23:01	00:01	01:01	02:01	03:01	04:01	05:01	06:01	07:01	08:01	09:01	10:01	11:01	12:01	13:01	14:01	15:01	16:01	17:01	18:01	19:01	20:01	21:01	22:01
11^{01}_{pm}	12^{01}_{am}	1^{01}_{am}	2^{01}_{am}	3^{01}_{am}	4^{01}_{am}	5^{01}_{am}	6^{01}_{am}	7^{01}_{am}	8^{01}_{am}	9^{01}_{am}	10^{01}_{am}	11^{01}_{am}	12^{01}_{pm}	1^{01}_{pm}	2^{01}_{pm}	3^{01}_{pm}	4^{01}_{pm}	5^{01}_{pm}	6^{01}_{pm}	7^{01}_{pm}	8^{01}_{pm}	9^{01}_{pm}	10^{01}_{pm}
Sun	Mon	Mon	Mon	Mon	Mon	Mon	Mon	Mon	Mon	Mon	Mon	Mon	Mon	Mon	Mon	Mon	Mon	Mon	Mon	Mon	Mon	Mon	Mon

Note: Advanced Time = Daylight Saving Time = Summer Time

SOVIET UNION *(Continued)*

TIME ZONE X
Note: *Includes Magadan and Sakhalin Island*

Standard Time
Period: *Last Sunday in September to Last Sunday in March*
Time Zone: *23:00 (+11hrs UTC)*

[a]	[b]	[c]	[d]	[e]	[f]	[g]	[h]	[i]	[j]	[k]	[l]	[m]	[n]	[o]	[p]	[q]	[r]	[s]	[t]	[u]	[v]	[w]	[x]
23:01	00:01	01:01	02:01	03:01	04:01	05:01	06:01	07:01	08:01	09:01	10:01	11:01	12:01	13:01	14:01	15:01	16:01	17:01	18:01	19:01	20:01	21:01	22:0(
11^{01}_{pm}	12^{01}_{am}	1^{01}_{am}	2^{01}_{am}	3^{01}_{am}	4^{01}_{am}	5^{01}_{am}	6^{01}_{am}	7^{01}_{am}	8^{01}_{am}	9^{01}_{am}	10^{01}_{am}	11^{01}_{am}	12^{01}_{pm}	1^{01}_{pm}	2^{01}_{pm}	3^{01}_{pm}	4^{01}_{pm}	5^{01}_{pm}	6^{01}_{pm}	7^{01}_{pm}	8^{01}_{pm}	9^{01}_{pm}	10
Sun	Mon	Mon	Mon	Mon	Mon	Mon	Mon	Mon	Mon	Mon	Mon	Mon	Mon	Mon	Mon	Mon	Mon	Mon	Mon	Mon	Mon	Mon	M

Advanced Time
Period: *Last Sunday in March to Last Sunday in September*
Time Zone: *24:00 (+12hrs UTC)*

[a]	[b]	[c]	[d]	[e]	[f]	[g]	[h]	[i]	[j]	[k]	[l]	[m]	[n]	[o]	[p]	[q]	[r]	[s]	[t]	[u]	[v]	[w]	[
00:01	01:01	02:01	03:01	04:01	05:01	06:01	07:01	08:01	09:01	10:01	11:01	12:01	13:01	14:01	15:01	16:01	17:01	18:01	19:01	20:01	21:01	22:01	23:
12^{01}_{am}	1^{01}_{am}	2^{01}_{am}	3^{01}_{am}	4^{01}_{am}	5^{01}_{am}	6^{01}_{am}	7^{01}_{am}	8^{01}_{am}	9^{01}_{am}	10^{01}_{am}	11^{01}_{am}	12^{01}_{pm}	1^{01}_{pm}	2^{01}_{pm}	3^{01}_{pm}	4^{01}_{pm}	5^{01}_{pm}	6^{01}_{pm}	7^{01}_{pm}	8^{01}_{pm}	9^{01}_{pm}	10^{01}_{pm}	11
Mon	Mon	Mon	Mon	Mon	Mon	Mon	Mon	Mon	Mon	Mon	Mon	Mon	Mon	Mon	Mon	Mon	Mon	Mon	Mon	Mon	Mon	Mon	M

TIME ZONE XI
Note: *Includes Petropavlovsk-Kamchatskiy*

Standard Time
Period: *Last Sunday in September to Last Sunday in March*
Time Zone: *24:00 (+12hrs UTC)*

[a]	[b]	[c]	[d]	[e]	[f]	[g]	[h]	[i]	[j]	[k]	[l]	[m]	[n]	[o]	[p]	[q]	[r]	[s]	[t]	[u]	[v]	[w]	[
00:01	01:01	02:01	03:01	04:01	05:01	06:01	07:01	08:01	09:01	10:01	11:01	12:01	13:01	14:01	15:01	16:01	17:01	18:01	19:01	20:01	21:01	22:01	23:
12^{01}_{am}	1^{01}_{am}	2^{01}_{am}	3^{01}_{am}	4^{01}_{am}	5^{01}_{am}	6^{01}_{am}	7^{01}_{am}	8^{01}_{am}	9^{01}_{am}	10^{01}_{am}	11^{01}_{am}	12^{01}_{pm}	1^{01}_{pm}	2^{01}_{pm}	3^{01}_{pm}	4^{01}_{pm}	5^{01}_{pm}	6^{01}_{pm}	7^{01}_{pm}	8^{01}_{pm}	9^{01}_{pm}	10^{01}_{pm}	11
Mon	Mon	Mon	Mon	Mon	Mon	Mon	Mon	Mon	Mon	Mon	Mon	Mon	Mon	Mon	Mon	Mon	Mon	Mon	Mon	Mon	Mon	Mon	M

Advanced Time
Period: *Last Sunday in March to Last Sunday in September*
Time Zone: *25:00 (+13hrs UTC)*

[a]	[b]	[c]	[d]	[e]	[f]	[g]	[h]	[i]	[j]	[k]	[l]	[m]	[n]	[o]	[p]	[q]	[r]	[s]	[t]	[u]	[v]	[w]	[
01:01	02:01	03:01	04:01	05:01	06:01	07:01	08:01	09:01	10:01	11:01	12:01	13:01	14:01	15:01	16:01	17:01	18:01	19:01	20:01	21:01	22:01	23:01	00:
1^{01}_{am}	2^{01}_{am}	3^{01}_{am}	4^{01}_{am}	5^{01}_{am}	6^{01}_{am}	7^{01}_{am}	8^{01}_{am}	9^{01}_{am}	10^{01}_{am}	11^{01}_{am}	12^{01}_{pm}	1^{01}_{pm}	2^{01}_{pm}	3^{01}_{pm}	4^{01}_{pm}	5^{01}_{pm}	6^{01}_{pm}	7^{01}_{pm}	8^{01}_{pm}	9^{01}_{pm}	10^{01}_{pm}	11^{01}_{pm}	12
Mon	Mon	Mon	Mon	Mon	Mon	Mon	Mon	Mon	Mon	Mon	Mon	Mon	Mon	Mon	Mon	Mon	Mon	Mon	Mon	Mon	Mon	Mon	T

Note: Advanced Time = Daylight Saving Time = Summer Time

SOVIET UNION *(Continued)*

TIME ZONE XII
Note: *Includes Anadyr*

Standard Time
Period: *Last Sunday in September to Last Sunday in March*
Time Zone: *25:00 (+13hrs UTC)*

[a]	[b]	[c]	[d]	[e]	[f]	[g]	[h]	[i]	[j]	[k]	[l]	[m]	[n]	[o]	[p]	[q]	[r]	[s]	[t]	[u]	[v]	[w]	[x]
01:01	02:01	03:01	04:01	05:01	06:01	07:01	08:01	09:01	10:01	11:01	12:01	13:01	14:01	15:01	16:01	17:01	18:01	19:01	20:01	21:01	22:01	23:01	00:01
1^{01}_{am}	2^{01}_{am}	3^{01}_{am}	4^{01}_{am}	5^{01}_{am}	6^{01}_{am}	7^{01}_{am}	8^{01}_{am}	9^{01}_{am}	10^{01}_{am}	11^{01}_{am}	12^{01}_{pm}	1^{01}_{pm}	2^{01}_{pm}	3^{01}_{pm}	4^{01}_{pm}	5^{01}_{pm}	6^{01}_{pm}	7^{01}_{pm}	8^{01}_{pm}	9^{01}_{pm}	10^{01}_{pm}	11^{01}_{pm}	12^{01}_{am}
Mon	Mon	Mon	Mon	Mon	Mon	Mon	Mon	Mon	Mon	Mon	Mon	Mon	Mon	Mon	Mon	Mon	Mon	Mon	Mon	Mon	Mon	Mon	Tue

Advanced Time
Period: *Last Sunday in March to Last Sunday in September*
Time Zone: *26:00 (+14hrs UTC)*

[a]	[b]	[c]	[d]	[e]	[f]	[g]	[h]	[i]	[j]	[k]	[l]	[m]	[n]	[o]	[p]	[q]	[r]	[s]	[t]	[u]	[v]	[w]	[x]
02:01	03:01	04:01	05:01	06:01	07:01	08:01	09:01	10:01	11:01	12:01	13:01	14:01	15:01	16:01	17:01	18:01	19:01	20:01	21:01	22:01	23:01	00:01	01:01
2^{01}_{am}	3^{01}_{am}	4^{01}_{am}	5^{01}_{am}	6^{01}_{am}	7^{01}_{am}	8^{01}_{am}	9^{01}_{am}	10^{01}_{am}	11^{01}_{am}	12^{01}_{pm}	1^{01}_{pm}	2^{01}_{pm}	3^{01}_{pm}	4^{01}_{pm}	5^{01}_{pm}	6^{01}_{pm}	7^{01}_{pm}	8^{01}_{pm}	9^{01}_{pm}	10^{01}_{pm}	11^{01}_{pm}	12^{01}_{am}	1^{01}_{am}
Mon	Mon	Mon	Mon	Mon	Mon	Mon	Mon	Mon	Mon	Mon	Mon	Mon	Mon	Mon	Mon	Mon	Mon	Mon	Mon	Mon	Mon	Tue	Tue

SPAIN
Number of Time Zones: *1*

Standard Time
Period: *Last Sunday in September to Last Sunday in March*
Time Zone: *13:00 (+1hr UTC)*

[a]	[b]	[c]	[d]	[e]	[f]	[g]	[h]	[i]	[j]	[k]	[l]	[m]	[n]	[o]	[p]	[q]	[r]	[s]	[t]	[u]	[v]	[w]	[x]
13:01	14:01	15:01	16:01	17:01	18:01	19:01	20:01	21:01	22:01	23:01	00:01	01:01	02:01	03:01	04:01	05:01	06:01	07:01	08:01	09:01	10:01	11:01	12:01
1^{01}_{pm}	2^{01}_{pm}	3^{01}_{pm}	4^{01}_{pm}	5^{01}_{pm}	6^{01}_{pm}	7^{01}_{pm}	8^{01}_{pm}	9^{01}_{pm}	10^{01}_{pm}	11^{01}_{pm}	12^{01}_{am}	1^{01}_{am}	2^{01}_{am}	3^{01}_{am}	4^{01}_{am}	5^{01}_{am}	6^{01}_{am}	7^{01}_{am}	8^{01}_{am}	9^{01}_{am}	10^{01}_{am}	11^{01}_{am}	12^{01}_{pm}
Sun	Sun	Sun	Sun	Sun	Sun	Sun	Sun	Sun	Sun	Sun	Mon	Mon	Mon	Mon	Mon	Mon	Mon	Mon	Mon	Mon	Mon	Mon	Mon

Advanced Time
Period: *Last Sunday in March to Last Sunday in September*
Time Zone: *14:00 (+2hrs UTC)*

[a]	[b]	[c]	[d]	[e]	[f]	[g]	[h]	[i]	[j]	[k]	[l]	[m]	[n]	[o]	[p]	[q]	[r]	[s]	[t]	[u]	[v]	[w]	[x]
14:01	15:01	16:01	17:01	18:01	19:01	20:01	21:01	22:01	23:01	00:01	01:01	02:01	03:01	04:01	05:01	06:01	07:01	08:01	09:01	10:01	11:01	12:01	13:01
2^{01}_{pm}	3^{01}_{pm}	4^{01}_{pm}	5^{01}_{pm}	6^{01}_{pm}	7^{01}_{pm}	8^{01}_{pm}	9^{01}_{pm}	10^{01}_{pm}	11^{01}_{pm}	12^{01}_{am}	1^{01}_{am}	2^{01}_{am}	3^{01}_{am}	4^{01}_{am}	5^{01}_{am}	6^{01}_{am}	7^{01}_{am}	8^{01}_{am}	9^{01}_{am}	10^{01}_{am}	11^{01}_{am}	12^{01}_{pm}	1^{01}_{pm}
Sun	Sun	Sun	Sun	Sun	Sun	Sun	Sun	Sun	Sun	Mon	Mon	Mon	Mon	Mon	Mon	Mon	Mon	Mon	Mon	Mon	Mon	Mon	Mon

Note: Advanced Time = Daylight Saving Time = Summer Time

SRI LANKA
Number of Time Zones: *1*
Standard Time: *Applicable for the entire year*
Advanced Time: *Not observed*
Time Zone: *17:30 (+5hrs 30mins UTC)*

[a]	[b]	[c]	[d]	[e]	[f]	[g]	[h]	[i]	[j]	[k]	[l]	[m]	[n]	[o]	[p]	[q]	[r]	[s]	[t]	[u]	[v]	[w]	[x]
17:31	18:31	19:31	20:31	21:31	22:31	23:31	00:31	01:31	02:31	03:31	04:31	05:31	06:31	07:31	08:31	09:31	10:31	11:31	12:31	13:31	14:31	15:31	16:31
5^{31}_{pm}	6^{31}_{pm}	7^{31}_{pm}	8^{31}_{pm}	9^{31}_{pm}	10^{31}_{pm}	11^{31}_{pm}	12^{31}_{am}	1^{31}_{am}	2^{31}_{am}	3^{31}_{am}	4^{31}_{am}	5^{31}_{am}	6^{31}_{am}	7^{31}_{am}	8^{31}_{am}	9^{31}_{am}	10^{31}_{am}	11^{31}_{am}	12^{31}_{pm}	1^{31}_{pm}	2^{31}_{pm}	3^{31}_{pm}	4^{31}_{pm}
Sun	Sun	Sun	Sun	Sun	Sun	Sun	Mon	Mon	Mon	Mon	Mon	Mon	Mon	Mon	Mon	Mon	Mon	Mon	Mon	Mon	Mon	Mon	Mon

SUDAN
Number of Time Zones: *1*
Standard Time: *Applicable for the entire year*
Advanced Time: *Not observed*
Time Zone: *14:00 (+2hrs UTC)*

[a]	[b]	[c]	[d]	[e]	[f]	[g]	[h]	[i]	[j]	[k]	[l]	[m]	[n]	[o]	[p]	[q]	[r]	[s]	[t]	[u]	[v]	[w]	[x]
14:01	15:01	16:01	17:01	18:01	19:01	20:01	21:01	22:01	23:01	00:01	01:01	02:01	03:01	04:01	05:01	06:01	07:01	08:01	09:01	10:01	11:01	12:01	13:01
2^{01}_{pm}	3^{01}_{pm}	4^{01}_{pm}	5^{01}_{pm}	6^{01}_{pm}	7^{01}_{pm}	8^{01}_{pm}	9^{01}_{pm}	10^{01}_{pm}	11^{01}_{pm}	12^{01}_{am}	1^{01}_{am}	2^{01}_{am}	3^{01}_{am}	4^{01}_{am}	5^{01}_{am}	6^{01}_{am}	7^{01}_{am}	8^{01}_{am}	9^{01}_{am}	10^{01}_{am}	11^{01}_{am}	12^{01}_{pm}	1^{0}_{pr}
Sun	Sun	Sun	Sun	Sun	Sun	Sun	Sun	Sun	Sun	Mon	Mon	Mon	Mon	Mon	Mon	Mon	Mon	Mon	Mon	Mon	Mon	Mon	Mon

SURINAME
Number of Time Zones: *1*
Standard Time: *Applicable for the entire year*
Advanced Time: *Not observed*
Time Zone: *09:00 (-3hrs UTC)*

[a]	[b]	[c]	[d]	[e]	[f]	[g]	[h]	[i]	[j]	[k]	[l]	[m]	[n]	[o]	[p]	[q]	[r]	[s]	[t]	[u]	[v]	[w]	[x]
09:01	10:01	11:01	12:01	13:01	14:01	15:01	16:01	17:01	18:01	19:01	20:01	21:01	22:01	23:01	00:01	01:01	02:01	03:01	04:01	05:01	06:01	07:01	08:0
9^{01}_{am}	10^{01}_{am}	11^{01}_{am}	12^{01}_{pm}	1^{01}_{pm}	2^{01}_{pm}	3^{01}_{pm}	4^{01}_{pm}	5^{01}_{pm}	6^{01}_{pm}	7^{01}_{pm}	8^{01}_{pm}	9^{01}_{pm}	10^{01}_{pm}	11^{01}_{pm}	12^{01}_{am}	1^{01}_{am}	2^{01}_{am}	3^{01}_{am}	4^{01}_{am}	5^{01}_{am}	6^{01}_{am}	7^{01}_{am}	8^{0}_{a}
Sun	Sun	Sun	Sun	Sun	Sun	Sun	Sun	Sun	Sun	Sun	Sun	Sun	Sun	Sun	Mon	Mon	Mon	Mon	Mon	Mon	Mon	Mon	Mo

Note: Advanced Time = Daylight Saving Time = Summer Time

SVALBARD ISLANDS
Number of Time Zones: *1*

Standard Time
Period: *Last Sunday in September to Last Sunday in March*
Time Zone: *13:00 (+1hr UTC)*

[a]	[b]	[c]	[d]	[e]	[f]	[g]	[h]	[i]	[j]	[k]	[l]	[m]	[n]	[o]	[p]	[q]	[r]	[s]	[t]	[u]	[v]	[w]	[x]
13:01	14:01	15:01	16:01	17:01	18:01	19:01	20:01	21:01	22:01	23:01	00:01	01:01	02:01	03:01	04:01	05:01	06:01	07:01	08:01	09:01	10:01	11:01	12:01
1^{01}_{pm}	2^{01}_{pm}	3^{01}_{pm}	4^{01}_{pm}	5^{01}_{pm}	6^{01}_{pm}	7^{01}_{pm}	8^{01}_{pm}	9^{01}_{pm}	10^{01}_{pm}	11^{01}_{pm}	12^{01}_{am}	1^{01}_{am}	2^{01}_{am}	3^{01}_{am}	4^{01}_{am}	5^{01}_{am}	6^{01}_{am}	7^{01}_{am}	8^{01}_{am}	9^{01}_{am}	10^{01}_{am}	11^{01}_{am}	12^{01}_{pm}
Sun	Sun	Sun	Sun	Sun	Sun	Sun	Sun	Sun	Sun	Sun	Mon	Mon	Mon	Mon	Mon	Mon	Mon	Mon	Mon	Mon	Mon	Mon	Mon

Advanced Time
Period: *Last Sunday in March to Last Sunday in September*
Time Zone: *14:00 (+2hrs UTC)*

[a]	[b]	[c]	[d]	[e]	[f]	[g]	[h]	[i]	[j]	[k]	[l]	[m]	[n]	[o]	[p]	[q]	[r]	[s]	[t]	[u]	[v]	[w]	[x]
14:01	15:01	16:01	17:01	18:01	19:01	20:01	21:01	22:01	23:01	00:01	01:01	02:01	03:01	04:01	05:01	06:01	07:01	08:01	09:01	10:01	11:01	12:01	13:01
2^{01}_{pm}	3^{01}_{pm}	4^{01}_{pm}	5^{01}_{pm}	6^{01}_{pm}	7^{01}_{pm}	8^{01}_{pm}	9^{01}_{pm}	10^{01}_{pm}	11^{01}_{pm}	12^{01}_{am}	1^{01}_{am}	2^{01}_{am}	3^{01}_{am}	4^{01}_{am}	5^{01}_{am}	6^{01}_{am}	7^{01}_{am}	8^{01}_{am}	9^{01}_{am}	10^{01}_{am}	11^{01}_{am}	12^{01}_{pm}	1^{01}_{pm}
Sun	Sun	Sun	Sun	Sun	Sun	Sun	Sun	Sun	Sun	Mon	Mon	Mon	Mon	Mon	Mon	Mon	Mon	Mon	Mon	Mon	Mon	Mon	Mon

SWAZILAND
Number of Time Zones: *1*
Standard Time: *Applicable for the entire year*
Advanced Time: *Not observed*
Time Zone: *14:00 (+2hrs UTC)*

[a]	[b]	[c]	[d]	[e]	[f]	[g]	[h]	[i]	[j]	[k]	[l]	[m]	[n]	[o]	[p]	[q]	[r]	[s]	[t]	[u]	[v]	[w]	[x]
14:01	15:01	16:01	17:01	18:01	19:01	20:01	21:01	22:01	23:01	00:01	01:01	02:01	03:01	04:01	05:01	06:01	07:01	08:01	09:01	10:01	11:01	12:01	13:01
2^{01}_{pm}	3^{01}_{pm}	4^{01}_{pm}	5^{01}_{pm}	6^{01}_{pm}	7^{01}_{pm}	8^{01}_{pm}	9^{01}_{pm}	10^{01}_{pm}	11^{01}_{pm}	12^{01}_{am}	1^{01}_{am}	2^{01}_{am}	3^{01}_{am}	4^{01}_{am}	5^{01}_{am}	6^{01}_{am}	7^{01}_{am}	8^{01}_{am}	9^{01}_{am}	10^{01}_{am}	11^{01}_{am}	12^{01}_{pm}	1^{01}_{pm}
Sun	Sun	Sun	Sun	Sun	Sun	Sun	Sun	Sun	Sun	Mon	Mon	Mon	Mon	Mon	Mon	Mon	Mon	Mon	Mon	Mon	Mon	Mon	Mon

Note: Advanced Time = Daylight Saving Time = Summer Time

SWEDEN
Number of Time Zones: *1*

Standard Time
Period: *Last Sunday in September to Last Sunday in March*
Time Zone: *13:00 (+1hr UTC)*

[a]	[b]	[c]	[d]	[e]	[f]	[g]	[h]	[i]	[j]	[k]	[l]	[m]	[n]	[o]	[p]	[q]	[r]	[s]	[t]	[u]	[v]	[w]	[x]
13:01	14:01	15:01	16:01	17:01	18:01	19:01	20:01	21:01	22:01	23:01	00:01	01:01	02:01	03:01	04:01	05:01	06:01	07:01	08:01	09:01	10:01	11:01	12:01
1^{01}_{pm}	2^{01}_{pm}	3^{01}_{pm}	4^{01}_{pm}	5^{01}_{pm}	6^{01}_{pm}	7^{01}_{pm}	8^{01}_{pm}	9^{01}_{pm}	10^{01}_{pm}	11^{01}_{pm}	12^{01}_{am}	1^{01}_{am}	2^{01}_{am}	3^{01}_{am}	4^{01}_{am}	5^{01}_{am}	6^{01}_{am}	7^{01}_{am}	8^{01}_{am}	9^{01}_{am}	10^{01}_{am}	11^{01}_{am}	12^{01}_{pm}
Sun	Sun	Sun	Sun	Sun	Sun	Sun	Sun	Sun	Sun	Sun	Mon	Mon	Mon	Mon	Mon	Mon	Mon	Mon	Mon	Mon	Mon	Mon	Mon

Advanced Time
Period: *Last Sunday in March to Last Sunday in September*
Time Zone: *14:00 (+2hrs UTC)*

[a]	[b]	[c]	[d]	[e]	[f]	[g]	[h]	[i]	[j]	[k]	[l]	[m]	[n]	[o]	[p]	[q]	[r]	[s]	[t]	[u]	[v]	[w]	[x]
14:01	15:01	16:01	17:01	18:01	19:01	20:01	21:01	22:01	23:01	00:01	01:01	02:01	03:01	04:01	05:01	06:01	07:01	08:01	09:01	10:01	11:01	12:01	13:01
2^{01}_{pm}	3^{01}_{pm}	4^{01}_{pm}	5^{01}_{pm}	6^{01}_{pm}	7^{01}_{pm}	8^{01}_{pm}	9^{01}_{pm}	10^{01}_{pm}	11^{01}_{pm}	12^{01}_{am}	1^{01}_{am}	2^{01}_{am}	3^{01}_{am}	4^{01}_{am}	5^{01}_{am}	6^{01}_{am}	7^{01}_{am}	8^{01}_{am}	9^{01}_{am}	10^{01}_{am}	11^{01}_{am}	12^{01}_{pm}	1^{01}_{pm}
Sun	Sun	Sun	Sun	Sun	Sun	Sun	Sun	Sun	Sun	Mon	Mon	Mon	Mon	Mon	Mon	Mon	Mon	Mon	Mon	Mon	Mon	Mon	Mon

SWITZERLAND
Number of Time Zones: *1*

Standard Time
Period: *Last Sunday in September to Last Sunday in March*
Time Zone: *13:00 (+1hr UTC)*

[a]	[b]	[c]	[d]	[e]	[f]	[g]	[h]	[i]	[j]	[k]	[l]	[m]	[n]	[o]	[p]	[q]	[r]	[s]	[t]	[u]	[v]	[w]	[x]
13:01	14:01	15:01	16:01	17:01	18:01	19:01	20:01	21:01	22:01	23:01	00:01	01:01	02:01	03:01	04:01	05:01	06:01	07:01	08:01	09:01	10:01	11:01	12:01
1^{01}_{pm}	2^{01}_{pm}	3^{01}_{pm}	4^{01}_{pm}	5^{01}_{pm}	6^{01}_{pm}	7^{01}_{pm}	8^{01}_{pm}	9^{01}_{pm}	10^{01}_{pm}	11^{01}_{pm}	12^{01}_{am}	1^{01}_{am}	2^{01}_{am}	3^{01}_{am}	4^{01}_{am}	5^{01}_{am}	6^{01}_{am}	7^{01}_{am}	8^{01}_{am}	9^{01}_{am}	10^{01}_{am}	11^{01}_{am}	12^{01}_{pm}
Sun	Sun	Sun	Sun	Sun	Sun	Sun	Sun	Sun	Sun	Sun	Mon	Mon	Mon	Mon	Mon	Mon	Mon	Mon	Mon	Mon	Mon	Mon	Mon

Advanced Time
Period: *Last Sunday in March to Last Sunday in September*
Time Zone: *14:00 (+2hrs UTC)*

[a]	[b]	[c]	[d]	[e]	[f]	[g]	[h]	[i]	[j]	[k]	[l]	[m]	[n]	[o]	[p]	[q]	[r]	[s]	[t]	[u]	[v]	[w]	[x]
14:01	15:01	16:01	17:01	18:01	19:01	20:01	21:01	22:01	23:01	00:01	01:01	02:01	03:01	04:01	05:01	06:01	07:01	08:01	09:01	10:01	11:01	12:01	13:01
2^{01}_{pm}	3^{01}_{pm}	4^{01}_{pm}	5^{01}_{pm}	6^{01}_{pm}	7^{01}_{pm}	8^{01}_{pm}	9^{01}_{pm}	10^{01}_{pm}	11^{01}_{pm}	12^{01}_{am}	1^{01}_{am}	2^{01}_{am}	3^{01}_{am}	4^{01}_{am}	5^{01}_{am}	6^{01}_{am}	7^{01}_{am}	8^{01}_{am}	9^{01}_{am}	10^{01}_{am}	11^{01}_{am}	12^{01}_{pm}	1^{01}_{pm}
Sun	Sun	Sun	Sun	Sun	Sun	Sun	Sun	Sun	Sun	Mon	Mon	Mon	Mon	Mon	Mon	Mon	Mon	Mon	Mon	Mon	Mon	Mon	Mon

Note: Advanced Time = Daylight Saving Time = Summer Time

SYRIA

Number of Time Zones: *1*

Standard Time

Period: *Varies: Late-October to Mid-March*
Time Zone: *14:00 (+2hrs UTC)*

[a]	[b]	[c]	[d]	[e]	[f]	[g]	[h]	[i]	[j]	[k]	[l]	[m]	[n]	[o]	[p]	[q]	[r]	[s]	[t]	[u]	[v]	[w]	[x]
14:01	15:01	16:01	17:01	18:01	19:01	20:01	21:01	22:01	23:01	00:01	01:01	02:01	03:01	04:01	05:01	06:01	07:01	08:01	09:01	10:01	11:01	12:01	13:01
2^{01}_{pm}	3^{01}_{pm}	4^{01}_{pm}	5^{01}_{pm}	6^{01}_{pm}	7^{01}_{pm}	8^{01}_{pm}	9^{01}_{pm}	10^{01}_{pm}	11^{01}_{pm}	12^{01}_{am}	1^{01}_{am}	2^{01}_{am}	3^{01}_{am}	4^{01}_{am}	5^{01}_{am}	6^{01}_{am}	7^{01}_{am}	8^{01}_{am}	9^{01}_{am}	10^{01}_{am}	11^{01}_{am}	12^{01}_{pm}	1^{01}_{pm}
Sun	Sun	Sun	Sun	Sun	Sun	Sun	Sun	Sun	Sun	Mon	Mon	Mon	Mon	Mon	Mon	Mon	Mon	Mon	Mon	Mon	Mon	Mon	Mon

Advanced Time

Period: *Varies: Mid-March to Late-October*
Time Zone: *15:00 (+3hrs UTC)*

[a]	[b]	[c]	[d]	[e]	[f]	[g]	[h]	[i]	[j]	[k]	[l]	[m]	[n]	[o]	[p]	[q]	[r]	[s]	[t]	[u]	[v]	[w]	[x]
15:01	16:01	17:01	18:01	19:01	20:01	21:01	22:01	23:01	00:01	01:01	02:01	03:01	04:01	05:01	06:01	07:01	08:01	09:01	10:01	11:01	12:01	13:01	14:01
3^{01}_{pm}	4^{01}_{pm}	5^{01}_{pm}	6^{01}_{pm}	7^{01}_{pm}	8^{01}_{pm}	9^{01}_{pm}	10^{01}_{pm}	11^{01}_{pm}	12^{01}_{am}	1^{01}_{am}	2^{01}_{am}	3^{01}_{am}	4^{01}_{am}	5^{01}_{am}	6^{01}_{am}	7^{01}_{am}	8^{01}_{am}	9^{01}_{am}	10^{01}_{am}	11^{01}_{am}	12^{01}_{pm}	1^{01}_{pm}	2^{01}_{pm}
Sun	Sun	Sun	Sun	Sun	Sun	Sun	Sun	Sun	Mon	Mon	Mon	Mon	Mon	Mon	Mon	Mon	Mon	Mon	Mon	Mon	Mon	Mon	Mon

TAIWAN

Number of Time Zones: *1*
Standard Time: *Applicable for the entire year*
Advanced Time: *Not observed*
Time Zone: *20:00 (+8hrs UTC)*

[a]	[b]	[c]	[d]	[e]	[f]	[g]	[h]	[i]	[j]	[k]	[l]	[m]	[n]	[o]	[p]	[q]	[r]	[s]	[t]	[u]	[v]	[w]	[x]
20:01	21:01	22:01	23:01	00:01	01:01	02:01	03:01	04:01	05:01	06:01	07:01	08:01	09:01	10:01	11:01	12:01	13:01	14:01	15:01	16:01	17:01	18:01	19:01
8^{01}_{pm}	9^{01}_{pm}	10^{01}_{pm}	11^{01}_{pm}	12^{01}_{am}	1^{01}_{am}	2^{01}_{am}	3^{01}_{am}	4^{01}_{am}	5^{01}_{am}	6^{01}_{am}	7^{01}_{am}	8^{01}_{am}	9^{01}_{am}	10^{01}_{am}	11^{01}_{am}	12^{01}_{pm}	1^{01}_{pm}	2^{01}_{pm}	3^{01}_{pm}	4^{01}_{pm}	5^{01}_{pm}	6^{01}_{pm}	7^{01}_{pm}
Sun	Sun	Sun	Sun	Mon	Mon	Mon	Mon	Mon	Mon	Mon	Mon	Mon	Mon	Mon	Mon	Mon	Mon	Mon	Mon	Mon	Mon	Mon	Mon

Note: Advanced Time = Daylight Saving Time = Summer Time

TANZANIA

Number of Time Zones: *1*
Standard Time: *Applicable for the entire year*
Advanced Time: *Not observed*
Time Zone: *15:00 (+3hrs UTC)*

[a]	[b]	[c]	[d]	[e]	[f]	[g]	[h]	[i]	[j]	[k]	[l]	[m]	[n]	[o]	[p]	[q]	[r]	[s]	[t]	[u]	[v]	[w]	[x]
15:01	16:01	17:01	18:01	19:01	20:01	21:01	22:01	23:01	00:01	01:01	02:01	03:01	04:01	05:01	06:01	07:01	08:01	09:01	10:01	11:01	12:01	13:01	14:01
3^{01}_{pm}	4^{01}_{pm}	5^{01}_{pm}	6^{01}_{pm}	7^{01}_{pm}	8^{01}_{pm}	9^{01}_{pm}	10^{01}_{pm}	11^{01}_{pm}	12^{01}_{am}	1^{01}_{am}	2^{01}_{am}	3^{01}_{am}	4^{01}_{am}	5^{01}_{am}	6^{01}_{am}	7^{01}_{am}	8^{01}_{am}	9^{01}_{am}	10^{01}_{am}	11^{01}_{am}	12^{01}_{pm}	1^{01}_{pm}	2^{01}_{pm}
Sun	Sun	Sun	Sun	Sun	Sun	Sun	Sun	Sun	Mon	Mon	Mon	Mon	Mon	Mon	Mon	Mon	Mon	Mon	Mon	Mon	Mon	Mon	Mon

THAILAND

Number of Time Zones: *1*
Standard Time: *Applicable for the entire year*
Advanced Time: *Not observed*
Time Zone: *19:00 (+7hrs UTC)*

[a]	[b]	[c]	[d]	[e]	[f]	[g]	[h]	[i]	[j]	[k]	[l]	[m]	[n]	[o]	[p]	[q]	[r]	[s]	[t]	[u]	[v]	[w]	[x]
19:01	20:01	21:01	22:01	23:01	00:01	01:01	02:01	03:01	04:01	05:01	06:01	07:01	08:01	09:01	10:01	11:01	12:01	13:01	14:01	15:01	16:01	17:01	18:01
7^{01}_{pm}	8^{01}_{pm}	9^{01}_{pm}	10^{01}_{pm}	11^{01}_{pm}	12^{01}_{am}	1^{01}_{am}	2^{01}_{am}	3^{01}_{am}	4^{01}_{am}	5^{01}_{am}	6^{01}_{am}	7^{01}_{am}	8^{01}_{am}	9^{01}_{am}	10^{01}_{am}	11^{01}_{am}	12^{01}_{pm}	1^{01}_{pm}	2^{01}_{pm}	3^{01}_{pm}	4^{01}_{pm}	5^{01}_{pm}	6^{01}_{pm}
Sun	Sun	Sun	Sun	Sun	Mon	Mon	Mon	Mon	Mon	Mon	Mon	Mon	Mon	Mon	Mon	Mon	Mon	Mon	Mon	Mon	Mon	Mon	Mon

TOBAGO

Number of Time Zones: *1*
Standard Time: *Applicable for the entire year*
Advanced Time: *Not observed*
Time Zone: *08:00 (-4hrs UTC)*

[a]	[b]	[c]	[d]	[e]	[f]	[g]	[h]	[i]	[j]	[k]	[l]	[m]	[n]	[o]	[p]	[q]	[r]	[s]	[t]	[u]	[v]	[w]	[x]
08:01	09:01	10:01	11:01	12:01	13:01	14:01	15:01	16:01	17:01	18:01	19:01	20:01	21:01	22:01	23:01	00:01	01:01	02:01	03:01	04:01	05:01	06:01	07:01
8^{01}_{am}	9^{01}_{am}	10^{01}_{am}	11^{01}_{am}	12^{01}_{pm}	1^{01}_{pm}	2^{01}_{pm}	3^{01}_{pm}	4^{01}_{pm}	5^{01}_{pm}	6^{01}_{pm}	7^{01}_{pm}	8^{01}_{pm}	9^{01}_{pm}	10^{01}_{pm}	11^{01}_{pm}	12^{01}_{am}	1^{01}_{am}	2^{01}_{am}	3^{01}_{am}	4^{01}_{am}	5^{01}_{am}	6^{01}_{am}	7^{01}_{am}
Sun	Sun	Sun	Sun	Sun	Sun	Sun	Sun	Sun	Sun	Sun	Sun	Sun	Sun	Sun	Sun	Sun	Mon	Mon	Mon	Mon	Mon	Mon	Mon

Note: Advanced Time = Daylight Saving Time = Summer Time

TOGO

Number of Time Zones: *1*
Standard Time: *Applicable for the entire year*
Advanced Time: *Not observed*
Time Zone: *12:00 (UTC)*

[a]	[b]	[c]	[d]	[e]	[f]	[g]	[h]	[i]	[j]	[k]	[l]	[m]	[n]	[o]	[p]	[q]	[r]	[s]	[t]	[u]	[v]	[w]	[x]
2:01	13:01	14:01	15:01	16:01	17:01	18:01	19:01	20:01	21:01	22:01	23:01	00:01	01:01	02:01	03:01	04:01	05:01	06:01	07:01	08:01	09:01	10:01	11:01
12^{01}_{pm}	1^{01}_{pm}	2^{01}_{pm}	3^{01}_{pm}	4^{01}_{pm}	5^{01}_{pm}	6^{01}_{pm}	7^{01}_{pm}	8^{01}_{pm}	9^{01}_{pm}	10^{01}_{pm}	11^{01}_{pm}	12^{01}_{am}	1^{01}_{am}	2^{01}_{am}	3^{01}_{am}	4^{01}_{am}	5^{01}_{am}	6^{01}_{am}	7^{01}_{am}	8^{01}_{am}	9^{01}_{am}	10^{01}_{am}	11^{01}_{am}
Sun	Sun	Sun	Sun	Sun	Sun	Sun	Sun	Sun	Sun	Sun	Sun	Mon	Mon	Mon	Mon	Mon	Mon	Mon	Mon	Mon	Mon	Mon	Mon

TOKELAU

Number of Time Zones: *1*
Standard Time: *Applicable for the entire year*
Advanced Time: *Not observed*
Time Zone: *01:00 (-11hrs UTC)*

[a]	[b]	[c]	[d]	[e]	[f]	[g]	[h]	[i]	[j]	[k]	[l]	[m]	[n]	[o]	[p]	[q]	[r]	[s]	[t]	[u]	[v]	[w]	[x]
1:01	02:01	03:01	04:01	05:01	06:01	07:01	08:01	09:01	10:01	11:01	12:01	13:01	14:01	15:01	16:01	17:01	18:01	19:01	20:01	21:01	22:01	23:01	00:01
1^{01}_{am}	2^{01}_{am}	3^{01}_{am}	4^{01}_{am}	5^{01}_{am}	6^{01}_{am}	7^{01}_{am}	8^{01}_{am}	9^{01}_{am}	10^{01}_{am}	11^{01}_{am}	12^{01}_{pm}	1^{01}_{pm}	2^{01}_{pm}	3^{01}_{pm}	4^{01}_{pm}	5^{01}_{pm}	6^{01}_{pm}	7^{01}_{pm}	8^{01}_{pm}	9^{01}_{pm}	10^{01}_{pm}	11^{01}_{pm}	12^{01}_{am}
Sun	Sun	Sun	Sun	Sun	Sun	Sun	Sun	Sun	Sun	Sun	Sun	Sun	Sun	Sun	Sun	Sun	Sun	Sun	Sun	Sun	Sun	Sun	Mon

TONGA

Number of Time Zones: *1*
Standard Time: *Applicable for the entire year*
Advanced Time: *Not observed*
Time Zone: *25:00 (+13hrs UTC)*

[a]	[b]	[c]	[d]	[e]	[f]	[g]	[h]	[i]	[j]	[k]	[l]	[m]	[n]	[o]	[p]	[q]	[r]	[s]	[t]	[u]	[v]	[w]	[x]
1:01	02:01	03:01	04:01	05:01	06:01	07:01	08:01	09:01	10:01	11:01	12:01	13:01	14:01	15:01	16:01	17:01	18:01	19:01	20:01	21:01	22:01	23:01	00:01
1^{01}_{am}	2^{01}_{am}	3^{01}_{am}	4^{01}_{am}	5^{01}_{am}	6^{01}_{am}	7^{01}_{am}	8^{01}_{am}	9^{01}_{am}	10^{01}_{am}	11^{01}_{am}	12^{01}_{pm}	1^{01}_{pm}	2^{01}_{pm}	3^{01}_{pm}	4^{01}_{pm}	5^{01}_{pm}	6^{01}_{pm}	7^{01}_{pm}	8^{01}_{pm}	9^{01}_{pm}	10^{01}_{pm}	11^{01}_{pm}	12^{01}_{am}
Mon	Mon	Mon	Mon	Mon	Mon	Mon	Mon	Mon	Mon	Mon	Mon	Mon	Mon	Mon	Mon	Mon	Mon	Mon	Mon	Mon	Mon	Mon	Tue

Note: Advanced Time = Daylight Saving Time = Summer Time

TRINIDAD AND TOBAGO

Number of Time Zones: *1*
Standard Time: *Applicable for the entire year*
Advanced Time: *Not observed*
Time Zone: *08:00 (-4hrs UTC)*

[a]	[b]	[c]	[d]	[e]	[f]	[g]	[h]	[i]	[j]	[k]	[l]	[m]	[n]	[o]	[p]	[q]	[r]	[s]	[t]	[u]	[v]	[w]	[x]
08:01	09:01	10:01	11:01	12:01	13:01	14:01	15:01	16:01	17:01	18:01	19:01	20:01	21:01	22:01	23:01	00:01	01:01	02:01	03:01	04:01	05:01	06:01	07:01
8^{01}_{am}	9^{01}_{am}	10^{01}_{am}	11^{01}_{am}	12^{01}_{pm}	1^{01}_{pm}	2^{01}_{pm}	3^{01}_{pm}	4^{01}_{pm}	5^{01}_{pm}	6^{01}_{pm}	7^{01}_{pm}	8^{01}_{pm}	9^{01}_{pm}	10^{01}_{pm}	11^{01}_{pm}	12^{01}_{am}	1^{01}_{am}	2^{01}_{am}	3^{01}_{am}	4^{01}_{am}	5^{01}_{am}	6^{01}_{am}	7^{01}_{am}
Sun	Sun	Sun	Sun	Sun	Sun	Sun	Sun	Sun	Sun	Sun	Sun	Sun	Sun	Sun	Sun	Mon	Mon	Mon	Mon	Mon	Mon	Mon	Mon

TRISTAN DA CUNHA

Number of Time Zones: *1*

Standard Time

Period: *Third Sunday in April to Second Sunday in September*
Time Zone: *12:00 (UTC)*

[a]	[b]	[c]	[d]	[e]	[f]	[g]	[h]	[i]	[j]	[k]	[l]	[m]	[n]	[o]	[p]	[q]	[r]	[s]	[t]	[u]	[v]	[w]	[x]
12:01	13:01	14:01	15:01	16:01	17:01	18:01	19:01	20:01	21:01	22:01	23:01	00:01	01:01	02:01	03:01	04:01	05:01	06:01	07:01	08:01	09:01	10:01	11:01
12^{01}_{pm}	1^{01}_{pm}	2^{01}_{pm}	3^{01}_{pm}	4^{01}_{pm}	5^{01}_{pm}	6^{01}_{pm}	7^{01}_{pm}	8^{01}_{pm}	9^{01}_{pm}	10^{01}_{pm}	11^{01}_{pm}	12^{01}_{am}	1^{01}_{am}	2^{01}_{am}	3^{01}_{am}	4^{01}_{am}	5^{01}_{am}	6^{01}_{am}	7^{01}_{am}	8^{01}_{am}	9^{01}_{am}	10^{01}_{am}	11^{01}_{am}
Sun	Sun	Sun	Sun	Sun	Sun	Sun	Sun	Sun	Sun	Sun	Sun	Mon	Mon	Mon	Mon	Mon	Mon	Mon	Mon	Mon	Mon	Mon	Mon

Advanced Time

Period: *Second Sunday in September to Third Sunday in April*
Time Zone: *13:00 (+1hr UTC)*

[a]	[b]	[c]	[d]	[e]	[f]	[g]	[h]	[i]	[j]	[k]	[l]	[m]	[n]	[o]	[p]	[q]	[r]	[s]	[t]	[u]	[v]	[w]	[x]
13:01	14:01	15:01	16:01	17:01	18:01	19:01	20:01	21:01	22:01	23:01	00:01	01:01	02:01	03:01	04:01	05:01	06:01	07:01	08:01	09:01	10:01	11:01	12:01
1^{01}_{pm}	2^{01}_{pm}	3^{01}_{pm}	4^{01}_{pm}	5^{01}_{pm}	6^{01}_{pm}	7^{01}_{pm}	8^{01}_{pm}	9^{01}_{pm}	10^{01}_{pm}	11^{01}_{pm}	12^{01}_{am}	1^{01}_{am}	2^{01}_{am}	3^{01}_{am}	4^{01}_{am}	5^{01}_{am}	6^{01}_{am}	7^{01}_{am}	8^{01}_{am}	9^{01}_{am}	10^{01}_{am}	11^{01}_{am}	12^{01}_{pm}
Sun	Sun	Sun	Sun	Sun	Sun	Sun	Sun	Sun	Sun	Sun	Mon	Mon	Mon	Mon	Mon	Mon	Mon	Mon	Mon	Mon	Mon	Mon	Mon

Note: Advanced Time = Daylight Saving Time = Summer Time

TUNISIA

Number of Time Zones: *1*

Standard Time

Period: *Last Sunday in September to Second Sunday in April*
Time Zone: *13:00 (+1hr UTC)*

[a]	[b]	[c]	[d]	[e]	[f]	[g]	[h]	[i]	[j]	[k]	[l]	[m]	[n]	[o]	[p]	[q]	[r]	[s]	[t]	[u]	[v]	[w]	[x]
…01	14:01	15:01	16:01	17:01	18:01	19:01	20:01	21:01	22:01	23:01	00:01	01:01	02:01	03:01	04:01	05:01	06:01	07:01	08:01	09:01	10:01	11:01	12:01
1^{01}_{pm}	2^{01}_{pm}	3^{01}_{pm}	4^{01}_{pm}	5^{01}_{pm}	6^{01}_{pm}	7^{01}_{pm}	8^{01}_{pm}	9^{01}_{pm}	10^{01}_{pm}	11^{01}_{pm}	12^{01}_{am}	1^{01}_{am}	2^{01}_{am}	3^{01}_{am}	4^{01}_{am}	5^{01}_{am}	6^{01}_{am}	7^{01}_{am}	8^{01}_{am}	9^{01}_{am}	10^{01}_{am}	11^{01}_{am}	12^{01}_{pm}
Sun	Sun	Sun	Sun	Sun	Sun	Sun	Sun	Sun	Sun	Sun	Mon	Mon	Mon	Mon	Mon	Mon	Mon	Mon	Mon	Mon	Mon	Mon	Mon

Advanced Time

Period: *Second Sunday in April to Last Sunday in September*
Time Zone: *14:00 (+2hrs UTC)*

[a]	[b]	[c]	[d]	[e]	[f]	[g]	[h]	[i]	[j]	[k]	[l]	[m]	[n]	[o]	[p]	[q]	[r]	[s]	[t]	[u]	[v]	[w]	[x]
…01	15:01	16:01	17:01	18:01	19:01	20:01	21:01	22:01	23:01	00:01	01:01	02:01	03:01	04:01	05:01	06:01	07:01	08:01	09:01	10:01	11:01	12:01	13:01
2^{01}_{pm}	3^{01}_{pm}	4^{01}_{pm}	5^{01}_{pm}	6^{01}_{pm}	7^{01}_{pm}	8^{01}_{pm}	9^{01}_{pm}	10^{01}_{pm}	11^{01}_{pm}	12^{01}_{am}	1^{01}_{am}	2^{01}_{am}	3^{01}_{am}	4^{01}_{am}	5^{01}_{am}	6^{01}_{am}	7^{01}_{am}	8^{01}_{am}	9^{01}_{am}	10^{01}_{am}	11^{01}_{am}	12^{01}_{pm}	1^{01}_{pm}
Sun	Sun	Sun	Sun	Sun	Sun	Sun	Sun	Sun	Sun	Sun	Mon	Mon	Mon	Mon	Mon	Mon	Mon	Mon	Mon	Mon	Mon	Mon	Mon

TURKEY

Number of Time Zones: *1*

Standard Time

Period: *Last Sunday in September to Last Sunday in March*
Time Zone: *14:00 (+2hrs UTC)*

[a]	[b]	[c]	[d]	[e]	[f]	[g]	[h]	[i]	[j]	[k]	[l]	[m]	[n]	[o]	[p]	[q]	[r]	[s]	[t]	[u]	[v]	[w]	[x]
…01	15:01	16:01	17:01	18:01	19:01	20:01	21:01	22:01	23:01	00:01	01:01	02:01	03:01	04:01	05:01	06:01	07:01	08:01	09:01	10:01	11:01	12:01	13:01
2^{01}_{pm}	3^{01}_{pm}	4^{01}_{pm}	5^{01}_{pm}	6^{01}_{pm}	7^{01}_{pm}	8^{01}_{pm}	9^{01}_{pm}	10^{01}_{pm}	11^{01}_{pm}	12^{01}_{am}	1^{01}_{am}	2^{01}_{am}	3^{01}_{am}	4^{01}_{am}	5^{01}_{am}	6^{01}_{am}	7^{01}_{am}	8^{01}_{am}	9^{01}_{am}	10^{01}_{am}	11^{01}_{am}	12^{01}_{pm}	1^{01}_{pm}
Sun	Sun	Sun	Sun	Sun	Sun	Sun	Sun	Sun	Sun	Sun	Mon	Mon	Mon	Mon	Mon	Mon	Mon	Mon	Mon	Mon	Mon	Mon	Mon

Advanced Time

Period: *Last Sunday in March to Last Sunday in September*
Time Zone: *15:00 (+3hrs UTC)*

[a]	[b]	[c]	[d]	[e]	[f]	[g]	[h]	[i]	[j]	[k]	[l]	[m]	[n]	[o]	[p]	[q]	[r]	[s]	[t]	[u]	[v]	[w]	[x]
…01	16:01	17:01	18:01	19:01	20:01	21:01	22:01	23:01	00:01	01:01	02:01	03:01	04:01	05:01	06:01	07:01	08:01	09:01	10:01	11:01	12:01	13:01	14:01
3^{01}_{pm}	4^{01}_{pm}	5^{01}_{pm}	6^{01}_{pm}	7^{01}_{pm}	8^{01}_{pm}	9^{01}_{pm}	10^{01}_{pm}	11^{01}_{pm}	12^{01}_{am}	1^{01}_{am}	2^{01}_{am}	3^{01}_{am}	4^{01}_{am}	5^{01}_{am}	6^{01}_{am}	7^{01}_{am}	8^{01}_{am}	9^{01}_{am}	10^{01}_{am}	11^{01}_{am}	12^{01}_{pm}	1^{01}_{pm}	2^{01}_{pm}
Sun	Sun	Sun	Sun	Sun	Sun	Sun	Sun	Sun	Sun	Sun	Mon	Mon	Mon	Mon	Mon	Mon	Mon	Mon	Mon	Mon	Mon	Mon	Mon

Note: Advanced Time = Daylight Saving Time = Summer Time

TURKS AND CAICOS ISLANDS
Number of Time Zones: *1*

Standard Time
Period: *Last Sunday in October to First Sunday in April*
Time Zone: *07:00 (-5hrs UTC)*

[a]	[b]	[c]	[d]	[e]	[f]	[g]	[h]	[i]	[j]	[k]	[l]	[m]	[n]	[o]	[p]	[q]	[r]	[s]	[t]	[u]	[v]	[w]	[x
07:01	08:01	09:01	10:01	11:01	12:01	13:01	14:01	15:01	16:01	17:01	18:01	19:01	20:01	21:01	22:01	23:01	00:01	01:01	02:01	03:01	04:01	05:01	06:0
7^{01}_{am}	8^{01}_{am}	9^{01}_{am}	10^{01}_{am}	11^{01}_{am}	12^{01}_{pm}	1^{01}_{pm}	2^{01}_{pm}	3^{01}_{pm}	4^{01}_{pm}	5^{01}_{pm}	6^{01}_{pm}	7^{01}_{pm}	8^{01}_{pm}	9^{01}_{pm}	10^{01}_{pm}	11^{01}_{pm}	12^{01}_{am}	1^{01}_{am}	2^{01}_{am}	3^{01}_{am}	4^{01}_{am}	5^{01}_{am}	6^{0}_{ar}
Sun	Sun	Sun	Sun	Sun	Sun	Sun	Sun	Sun	Sun	Sun	Sun	Sun	Sun	Sun	Sun	Sun	Sun	Mon	Mon	Mon	Mon	Mon	Mo

Advanced Time
Period: *First Sunday in April to Last Sunday in October*
Time Zone: *08:00 (-4hrs UTC)*

[a]	[b]	[c]	[d]	[e]	[f]	[g]	[h]	[i]	[j]	[k]	[l]	[m]	[n]	[o]	[p]	[q]	[r]	[s]	[t]	[u]	[v]	[w]	[x
08:01	09:01	10:01	11:01	12:01	13:01	14:01	15:01	16:01	17:01	18:01	19:01	20:01	21:01	22:01	23:01	00:01	01:01	02:01	03:01	04:01	05:01	06:01	07:0
8^{01}_{am}	9^{01}_{am}	10^{01}_{am}	11^{01}_{am}	12^{01}_{pm}	1^{01}_{pm}	2^{01}_{pm}	3^{01}_{pm}	4^{01}_{pm}	5^{01}_{pm}	6^{01}_{pm}	7^{01}_{pm}	8^{01}_{pm}	9^{01}_{pm}	10^{01}_{pm}	11^{01}_{pm}	12^{01}_{am}	1^{01}_{am}	2^{01}_{am}	3^{01}_{am}	4^{01}_{am}	5^{01}_{am}	6^{01}_{am}	7^{0}_{a}
Sun	Sun	Sun	Sun	Sun	Sun	Sun	Sun	Sun	Sun	Sun	Sun	Sun	Sun	Sun	Sun	Mon	Mon	Mon	Mon	Mon	Mon	Mon	Mo

TUVALU
Number of Time Zones: *1*
Standard Time: *Applicable for the entire year*
Advanced Time: *Not observed*
Time Zone: *24:00 (+12hrs UTC)*

[a]	[b]	[c]	[d]	[e]	[f]	[g]	[h]	[i]	[j]	[k]	[l]	[m]	[n]	[o]	[p]	[q]	[r]	[s]	[t]	[u]	[v]	[w]	[x
00:01	01:01	02:01	03:01	04:01	05:01	06:01	07:01	08:01	09:01	10:01	11:01	12:01	13:01	14:01	15:01	16:01	17:01	18:01	19:01	20:01	21:01	22:01	23:0
12^{01}_{am}	1^{01}_{am}	2^{01}_{am}	3^{01}_{am}	4^{01}_{am}	5^{01}_{am}	6^{01}_{am}	7^{01}_{am}	8^{01}_{am}	9^{01}_{am}	10^{01}_{am}	11^{01}_{am}	12^{01}_{pm}	1^{01}_{pm}	2^{01}_{pm}	3^{01}_{pm}	4^{01}_{pm}	5^{01}_{pm}	6^{01}_{pm}	7^{01}_{pm}	8^{01}_{pm}	9^{01}_{pm}	10^{01}_{pm}	11^{0}
Mon	Mon	Mon	Mon	Mon	Mon	Mon	Mon	Mon	Mon	Mon	Mon	Mon	Mon	Mon	Mon	Mon	Mon	Mon	Mon	Mon	Mon	Mon	Mc

UGANDA
Number of Time Zones: *1*
Standard Time: *Applicable for the entire year*
Advanced Time: *Not observed*
Time Zone: *15:00 (+3hrs UTC)*

[a]	[b]	[c]	[d]	[e]	[f]	[g]	[h]	[i]	[j]	[k]	[l]	[m]	[n]	[o]	[p]	[q]	[r]	[s]	[t]	[u]	[v]	[w]	[x
15:01	16:01	17:01	18:01	19:01	20:01	21:01	22:01	23:01	00:01	01:01	02:01	03:01	04:01	05:01	06:01	07:01	08:01	09:01	10:01	11:01	12:01	13:01	14:
3^{01}_{pm}	4^{01}_{pm}	5^{01}_{pm}	6^{01}_{pm}	7^{01}_{pm}	8^{01}_{pm}	9^{01}_{pm}	10^{01}_{pm}	11^{01}_{pm}	12^{01}_{am}	1^{01}_{am}	2^{01}_{am}	3^{01}_{am}	4^{01}_{am}	5^{01}_{am}	6^{01}_{am}	7^{01}_{am}	8^{01}_{am}	9^{01}_{am}	10^{01}_{am}	11^{01}_{am}	12^{01}_{pm}	1^{01}_{pm}	2_{p}
Sun	Sun	Sun	Sun	Sun	Sun	Sun	Sun	Sun	Mon	Mon	Mon	Mon	Mon	Mon	Mon	Mon	Mon	Mon	Mon	Mon	Mon	Mon	Mc

Note: Advanced Time = Daylight Saving Time = Summer Time

UNITED ARAB EMIRATES
Number of Time Zones: *1*
Standard Time: *Applicable for the entire year*
Advanced Time: *Not observed*
Time Zone: *16:00 (+4hrs UTC)*

[a]	[b]	[c]	[d]	[e]	[f]	[g]	[h]	[i]	[j]	[k]	[l]	[m]	[n]	[o]	[p]	[q]	[r]	[s]	[t]	[u]	[v]	[w]	[x]
16:01	17:01	18:01	19:01	20:01	21:01	22:01	23:01	00:01	01:01	02:01	03:01	04:01	05:01	06:01	07:01	08:01	09:01	10:01	11:01	12:01	13:01	14:01	15:01
4:01pm	5:01pm	6:01pm	7:01pm	8:01pm	9:01pm	10:01pm	11:01pm	12:01am	1:01am	2:01am	3:01am	4:01am	5:01am	6:01am	7:01am	8:01am	9:01am	10:01am	11:01am	12:01pm	1:01pm	2:01pm	3:01pm
Sun	Sun	Sun	Sun	Sun	Sun	Sun	Sun	Mon	Mon	Mon	Mon	Mon	Mon	Mon	Mon	Mon	Mon	Mon	Mon	Mon	Mon	Mon	Mon

UNITED KINGDOM
Number of Time Zones: *1*

Standard Time
Period: *Fourth Sunday in October to Last Sunday in March*
Time Zone: *12:00 (UTC)*

[a]	[b]	[c]	[d]	[e]	[f]	[g]	[h]	[i]	[j]	[k]	[l]	[m]	[n]	[o]	[p]	[q]	[r]	[s]	[t]	[u]	[v]	[w]	[x]
12:01	13:01	14:01	15:01	16:01	17:01	18:01	19:01	20:01	21:01	22:01	23:01	00:01	01:01	02:01	03:01	04:01	05:01	06:01	07:01	08:01	09:01	10:01	11:01
12:01pm	1:01pm	2:01pm	3:01pm	4:01pm	5:01pm	6:01pm	7:01pm	8:01pm	9:01pm	10:01pm	11:01pm	12:01am	1:01am	2:01am	3:01am	4:01am	5:01am	6:01am	7:01am	8:01am	9:01am	10:01am	11:01am
Sun	Sun	Sun	Sun	Sun	Sun	Sun	Sun	Sun	Sun	Sun	Sun	Mon	Mon	Mon	Mon	Mon	Mon	Mon	Mon	Mon	Mon	Mon	Mon

Advanced Time
Period: *Last Sunday in March to Fourth Sunday in October*
Time Zone: *13:00 (+1hr UTC)*

[a]	[b]	[c]	[d]	[e]	[f]	[g]	[h]	[i]	[j]	[k]	[l]	[m]	[n]	[o]	[p]	[q]	[r]	[s]	[t]	[u]	[v]	[w]	[x]
13:01	14:01	15:01	16:01	17:01	18:01	19:01	20:01	21:01	22:01	23:01	00:01	01:01	02:01	03:01	04:01	05:01	06:01	07:01	08:01	09:01	10:01	11:01	12:01
1:01pm	2:01pm	3:01pm	4:01pm	5:01pm	6:01pm	7:01pm	8:01pm	9:01pm	10:01pm	11:01pm	12:01am	1:01am	2:01am	3:01am	4:01am	5:01am	6:01am	7:01am	8:01am	9:01am	10:01am	11:01am	12:01pm
Sun	Sun	Sun	Sun	Sun	Sun	Sun	Sun	Sun	Sun	Sun	Mon	Mon	Mon	Mon	Mon	Mon	Mon	Mon	Mon	Mon	Mon	Mon	Mon

Note: Advanced Time = Daylight Saving Time = Summer Time

UNITED STATES

Number of Time Zones: *6*
Notes: *Advanced Time observed irregularly;*
See Reference Map I for graphic depiction of time zones

EASTERN TIME ZONE

Note: *Comprises Connecticut, Delaware, District of Columbia, Florida,
Georgia, Indiana except for six northwestern and five southwestern
counties, eastern half of Kentucky, Maine, Maryland, Massachusetts,
Michigan, New Jersey, New York, North Carolina, Pennsylvania, Rhode Island,
South Carolina, eastern third of Tennessee, and Vermont*

Standard Time

Period: *Last Sunday in October to First Sunday in April*
Time Zone: *07:00 (-5hrs UTC)*

[a]	[b]	[c]	[d]	[e]	[f]	[g]	[h]	[i]	[j]	[k]	[l]	[m]	[n]	[o]	[p]	[q]	[r]	[s]	[t]	[u]	[v]	[w]	[
07:01	08:01	09:01	10:01	11:01	12:01	13:01	14:01	15:01	16:01	17:01	18:01	19:01	20:01	21:01	22:01	23:01	00:01	01:01	02:01	03:01	04:01	05:01	06:
7^{01}_{am}	8^{01}_{am}	9^{01}_{am}	10^{01}_{am}	11^{01}_{am}	12^{01}_{pm}	1^{01}_{pm}	2^{01}_{pm}	3^{01}_{pm}	4^{01}_{pm}	5^{01}_{pm}	6^{01}_{pm}	7^{01}_{pm}	8^{01}_{pm}	9^{01}_{pm}	10^{01}_{pm}	11^{01}_{pm}	12^{01}_{am}	1^{01}_{am}	2^{01}_{am}	3^{01}_{am}	4^{01}_{am}	5^{01}_{am}	6
Sun	Sun	Sun	Sun	Sun	Sun	Sun	Sun	Sun	Sun	Sun	Sun	Sun	Sun	Sun	Sun	Sun	Mon	Mon	Mon	Mon	Mon	Mon	M

Advanced Time

Period: *First Sunday in April to Last Sunday in October*
Note: *The portion of Indiana that is in Eastern Time Zone does not
observe Advanced Time; all other areas listed above do observe Advanced
Time*
Time Zone: *08:00 (-4hrs UTC)*

[a]	[b]	[c]	[d]	[e]	[f]	[g]	[h]	[i]	[j]	[k]	[l]	[m]	[n]	[o]	[p]	[q]	[r]	[s]	[t]	[u]	[v]	[w]	[
08:01	09:01	10:01	11:01	12:01	13:01	14:01	15:01	16:01	17:01	18:01	19:01	20:01	21:01	22:01	23:01	00:01	01:01	02:01	03:01	04:01	05:01	06:01	07:
8^{01}_{am}	9^{01}_{am}	10^{01}_{am}	11^{01}_{am}	12^{01}_{pm}	1^{01}_{pm}	2^{01}_{pm}	3^{01}_{pm}	4^{01}_{pm}	5^{01}_{pm}	6^{01}_{pm}	7^{01}_{pm}	8^{01}_{pm}	9^{01}_{pm}	10^{01}_{pm}	11^{01}_{pm}	12^{01}_{am}	1^{01}_{am}	2^{01}_{am}	3^{01}_{am}	4^{01}_{am}	5^{01}_{am}	6^{01}_{am}	7
Sun	Sun	Sun	Sun	Sun	Sun	Sun	Sun	Sun	Sun	Sun	Sun	Sun	Sun	Sun	Sun	Mon	Mon	Mon	Mon	Mon	Mon	Mon	M

Note: Advanced Time = Daylight Saving Time = Summer Time

UNITED STATES *(Continued)*

CENTRAL TIME ZONE

Note: *Comprises Alabama, Arkansas, Illinois, six northwestern and five southwestern counties of Indiana, Iowa, Kansas except for five western counties, western half of Kentucky, Louisiana, Minnesota, Mississippi, Missouri, eastern two thirds of Nebraska, North Dakota except for southwestern quarter, eastern half of South Dakota, western two-thirds of Tennessee, Texas except for two westernmost counties, and Wisconsin*

Standard Time

Period: *Last Sunday in October to First Sunday in April*
Time Zone: *06:00 (-6hrs UTC)*

[a]	[b]	[c]	[d]	[e]	[f]	[g]	[h]	[i]	[j]	[k]	[l]	[m]	[n]	[o]	[p]	[q]	[r]	[s]	[t]	[u]	[v]	[w]	[x]
06:01	07:01	08:01	09:01	10:01	11:01	12:01	13:01	14:01	15:01	16:01	17:01	18:01	19:01	20:01	21:01	22:01	23:01	00:01	01:01	02:01	03:01	04:01	05:01
6^{01}_{am}	7^{01}_{am}	8^{01}_{am}	9^{01}_{am}	10^{01}_{am}	11^{01}_{am}	12^{01}_{pm}	1^{01}_{pm}	2^{01}_{pm}	3^{01}_{pm}	4^{01}_{pm}	5^{01}_{pm}	6^{01}_{pm}	7^{01}_{pm}	8^{01}_{pm}	9^{01}_{pm}	10^{01}_{pm}	11^{01}_{pm}	12^{01}_{am}	1^{01}_{am}	2^{01}_{am}	3^{01}_{am}	4^{01}_{am}	5^{01}_{am}
Sun	Sun	Sun	Sun	Sun	Sun	Sun	Sun	Sun	Sun	Sun	Sun	Sun	Sun	Sun	Sun	Sun	Sun	Mon	Mon	Mon	Mon	Mon	Mon

Advanced Time

Period: *First Sunday in April to Last Sunday in October*
Time Zone: *07:00 (-5hrs UTC)*

[a]	[b]	[c]	[d]	[e]	[f]	[g]	[h]	[i]	[j]	[k]	[l]	[m]	[n]	[o]	[p]	[q]	[r]	[s]	[t]	[u]	[v]	[w]	[x]
07:01	08:01	09:01	10:01	11:01	12:01	13:01	14:01	15:01	16:01	17:01	18:01	19:01	20:01	21:01	22:01	23:01	00:01	01:01	02:01	03:01	04:01	05:01	06:01
7^{01}_{am}	8^{01}_{am}	9^{01}_{am}	10^{01}_{am}	11^{01}_{am}	12^{01}_{pm}	1^{01}_{pm}	2^{01}_{pm}	3^{01}_{pm}	4^{01}_{pm}	5^{01}_{pm}	6^{01}_{pm}	7^{01}_{pm}	8^{01}_{pm}	9^{01}_{pm}	10^{01}_{pm}	11^{01}_{pm}	12^{01}_{am}	1^{01}_{am}	2^{01}_{am}	3^{01}_{am}	4^{01}_{am}	5^{01}_{am}	6^{01}_{am}
Sun	Sun	Sun	Sun	Sun	Sun	Sun	Sun	Sun	Sun	Sun	Sun	Sun	Sun	Sun	Sun	Sun	Mon	Mon	Mon	Mon	Mon	Mon	Mon

Note: Advanced Time = Daylight Saving Time = Summer Time

UNITED STATES *(Continued)*

MOUNTAIN TIME ZONE

Note: *Comprises Arizona, Colorado, southern half of Idaho, five western counties of Kansas, Montana, western third of Nebraska, New Mexico, southwestern quarter of North Dakota, northern four-fifths of Malheur County in Oregon, western half of South Dakota, and Wyoming.*

Standard Time

Period: *Last Sunday in October to First Sunday in April*
Time Zone: *05:00 (-7hrs UTC)*

[a]	[b]	[c]	[d]	[e]	[f]	[g]	[h]	[i]	[j]	[k]	[l]	[m]	[n]	[o]	[p]	[q]	[r]	[s]	[t]	[u]	[v]	[w]	[x]
05:01	06:01	07:01	08:01	09:01	10:01	11:01	12:01	13:01	14:01	15:01	16:01	17:01	18:01	19:01	20:01	21:01	22:01	23:01	00:01	01:01	02:01	03:01	04:01
5^{01}_{am}	6^{01}_{am}	7^{01}_{am}	8^{01}_{am}	9^{01}_{am}	10^{01}_{am}	11^{01}_{am}	12^{01}_{pm}	1^{01}_{pm}	2^{01}_{pm}	3^{01}_{pm}	4^{01}_{pm}	5^{01}_{pm}	6^{01}_{pm}	7^{01}_{pm}	8^{01}_{pm}	9^{01}_{pm}	10^{01}_{pm}	11^{01}_{pm}	12^{01}_{am}	1^{01}_{am}	2^{01}_{am}	3^{01}_{am}	4^{01}_{am}
Sun	Sun	Sun	Sun	Sun	Sun	Sun	Sun	Sun	Sun	Sun	Sun	Sun	Sun	Sun	Sun	Sun	Sun	Sun	Sun	Mon	Mon	Mon	Mon	Mon

Advanced Time

Period: *First Sunday in April to Last Sunday in October*
Note: *Arizona does not observe Advanced Time; all other areas listed above do*
Time Zone: *06:00 (-6hrs UTC)*

[a]	[b]	[c]	[d]	[e]	[f]	[g]	[h]	[i]	[j]	[k]	[l]	[m]	[n]	[o]	[p]	[q]	[r]	[s]	[t]	[u]	[v]	[w]	[x]
06:01	07:01	08:01	09:01	10:01	11:01	12:01	13:01	14:01	15:01	16:01	17:01	18:01	19:01	20:01	21:01	22:01	23:01	00:01	01:01	02:01	03:01	04:01	05:01
6^{01}_{am}	7^{01}_{am}	8^{01}_{am}	9^{01}_{am}	10^{01}_{am}	11^{01}_{am}	12^{01}_{pm}	1^{01}_{pm}	2^{01}_{pm}	3^{01}_{pm}	4^{01}_{pm}	5^{01}_{pm}	6^{01}_{pm}	7^{01}_{pm}	8^{01}_{pm}	9^{01}_{pm}	10^{01}_{pm}	11^{01}_{pm}	12^{01}_{am}	1^{01}_{am}	2^{01}_{am}	3^{01}_{am}	4^{01}_{am}	5^{01}_{am}
Sun	Sun	Sun	Sun	Sun	Sun	Sun	Sun	Sun	Sun	Sun	Sun	Sun	Sun	Sun	Sun	Sun	Sun	Mon	Mon	Mon	Mon	Mon	Mon

Note: Advanced Time = Daylight Saving Time = Summer Time

UNITED STATES *(Continued)*

PACIFIC TIME ZONE
Note: *Comprises California, northern half of Idaho, Nevada, Oregon except for northern four-fifths of Malheur County, and Washington*

Standard Time
Period: *Last Sunday in October to First Sunday in April*
Time Zone: *04:00 (-8hrs UTC)*

[a]	[b]	[c]	[d]	[e]	[f]	[g]	[h]	[i]	[j]	[k]	[l]	[m]	[n]	[o]	[p]	[q]	[r]	[s]	[t]	[u]	[v]	[w]	[x]
4:01	05:01	06:01	07:01	08:01	09:01	10:01	11:01	12:01	13:01	14:01	15:01	16:01	17:01	18:01	19:01	20:01	21:01	22:01	23:01	00:01	01:01	02:01	03:01
4^{01}_{am}	5^{01}_{am}	6^{01}_{am}	7^{01}_{am}	8^{01}_{am}	9^{01}_{am}	10^{01}_{am}	11^{01}_{am}	12^{01}_{pm}	1^{01}_{pm}	2^{01}_{pm}	3^{01}_{pm}	4^{01}_{pm}	5^{01}_{pm}	6^{01}_{pm}	7^{01}_{pm}	8^{01}_{pm}	9^{01}_{pm}	10^{01}_{pm}	11^{01}_{pm}	12^{01}_{am}	1^{01}_{am}	2^{01}_{am}	3^{01}_{am}
Sun	Sun	Sun	Sun	Sun	Sun	Sun	Sun	Sun	Sun	Sun	Sun	Sun	Sun	Sun	Sun	Sun	Sun	Sun	Sun	Mon	Mon	Mon	Mon

Advanced Time
Period: *First Sunday in April to Last Sunday in October*
Time Zone: *05:00 (-7hrs UTC)*

[a]	[b]	[c]	[d]	[e]	[f]	[g]	[h]	[i]	[j]	[k]	[l]	[m]	[n]	[o]	[p]	[q]	[r]	[s]	[t]	[u]	[v]	[w]	[x]
5:01	06:01	07:01	08:01	09:01	10:01	11:01	12:01	13:01	14:01	15:01	16:01	17:01	18:01	19:01	20:01	21:01	22:01	23:01	00:01	01:01	02:01	03:01	04:01
5^{01}_{am}	6^{01}_{am}	7^{01}_{am}	8^{01}_{am}	9^{01}_{am}	10^{01}_{am}	11^{01}_{am}	12^{01}_{pm}	1^{01}_{pm}	2^{01}_{pm}	3^{01}_{pm}	4^{01}_{pm}	5^{01}_{pm}	6^{01}_{pm}	7^{01}_{pm}	8^{01}_{pm}	9^{01}_{pm}	10^{01}_{pm}	11^{01}_{pm}	12^{01}_{am}	1^{01}_{am}	2^{01}_{am}	3^{01}_{am}	4^{01}_{am}
Sun	Sun	Sun	Sun	Sun	Sun	Sun	Sun	Sun	Sun	Sun	Sun	Sun	Sun	Sun	Sun	Sun	Sun	Sun	Sun	Mon	Mon	Mon	Mon

ALASKA TIME ZONE
Note: *Comprises Alaska except for Aleutian Islands west of 170th meridian*

Standard Time
Period: *Last Sunday in October to First Sunday in April*
Time Zone: *03:00 (-9hrs UTC)*

[a]	[b]	[c]	[d]	[e]	[f]	[g]	[h]	[i]	[j]	[k]	[l]	[m]	[n]	[o]	[p]	[q]	[r]	[s]	[t]	[u]	[v]	[w]	[x]
3:01	04:01	05:01	06:01	07:01	08:01	09:01	10:01	11:01	12:01	13:01	14:01	15:01	16:01	17:01	18:01	19:01	20:01	21:01	22:01	23:01	00:01	01:01	02:01
3^{01}_{am}	4^{01}_{am}	5^{01}_{am}	6^{01}_{am}	7^{01}_{am}	8^{01}_{am}	9^{01}_{am}	10^{01}_{am}	11^{01}_{am}	12^{01}_{pm}	1^{01}_{pm}	2^{01}_{pm}	3^{01}_{pm}	4^{01}_{pm}	5^{01}_{pm}	6^{01}_{pm}	7^{01}_{pm}	8^{01}_{pm}	9^{01}_{pm}	10^{01}_{pm}	11^{01}_{pm}	12^{01}_{am}	1^{01}_{am}	2^{01}_{am}
Sun	Sun	Sun	Sun	Sun	Sun	Sun	Sun	Sun	Sun	Sun	Sun	Sun	Sun	Sun	Sun	Sun	Sun	Sun	Sun	Sun	Mon	Mon	Mon

Advanced Time
Period: *First Sunday in April to Last Sunday in October*
Time Zone: *04:00 (-8hrs UTC)*

[a]	[b]	[c]	[d]	[e]	[f]	[g]	[h]	[i]	[j]	[k]	[l]	[m]	[n]	[o]	[p]	[q]	[r]	[s]	[t]	[u]	[v]	[w]	[x]
4:01	05:01	06:01	07:01	08:01	09:01	10:01	11:01	12:01	13:01	14:01	15:01	16:01	17:01	18:01	19:01	20:01	21:01	22:01	23:01	00:01	01:01	02:01	03:01
4^{01}_{am}	5^{01}_{am}	6^{01}_{am}	7^{01}_{am}	8^{01}_{am}	9^{01}_{am}	10^{01}_{am}	11^{01}_{am}	12^{01}_{pm}	1^{01}_{pm}	2^{01}_{pm}	3^{01}_{pm}	4^{01}_{pm}	5^{01}_{pm}	6^{01}_{pm}	7^{01}_{pm}	8^{01}_{pm}	9^{01}_{pm}	10^{01}_{pm}	11^{01}_{pm}	12^{01}_{am}	1^{01}_{am}	2^{01}_{am}	3^{01}_{am}
Sun	Sun	Sun	Sun	Sun	Sun	Sun	Sun	Sun	Sun	Sun	Sun	Sun	Sun	Sun	Sun	Sun	Sun	Sun	Sun	Mon	Mon	Mon	Mon

Note: Advanced Time = Daylight Saving Time = Summer Time

UNITED STATES *(Continued)*

HAWAII-ALEUTIAN TIME ZONE

Note: *Comprises the Aleutian Islands west of the 170th meridian and the major islands of Hawaii from Hawaii in the southeast to Laysan Island in the northwest*

Standard Time

Note: *Applies for the entire year for Hawaii*
Period: *Last Sunday in October to First Sunday in April for Aleutian Islands west of the 170th meridian*
Time Zone: *02:00 (-10hrs UTC)*

Advanced Time

Note: *Applies only to Aleutian Islands west of the 170th meridian*
Period: *First Sunday in April to Last Sunday in October*
Time Zone: *03:00 (-9hrs UTC)*

[a]	[b]	[c]	[d]	[e]	[f]	[g]	[h]	[i]	[j]	[k]	[l]	[m]	[n]	[o]	[p]	[q]	[r]	[s]	[t]	[u]	[v]	[w]	[x]
03:01	04:01	05:01	06:01	07:01	08:01	09:01	10:01	11:01	12:01	13:01	14:01	15:01	16:01	17:01	18:01	19:01	20:01	21:01	22:01	23:01	00:01	01:01	02:0
3^{01}_{am}	4^{01}_{am}	5^{01}_{am}	6^{01}_{am}	7^{01}_{am}	8^{01}_{am}	9^{01}_{am}	10^{01}_{am}	11^{01}_{am}	12^{01}_{pm}	1^{01}_{pm}	2^{01}_{pm}	3^{01}_{pm}	4^{01}_{pm}	5^{01}_{pm}	6^{01}_{pm}	7^{01}_{pm}	8^{01}_{pm}	9^{01}_{pm}	10^{01}_{pm}	11^{01}_{pm}	12^{01}_{am}	1^{01}_{am}	2^0_a
Sun	Sun	Sun	Sun	Sun	Sun	Sun	Sun	Sun	Sun	Sun	Sun	Sun	Sun	Sun	Sun	Sun	Sun	Sun	Sun	Sun	Sun	Mon	Mon	Mo

BERING TIME ZONE

Note: *Comprises northwestern islands of Hawaii*
Standard Time: *Applicable for the entire year*
Advanced Time: *Not observed*
Time Zone: *01:00 (-11hrs UTC)*

[a]	[b]	[c]	[d]	[e]	[f]	[g]	[h]	[i]	[j]	[k]	[l]	[m]	[n]	[o]	[p]	[q]	[r]	[s]	[t]	[u]	[v]	[w]	[x]
01:01	02:01	03:01	04:01	05:01	06:01	07:01	08:01	09:01	10:01	11:01	12:01	13:01	14:01	15:01	16:01	17:01	18:01	19:01	20:01	21:01	22:01	23:01	00:0
1^{01}_{am}	2^{01}_{am}	3^{01}_{am}	4^{01}_{am}	5^{01}_{am}	6^{01}_{am}	7^{01}_{am}	8^{01}_{am}	9^{01}_{am}	10^{01}_{am}	11^{01}_{am}	12^{01}_{pm}	1^{01}_{pm}	2^{01}_{pm}	3^{01}_{pm}	4^{01}_{pm}	5^{01}_{pm}	6^{01}_{pm}	7^{01}_{pm}	8^{01}_{pm}	9^{01}_{pm}	10^{01}_{pm}	11^{01}_{pm}	12^0_a
Sun	Sun	Sun	Sun	Sun	Sun	Sun	Sun	Sun	Sun	Sun	Sun	Sun	Sun	Sun	Sun	Sun	Sun	Sun	Sun	Sun	Sun	Sun	Mor

Note: Advanced Time = Daylight Saving Time = Summer Time

URUGUAY

Number of Time Zones: *1*

Standard Time
Period: *Last Sunday in February to Second Sunday in December*
Time Zone: *09:00 (-3hrs UTC)*

[a]	[b]	[c]	[d]	[e]	[f]	[g]	[h]	[i]	[j]	[k]	[l]	[m]	[n]	[o]	[p]	[q]	[r]	[s]	[t]	[u]	[v]	[w]	[x]
09:01	10:01	11:01	12:01	13:01	14:01	15:01	16:01	17:01	18:01	19:01	20:01	21:01	22:01	23:01	00:01	01:01	02:01	03:01	04:01	05:01	06:01	07:01	08:01
9^{01}_{am}	10^{01}_{am}	11^{01}_{am}	12^{01}_{pm}	1^{01}_{pm}	2^{01}_{pm}	3^{01}_{pm}	4^{01}_{pm}	5^{01}_{pm}	6^{01}_{pm}	7^{01}_{pm}	8^{01}_{pm}	9^{01}_{pm}	10^{01}_{pm}	11^{01}_{pm}	12^{01}_{am}	1^{01}_{am}	2^{01}_{am}	3^{01}_{am}	4^{01}_{am}	5^{01}_{am}	6^{01}_{am}	7^{01}_{am}	8^{01}_{am}
Sun	Sun	Sun	Sun	Sun	Sun	Sun	Sun	Sun	Sun	Sun	Sun	Sun	Sun	Sun	Mon	Mon	Mon	Mon	Mon	Mon	Mon	Mon	Mon

Advanced Time
Period: *Second Sunday in December to Last Sunday in February*
Time Zone: *10:00 (-2hrs UTC)*

[a]	[b]	[c]	[d]	[e]	[f]	[g]	[h]	[i]	[j]	[k]	[l]	[m]	[n]	[o]	[p]	[q]	[r]	[s]	[t]	[u]	[v]	[w]	[x]
10:01	11:01	12:01	13:01	14:01	15:01	16:01	17:01	18:01	19:01	20:01	21:01	22:01	23:01	00:01	01:01	02:01	03:01	04:01	05:01	06:01	07:01	08:01	09:01
10^{01}_{am}	11^{01}_{am}	12^{01}_{pm}	1^{01}_{pm}	2^{01}_{pm}	3^{01}_{pm}	4^{01}_{pm}	5^{01}_{pm}	6^{01}_{pm}	7^{01}_{pm}	8^{01}_{pm}	9^{01}_{pm}	10^{01}_{pm}	11^{01}_{pm}	12^{01}_{am}	1^{01}_{am}	2^{01}_{am}	3^{01}_{am}	4^{01}_{am}	5^{01}_{am}	6^{01}_{am}	7^{01}_{am}	8^{01}_{am}	9^{01}_{am}
Sun	Sun	Sun	Sun	Sun	Sun	Sun	Sun	Sun	Sun	Sun	Sun	Sun	Sun	Sun	Mon	Mon	Mon	Mon	Mon	Mon	Mon	Mon	Mon

VANUATU

Number of Time Zones: *1*

Standard Time
Period: *Last Sunday in March to Last Sunday in September*
Time Zone: *23:00 (+11hrs UTC)*

[a]	[b]	[c]	[d]	[e]	[f]	[g]	[h]	[i]	[j]	[k]	[l]	[m]	[n]	[o]	[p]	[q]	[r]	[s]	[t]	[u]	[v]	[w]	[x]
23:01	00:01	01:01	02:01	03:01	04:01	05:01	06:01	07:01	08:01	09:01	10:01	11:01	12:01	13:01	14:01	15:01	16:01	17:01	18:01	19:01	20:01	21:01	22:01
11^{01}_{pm}	12^{01}_{am}	1^{01}_{am}	2^{01}_{am}	3^{01}_{am}	4^{01}_{am}	5^{01}_{am}	6^{01}_{am}	7^{01}_{am}	8^{01}_{am}	9^{01}_{am}	10^{01}_{am}	11^{01}_{am}	12^{01}_{pm}	1^{01}_{pm}	2^{01}_{pm}	3^{01}_{pm}	4^{01}_{pm}	5^{01}_{pm}	6^{01}_{pm}	7^{01}_{pm}	8^{01}_{pm}	9^{01}_{pm}	10^{01}_{pm}
Sun	Mon	Mon	Mon	Mon	Mon	Mon	Mon	Mon	Mon	Mon	Mon	Mon	Mon	Mon	Mon	Mon	Mon	Mon	Mon	Mon	Mon	Mon	Mon

Advanced Time
Period: *Last Sunday in September to Last Sunday in March*
Time Zone: *24:00 (+12hrs UTC)*

[a]	[b]	[c]	[d]	[e]	[f]	[g]	[h]	[i]	[j]	[k]	[l]	[m]	[n]	[o]	[p]	[q]	[r]	[s]	[t]	[u]	[v]	[w]	[x]
00:01	01:01	02:01	03:01	04:01	05:01	06:01	07:01	08:01	09:01	10:01	11:01	12:01	13:01	14:01	15:01	16:01	17:01	18:01	19:01	20:01	21:01	22:01	23:01
12^{01}_{am}	1^{01}_{am}	2^{01}_{am}	3^{01}_{am}	4^{01}_{am}	5^{01}_{am}	6^{01}_{am}	7^{01}_{am}	8^{01}_{am}	9^{01}_{am}	10^{01}_{am}	11^{01}_{am}	12^{01}_{pm}	1^{01}_{pm}	2^{01}_{pm}	3^{01}_{pm}	4^{01}_{pm}	5^{01}_{pm}	6^{01}_{pm}	7^{01}_{pm}	8^{01}_{pm}	9^{01}_{pm}	10^{01}_{pm}	11^{01}_{pm}
Mon	Mon	Mon	Mon	Mon	Mon	Mon	Mon	Mon	Mon	Mon	Mon	Mon	Mon	Mon	Mon	Mon	Mon	Mon	Mon	Mon	Mon	Mon	Mon

Note: Advanced Time = Daylight Saving Time = Summer Time

VATICAN CITY
Number of Time Zones: *1*

Standard Time
Period: *Last Sunday in September to Last Sunday in March*
Time Zone: *13:00 (+1hr UTC)*

[a]	[b]	[c]	[d]	[e]	[f]	[g]	[h]	[i]	[j]	[k]	[l]	[m]	[n]	[o]	[p]	[q]	[r]	[s]	[t]	[u]	[v]	[w]	[x]
13:01	14:01	15:01	16:01	17:01	18:01	19:01	20:01	21:01	22:01	23:01	00:01	01:01	02:01	03:01	04:01	05:01	06:01	07:01	08:01	09:01	10:01	11:01	12:01
1^{01}_{pm}	2^{01}_{pm}	3^{01}_{pm}	4^{01}_{pm}	5^{01}_{pm}	6^{01}_{pm}	7^{01}_{pm}	8^{01}_{pm}	9^{01}_{pm}	10^{01}_{pm}	11^{01}_{pm}	12^{01}_{am}	1^{01}_{am}	2^{01}_{am}	3^{01}_{am}	4^{01}_{am}	5^{01}_{am}	6^{01}_{am}	7^{01}_{am}	8^{01}_{am}	9^{01}_{am}	10^{01}_{am}	11^{01}_{am}	12^{01}_{pm}
Sun	Sun	Sun	Sun	Sun	Sun	Sun	Sun	Sun	Sun	Sun	Mon	Mon	Mon	Mon	Mon	Mon	Mon	Mon	Mon	Mon	Mon	Mon	Mon

Advanced Time
Period: *Last Sunday in March to Last Sunday in September*
Time Zone: *14:00 (+2hrs UTC)*

[a]	[b]	[c]	[d]	[e]	[f]	[g]	[h]	[i]	[j]	[k]	[l]	[m]	[n]	[o]	[p]	[q]	[r]	[s]	[t]	[u]	[v]	[w]	[x]
14:01	15:01	16:01	17:01	18:01	19:01	20:01	21:01	22:01	23:01	00:01	01:01	02:01	03:01	04:01	05:01	06:01	07:01	08:01	09:01	10:01	11:01	12:01	13:01
2^{01}_{pm}	3^{01}_{pm}	4^{01}_{pm}	5^{01}_{pm}	6^{01}_{pm}	7^{01}_{pm}	8^{01}_{pm}	9^{01}_{pm}	10^{01}_{pm}	11^{01}_{pm}	12^{01}_{am}	1^{01}_{am}	2^{01}_{am}	3^{01}_{am}	4^{01}_{am}	5^{01}_{am}	6^{01}_{am}	7^{01}_{am}	8^{01}_{am}	9^{01}_{am}	10^{01}_{am}	11^{01}_{am}	12^{01}_{pm}	1^{01}_{pm}
Sun	Sun	Sun	Sun	Sun	Sun	Sun	Sun	Sun	Sun	Mon	Mon	Mon	Mon	Mon	Mon	Mon	Mon	Mon	Mon	Mon	Mon	Mon	Mon

VENEZUELA
Number of Time Zones: *1*
Standard Time: *Applicable for the entire year*
Advanced Time: *Not observed*
Time Zone: *08:00 (-4hrs UTC)*

[a]	[b]	[c]	[d]	[e]	[f]	[g]	[h]	[i]	[j]	[k]	[l]	[m]	[n]	[o]	[p]	[q]	[r]	[s]	[t]	[u]	[v]	[w]	[x]
08:01	09:01	10:01	11:01	12:01	13:01	14:01	15:01	16:01	17:01	18:01	19:01	20:01	21:01	22:01	23:01	00:01	01:01	02:01	03:01	04:01	05:01	06:01	07:01
8^{01}_{am}	9^{01}_{am}	10^{01}_{am}	11^{01}_{am}	12^{01}_{pm}	1^{01}_{pm}	2^{01}_{pm}	3^{01}_{pm}	4^{01}_{pm}	5^{01}_{pm}	6^{01}_{pm}	7^{01}_{pm}	8^{01}_{pm}	9^{01}_{pm}	10^{01}_{pm}	11^{01}_{pm}	12^{01}_{am}	1^{01}_{am}	2^{01}_{am}	3^{01}_{am}	4^{01}_{am}	5^{01}_{am}	6^{01}_{am}	7^{01}_{am}
Sun	Sun	Sun	Sun	Sun	Sun	Sun	Sun	Sun	Sun	Sun	Sun	Sun	Sun	Sun	Sun	Sun	Mon	Mon	Mon	Mon	Mon	Mon	Mon

VIETNAM
Number of Time Zones: *1*
Standard Time: *Applicable for the entire year*
Advanced Time: *Not observed*
Time Zone: *19:00 (+7hrs UTC)*

[a]	[b]	[c]	[d]	[e]	[f]	[g]	[h]	[i]	[j]	[k]	[l]	[m]	[n]	[o]	[p]	[q]	[r]	[s]	[t]	[u]	[v]	[w]	[x]
19:01	20:01	21:01	22:01	23:01	00:01	01:01	02:01	03:01	04:01	05:01	06:01	07:01	08:01	09:01	10:01	11:01	12:01	13:01	14:01	15:01	16:01	17:01	18:01
7^{01}_{pm}	8^{01}_{pm}	9^{01}_{pm}	10^{01}_{pm}	11^{01}_{pm}	12^{01}_{am}	1^{01}_{am}	2^{01}_{am}	3^{01}_{am}	4^{01}_{am}	5^{01}_{am}	6^{01}_{am}	7^{01}_{am}	8^{01}_{am}	9^{01}_{am}	10^{01}_{am}	11^{01}_{am}	12^{01}_{pm}	1^{01}_{pm}	2^{01}_{pm}	3^{01}_{pm}	4^{01}_{pm}	5^{01}_{pm}	6^{01}_{pm}
Sun	Sun	Sun	Sun	Sun	Mon	Mon	Mon	Mon	Mon	Mon	Mon	Mon	Mon	Mon	Mon	Mon	Mon	Mon	Mon	Mon	Mon	Mon	Mon

Note: Advanced Time = Daylight Saving Time = Summer Time

VIRGIN ISLANDS, BRITISH

Number of Time Zones: *1*
Standard Time: *Applicable for the entire year*
Advanced Time: *Not observed*
Time Zone: *08:00 (-4hrs UTC)*

[a]	[b]	[c]	[d]	[e]	[f]	[g]	[h]	[i]	[j]	[k]	[l]	[m]	[n]	[o]	[p]	[q]	[r]	[s]	[t]	[u]	[v]	[w]	[x]
08:01	09:01	10:01	11:01	12:01	13:01	14:01	15:01	16:01	17:01	18:01	19:01	20:01	21:01	22:01	23:01	00:01	01:01	02:01	03:01	04:01	05:01	06:01	07:01
8^{01}_{am}	9^{01}_{am}	10^{01}_{am}	11^{01}_{am}	12^{01}_{pm}	1^{01}_{pm}	2^{01}_{pm}	3^{01}_{pm}	4^{01}_{pm}	5^{01}_{pm}	6^{01}_{pm}	7^{01}_{pm}	8^{01}_{pm}	9^{01}_{pm}	10^{01}_{pm}	11^{01}_{pm}	12^{01}_{am}	1^{01}_{am}	2^{01}_{am}	3^{01}_{am}	4^{01}_{am}	5^{01}_{am}	6^{01}_{am}	7^{01}_{am}
Sun	Sun	Sun	Sun	Sun	Sun	Sun	Sun	Sun	Sun	Sun	Sun	Sun	Sun	Sun	Sun	Mon	Mon	Mon	Mon	Mon	Mon	Mon	Mon

VIRGIN ISLANDS, UNITED STATES

Number of Time Zones: *1*
Standard Time: *Applicable for the entire year*
Advanced Time: *Not observed*
Time Zone: *08:00 (-4hrs UTC)*

[a]	[b]	[c]	[d]	[e]	[f]	[g]	[h]	[i]	[j]	[k]	[l]	[m]	[n]	[o]	[p]	[q]	[r]	[s]	[t]	[u]	[v]	[w]	[x]
08:01	09:01	10:01	11:01	12:01	13:01	14:01	15:01	16:01	17:01	18:01	19:01	20:01	21:01	22:01	23:01	00:01	01:01	02:01	03:01	04:01	05:01	06:01	07:01
8^{01}_{am}	9^{01}_{am}	10^{01}_{am}	11^{01}_{am}	12^{01}_{pm}	1^{01}_{pm}	2^{01}_{pm}	3^{01}_{pm}	4^{01}_{pm}	5^{01}_{pm}	6^{01}_{pm}	7^{01}_{pm}	8^{01}_{pm}	9^{01}_{pm}	10^{01}_{pm}	11^{01}_{pm}	12^{01}_{am}	1^{01}_{am}	2^{01}_{am}	3^{01}_{am}	4^{01}_{am}	5^{01}_{am}	6^{01}_{am}	7^{01}_{am}
Sun	Sun	Sun	Sun	Sun	Sun	Sun	Sun	Sun	Sun	Sun	Sun	Sun	Sun	Sun	Sun	Mon	Mon	Mon	Mon	Mon	Mon	Mon	Mon

VOLCANO ISLANDS

Number of Time Zones: *1*
Standard Time: *Applicable for the entire year*
Advanced Time: *Not observed*
Time Zone: *22:00 (+10hrs UTC)*

[a]	[b]	[c]	[d]	[e]	[f]	[g]	[h]	[i]	[j]	[k]	[l]	[m]	[n]	[o]	[p]	[q]	[r]	[s]	[t]	[u]	[v]	[w]	[x]
22:01	23:01	00:01	01:01	02:01	03:01	04:01	05:01	06:01	07:01	08:01	09:01	10:01	11:01	12:01	13:01	14:01	15:01	16:01	17:01	18:01	19:01	20:01	21:01
10^{01}_{pm}	11^{01}_{pm}	12^{01}_{am}	1^{01}_{am}	2^{01}_{am}	3^{01}_{am}	4^{01}_{am}	5^{01}_{am}	6^{01}_{am}	7^{01}_{am}	8^{01}_{am}	9^{01}_{am}	10^{01}_{am}	11^{01}_{am}	12^{01}_{pm}	1^{01}_{pm}	2^{01}_{pm}	3^{01}_{pm}	4^{01}_{pm}	5^{01}_{pm}	6^{01}_{pm}	7^{01}_{pm}	8^{01}_{pm}	9^{01}_{pm}
Sun	Sun	Mon	Mon	Mon	Mon	Mon	Mon	Mon	Mon	Mon	Mon	Mon	Mon	Mon	Mon	Mon	Mon	Mon	Mon	Mon	Mon	Mon	Mon

WAKE ISLAND

Number of Time Zones: *1*
Standard Time: *Applicable for the entire year*
Advanced Time: *Not observed*
Time Zone: *24:00 (+12hrs UTC)*

[a]	[b]	[c]	[d]	[e]	[f]	[g]	[h]	[i]	[j]	[k]	[l]	[m]	[n]	[o]	[p]	[q]	[r]	[s]	[t]	[u]	[v]	[w]	[x]
00:01	01:01	02:01	03:01	04:01	05:01	06:01	07:01	08:01	09:01	10:01	11:01	12:01	13:01	14:01	15:01	16:01	17:01	18:01	19:01	20:01	21:01	22:01	23:01
12^{01}_{am}	1^{01}_{am}	2^{01}_{am}	3^{01}_{am}	4^{01}_{am}	5^{01}_{am}	6^{01}_{am}	7^{01}_{am}	8^{01}_{am}	9^{01}_{am}	10^{01}_{am}	11^{01}_{am}	12^{01}_{pm}	1^{01}_{pm}	2^{01}_{pm}	3^{01}_{pm}	4^{01}_{pm}	5^{01}_{pm}	6^{01}_{pm}	7^{01}_{pm}	8^{01}_{pm}	9^{01}_{pm}	10^{01}_{pm}	11^{01}_{pm}
Mon	Mon	Mon	Mon	Mon	Mon	Mon	Mon	Mon	Mon	Mon	Mon	Mon	Mon	Mon	Mon	Mon	Mon	Mon	Mon	Mon	Mon	Mon	Mon

Note: Advanced Time = Daylight Saving Time = Summer Time

WALLIS AND FUTUNA
Number of Time Zones: *1*
Standard Time: *Applicable for the entire year*
Advanced Time: *Not observed*
Time Zone: *24:00 (+12hrs UTC)*

[a]	[b]	[c]	[d]	[e]	[f]	[g]	[h]	[i]	[j]	[k]	[l]	[m]	[n]	[o]	[p]	[q]	[r]	[s]	[t]	[u]	[v]	[w]	[x]
00:01	01:01	02:01	03:01	04:01	05:01	06:01	07:01	08:01	09:01	10:01	11:01	12:01	13:01	14:01	15:01	16:01	17:01	18:01	19:01	20:01	21:01	22:01	23:01
12^{01}_{am}	1^{01}_{am}	2^{01}_{am}	3^{01}_{am}	4^{01}_{am}	5^{01}_{am}	6^{01}_{am}	7^{01}_{am}	8^{01}_{am}	9^{01}_{am}	10^{01}_{am}	11^{01}_{am}	12^{01}_{pm}	1^{01}_{pm}	2^{01}_{pm}	3^{01}_{pm}	4^{01}_{pm}	5^{01}_{pm}	6^{01}_{pm}	7^{01}_{pm}	8^{01}_{pm}	9^{01}_{pm}	10^{01}_{pm}	11^{01}_{pm}
Mon	Mon	Mon	Mon	Mon	Mon	Mon	Mon	Mon	Mon	Mon	Mon	Mon	Mon	Mon	Mon	Mon	Mon	Mon	Mon	Mon	Mon	Mon	Mon

WESTERN SAHARA
Number of Time Zones: *1*
Standard Time: *Applicable for the entire year*
Advanced Time: *Not observed*
Time Zone: *12:00 (UTC)*

[a]	[b]	[c]	[d]	[e]	[f]	[g]	[h]	[i]	[j]	[k]	[l]	[m]	[n]	[o]	[p]	[q]	[r]	[s]	[t]	[u]	[v]	[w]	[x]
12:01	13:01	14:01	15:01	16:01	17:01	18:01	19:01	20:01	21:01	22:01	23:01	00:01	01:01	02:01	03:01	04:01	05:01	06:01	07:01	08:01	09:01	10:01	11:01
12^{01}_{pm}	1^{01}_{pm}	2^{01}_{pm}	3^{01}_{pm}	4^{01}_{pm}	5^{01}_{pm}	6^{01}_{pm}	7^{01}_{pm}	8^{01}_{pm}	9^{01}_{pm}	10^{01}_{pm}	11^{01}_{pm}	12^{01}_{am}	1^{01}_{am}	2^{01}_{am}	3^{01}_{am}	4^{01}_{am}	5^{01}_{am}	6^{01}_{am}	7^{01}_{am}	8^{01}_{am}	9^{01}_{am}	10^{01}_{am}	11^{01}_{am}
Sun	Sun	Sun	Sun	Sun	Sun	Sun	Sun	Sun	Sun	Sun	Sun	Mon	Mon	Mon	Mon	Mon	Mon	Mon	Mon	Mon	Mon	Mon	Mon

WESTERN SAMOA
Number of Time Zones: *1*
Standard Time: *Applicable for the entire year*
Advanced Time: *Not observed*
Time Zone: *01:00 (-11hrs UTC)*

[a]	[b]	[c]	[d]	[e]	[f]	[g]	[h]	[i]	[j]	[k]	[l]	[m]	[n]	[o]	[p]	[q]	[r]	[s]	[t]	[u]	[v]	[w]	[x]
01:01	02:01	03:01	04:01	05:01	06:01	07:01	08:01	09:01	10:01	11:01	12:01	13:01	14:01	15:01	16:01	17:01	18:01	19:01	20:01	21:01	22:01	23:01	00:01
1^{01}_{am}	2^{01}_{am}	3^{01}_{am}	4^{01}_{am}	5^{01}_{am}	6^{01}_{am}	7^{01}_{am}	8^{01}_{am}	9^{01}_{am}	10^{01}_{am}	11^{01}_{am}	12^{01}_{pm}	1^{01}_{pm}	2^{01}_{pm}	3^{01}_{pm}	4^{01}_{pm}	5^{01}_{pm}	6^{01}_{pm}	7^{01}_{pm}	8^{01}_{pm}	9^{01}_{pm}	10^{01}_{pm}	11^{01}_{pm}	12^{01}_{am}
Sun	Sun	Sun	Sun	Sun	Sun	Sun	Sun	Sun	Sun	Sun	Sun	Sun	Sun	Sun	Sun	Sun	Sun	Sun	Sun	Sun	Sun	Sun	Mon

YEMEN, NORTH
Number of Time Zones: *1*
Standard Time: *Applicable for the entire year*
Advanced Time: *Not observed*
Time Zone: *15:00 (+3hrs UTC)*

[a]	[b]	[c]	[d]	[e]	[f]	[g]	[h]	[i]	[j]	[k]	[l]	[m]	[n]	[o]	[p]	[q]	[r]	[s]	[t]	[u]	[v]	[w]	[x]
15:01	16:01	17:01	18:01	19:01	20:01	21:01	22:01	23:01	00:01	01:01	02:01	03:01	04:01	05:01	06:01	07:01	08:01	09:01	10:01	11:01	12:01	13:01	14:01
3^{01}_{pm}	4^{01}_{pm}	5^{01}_{pm}	6^{01}_{pm}	7^{01}_{pm}	8^{01}_{pm}	9^{01}_{pm}	10^{01}_{pm}	11^{01}_{pm}	12^{01}_{am}	1^{01}_{am}	2^{01}_{am}	3^{01}_{am}	4^{01}_{am}	5^{01}_{am}	6^{01}_{am}	7^{01}_{am}	8^{01}_{am}	9^{01}_{am}	10^{01}_{am}	11^{01}_{am}	12^{01}_{pm}	1^{01}_{pm}	2^{01}_{pm}
Sun	Sun	Sun	Sun	Sun	Sun	Sun	Sun	Sun	Mon	Mon	Mon	Mon	Mon	Mon	Mon	Mon	Mon	Mon	Mon	Mon	Mon	Mon	Mon

Note: Advanced Time = Daylight Saving Time = Summer Time

YEMEN, SOUTH

Number of Time Zones: *1*
Standard Time: *Applicable for the entire year*
Advanced Time: *Not observed*
Time Zone: *15:00 (+3hrs UTC)*

[a]	[b]	[c]	[d]	[e]	[f]	[g]	[h]	[i]	[j]	[k]	[l]	[m]	[n]	[o]	[p]	[q]	[r]	[s]	[t]	[u]	[v]	[w]	[x]
15:01	16:01	17:01	18:01	19:01	20:01	21:01	22:01	23:01	00:01	01:01	02:01	03:01	04:01	05:01	06:01	07:01	08:01	09:01	10:01	11:01	12:01	13:01	14:01
3:01pm	4:01pm	5:01pm	6:01pm	7:01pm	8:01pm	9:01pm	10:01pm	11:01pm	12:01am	1:01am	2:01am	3:01am	4:01am	5:01am	6:01am	7:01am	8:01am	9:01am	10:01am	11:01am	12:01pm	1:01pm	2:01pm
Sun	Sun	Sun	Sun	Sun	Sun	Sun	Sun	Sun	Mon	Mon	Mon	Mon	Mon	Mon	Mon	Mon	Mon	Mon	Mon	Mon	Mon	Mon	Mon

YUGOSLAVIA

Number of Time Zones: *1*

Standard Time

Period: *Last Sunday in September to Last Sunday in March*
Time Zone: *13:00 (+1hr UTC)*

[a]	[b]	[c]	[d]	[e]	[f]	[g]	[h]	[i]	[j]	[k]	[l]	[m]	[n]	[o]	[p]	[q]	[r]	[s]	[t]	[u]	[v]	[w]	[x]
13:01	14:01	15:01	16:01	17:01	18:01	19:01	20:01	21:01	22:01	23:01	00:01	01:01	02:01	03:01	04:01	05:01	06:01	07:01	08:01	09:01	10:01	11:01	12:01
1:01pm	2:01pm	3:01pm	4:01pm	5:01pm	6:01pm	7:01pm	8:01pm	9:01pm	10:01pm	11:01pm	12:01am	1:01am	2:01am	3:01am	4:01am	5:01am	6:01am	7:01am	8:01am	9:01am	10:01am	11:01am	12:01pm
Sun	Sun	Sun	Sun	Sun	Sun	Sun	Sun	Sun	Sun	Sun	Mon	Mon	Mon	Mon	Mon	Mon	Mon	Mon	Mon	Mon	Mon	Mon	Mon

Advanced Time

Period: *Last Sunday in March to Last Sunday in September*
Time Zone: *14:00 (+2hrs UTC)*

[a]	[b]	[c]	[d]	[e]	[f]	[g]	[h]	[i]	[j]	[k]	[l]	[m]	[n]	[o]	[p]	[q]	[r]	[s]	[t]	[u]	[v]	[w]	[x]
14:01	15:01	16:01	17:01	18:01	19:01	20:01	21:01	22:01	23:01	00:01	01:01	02:01	03:01	04:01	05:01	06:01	07:01	08:01	09:01	10:01	11:01	12:01	13:01
2:01pm	3:01pm	4:01pm	5:01pm	6:01pm	7:01pm	8:01pm	9:01pm	10:01pm	11:01pm	12:01am	1:01am	2:01am	3:01am	4:01am	5:01am	6:01am	7:01am	8:01am	9:01am	10:01am	11:01am	12:01pm	1:01pm
Sun	Sun	Sun	Sun	Sun	Sun	Sun	Sun	Sun	Sun	Mon	Mon	Mon	Mon	Mon	Mon	Mon	Mon	Mon	Mon	Mon	Mon	Mon	Mon

Note: Advanced Time = Daylight Saving Time = Summer Time

ZAIRE

Number of Time Zones: *2*
Note: *Advanced Time not observed;*
See Reference Map I for graphic depiction of time zones

EASTERN TIME ZONE

Note: *Comprises Upper Zaire, East Kasai, West Kasai, Shaba*
Standard Time: *Applicable for the entire year*
Time Zone: *14:00 (+2hrs UTC)*

[a]	[b]	[c]	[d]	[e]	[f]	[g]	[h]	[i]	[j]	[k]	[l]	[m]	[n]	[o]	[p]	[q]	[r]	[s]	[t]	[u]	[v]	[w]	[
14:01	15:01	16:01	17:01	18:01	19:01	20:01	21:01	22:01	23:01	00:01	01:01	02:01	03:01	04:01	05:01	06:01	07:01	08:01	09:01	10:01	11:01	12:01	13:
2^{01}_{pm}	3^{01}_{pm}	4^{01}_{pm}	5^{01}_{pm}	6^{01}_{pm}	7^{01}_{pm}	8^{01}_{pm}	9^{01}_{pm}	10^{01}_{pm}	11^{01}_{pm}	12^{01}_{am}	1^{01}_{am}	2^{01}_{am}	3^{01}_{am}	4^{01}_{am}	5^{01}_{am}	6^{01}_{am}	7^{01}_{am}	8^{01}_{am}	9^{01}_{am}	10^{01}_{am}	11^{01}_{am}	12^{01}_{pm}	1
Sun	Sun	Sun	Sun	Sun	Sun	Sun	Sun	Sun	Sun	Mon	Mon	Mon	Mon	Mon	Mon	Mon	Mon	Mon	Mon	Mon	Mon	Mon	M

WESTERN TIME ZONE

Note: *Comprises Kinshasa (Capital), Lower Zaire, Bandundu, and Equator*
Standard Time: *Applicable for the entire year*
Time Zone: *13:00 (+1hr UTC)*

[a]	[b]	[c]	[d]	[e]	[f]	[g]	[h]	[i]	[j]	[k]	[l]	[m]	[n]	[o]	[p]	[q]	[r]	[s]	[t]	[u]	[v]	[w]	[
13:01	14:01	15:01	16:01	17:01	18:01	19:01	20:01	21:01	22:01	23:01	00:01	01:01	02:01	03:01	04:01	05:01	06:01	07:01	08:01	09:01	10:01	11:01	12:
1^{01}_{pm}	2^{01}_{pm}	3^{01}_{pm}	4^{01}_{pm}	5^{01}_{pm}	6^{01}_{pm}	7^{01}_{pm}	8^{01}_{pm}	9^{01}_{pm}	10^{01}_{pm}	11^{01}_{pm}	12^{01}_{am}	1^{01}_{am}	2^{01}_{am}	3^{01}_{am}	4^{01}_{am}	5^{01}_{am}	6^{01}_{am}	7^{01}_{am}	8^{01}_{am}	9^{01}_{am}	10^{01}_{am}	11^{01}_{am}	12^{0}
Sun	Sun	Sun	Sun	Sun	Sun	Sun	Sun	Sun	Sun	Sun	Mon	Mon	Mon	Mon	Mon	Mon	Mon	Mon	Mon	Mon	Mon	Mon	M

ZAMBIA

Number of Time Zones: *1*
Standard Time: *Applicable for the entire year*
Advanced Time: *Not observed*
Time Zone: *14:00 (+2hrs UTC)*

[a]	[b]	[c]	[d]	[e]	[f]	[g]	[h]	[i]	[j]	[k]	[l]	[m]	[n]	[o]	[p]	[q]	[r]	[s]	[t]	[u]	[v]	[w]	[
14:01	15:01	16:01	17:01	18:01	19:01	20:01	21:01	22:01	23:01	00:01	01:01	02:01	03:01	04:01	05:01	06:01	07:01	08:01	09:01	10:01	11:01	12:01	13:
2^{01}_{pm}	3^{01}_{pm}	4^{01}_{pm}	5^{01}_{pm}	6^{01}_{pm}	7^{01}_{pm}	8^{01}_{pm}	9^{01}_{pm}	10^{01}_{pm}	11^{01}_{pm}	12^{01}_{am}	1^{01}_{am}	2^{01}_{am}	3^{01}_{am}	4^{01}_{am}	5^{01}_{am}	6^{01}_{am}	7^{01}_{am}	8^{01}_{am}	9^{01}_{am}	10^{01}_{am}	11^{01}_{am}	12^{01}_{pm}	1
Sun	Sun	Sun	Sun	Sun	Sun	Sun	Sun	Sun	Sun	Mon	Mon	Mon	Mon	Mon	Mon	Mon	Mon	Mon	Mon	Mon	Mon	Mon	M

ZIMBABWE

Number of Time Zones: *1*
Standard Time: *Applicable for the entire year*
Advanced Time: *Not observed*
Time Zone: *14:00 (+2hrs UTC)*

[a]	[b]	[c]	[d]	[e]	[f]	[g]	[h]	[i]	[j]	[k]	[l]	[m]	[n]	[o]	[p]	[q]	[r]	[s]	[t]	[u]	[v]	[w]	[
14:01	15:01	16:01	17:01	18:01	19:01	20:01	21:01	22:01	23:01	00:01	01:01	02:01	03:01	04:01	05:01	06:01	07:01	08:01	09:01	10:01	11:01	12:01	13:0
2^{01}_{pm}	3^{01}_{pm}	4^{01}_{pm}	5^{01}_{pm}	6^{01}_{pm}	7^{01}_{pm}	8^{01}_{pm}	9^{01}_{pm}	10^{01}_{pm}	11^{01}_{pm}	12^{01}_{am}	1^{01}_{am}	2^{01}_{am}	3^{01}_{am}	4^{01}_{am}	5^{01}_{am}	6^{01}_{am}	7^{01}_{am}	8^{01}_{am}	9^{01}_{am}	10^{01}_{am}	11^{01}_{am}	12^{01}_{pm}	1
Sun	Sun	Sun	Sun	Sun	Sun	Sun	Sun	Sun	Sun	Mon	Mon	Mon	Mon	Mon	Mon	Mon	Mon	Mon	Mon	Mon	Mon	Mon	M

Note: Advanced Time = Daylight Saving Time = Summer Time

Standard Time Zones of the World

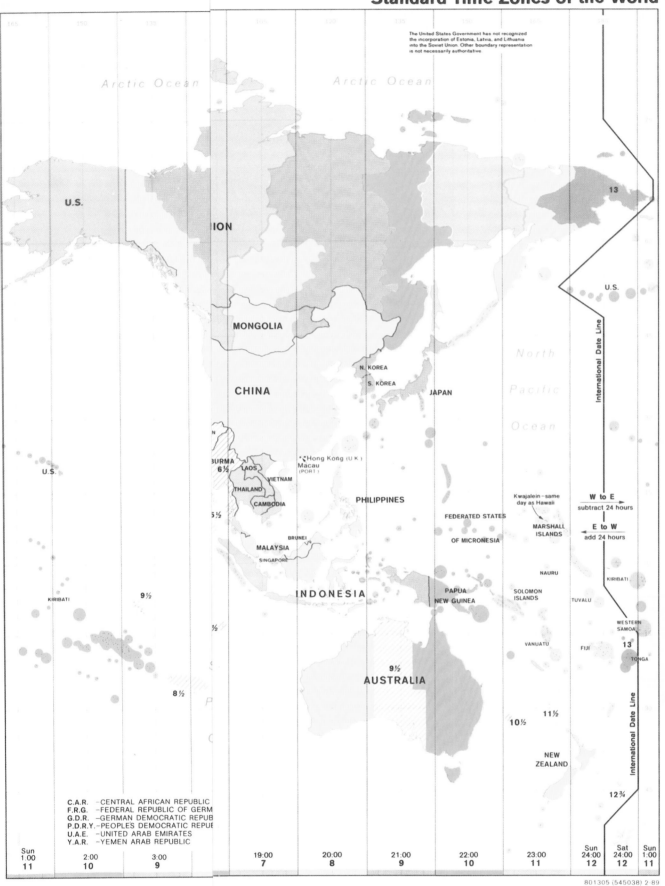

The United States Government has not recognized the incorporation of Estonia, Latvia, and Lithuania into the Soviet Union. Other boundary representation is not necessarily authoritative.

Arctic Ocean

Arctic Ocean

U.S.

ION

13

MONGOLIA

U.S.

International Date Line

N. KOREA

S. KOREA

North

CHINA

JAPAN

Pacific

Ocean

BURMA 6½

*Hong Kong (U K)
Macau
(PORT)

LAOS

VIETNAM

THAILAND

CAMBODIA

5½

PHILIPPINES

Kwajalein – same
day as Hawaii

W to E
subtract 24 hours

E to W
add 24 hours

BRUNEI

MALAYSIA

SINGAPORE

FEDERATED STATES

OF MICRONESIA

MARSHALL
ISLANDS

NAURU

KIRIBATI

U.S.

KIRIBATI

9½

INDONESIA

PAPUA
NEW GUINEA

SOLOMON
ISLANDS

TUVALU

½

WESTERN
SAMOA

13

VANUATU

FIJI

TONGA

8½

9½

AUSTRALIA

10½

11½

12¾

NEW
ZEALAND

International Date Line

C.A.R. –CENTRAL AFRICAN REPUBLIC
F.R.G. –FEDERAL REPUBLIC OF GERM
G.D.R. –GERMAN DEMOCRATIC REPUB
P.D.R.Y.–PEOPLES DEMOCRATIC REPUE
U.A.E. –UNITED ARAB EMIRATES
Y.A.R. –YEMEN ARAB REPUBLIC

Sun 1:00 11	2:00 10	3:00 9	19:00 7	20:00 8	21:00 9	22:00 10	23:00 11	Sun 24:00 12	Sat 24:00 12	Sun 1:00 11

801305 (545038) 2-89